WE DANCED ON OUR DESKS

WE DANCED
ON OUR DESKS

Brilliance and backstabbing at the Sixties'
most influential magazine

PHILIP NORMAN

MENSCH PUBLISHING

First published in Great Britain in 2023 by Mensch Publishing
51 Northchurch Road, London N1 4EE, UK

A CIP catalogue record for this book is available from the British Library.

ISBN 9781912914463
EBOOK 9781912914470

Design and Typeset by The Invisible Man
Cover by Phillip Beresford

Printed and bound by Ingram

https://menschpublishing.com/

To the memory of Nick Mason
Brilliance without backstabbing

Contents

Part Four

*   *   *

Part One

* * *

1

What's a byline?

The letter came on May 11th, 1966, a month after my 23rd birthday. A creamy envelope with a London postmark and **THE SUNDAY TIMES** shinily embossed on its flap. No, I thought, it couldn't be. It couldn't possibly be …

It was.

Dear Mr Norman

I am delighted to tell you that you have won our Writers' Contest. The cheque will follow in a few days.

Would you kindly telephone my colleague, Mrs Susan Raven, reversing the charges, so that we can find something out about you before we make the announcement.

Many congratulations

Yours sincerely

Godfrey Smith
Magazine editor

This early in the morning, the *Northern Echo's* Newcastle-upon-Tyne bureau was deserted but for me and Anita, the receptionist-cum-switchboard operator. Editorial and Advertising had only three telephone lines between them and more often than not one picked up the receiver to hear 'There's noah line,' in her plaintive Geordie accent.

'Fuck me!' I gasped, reading the letter again and then, seeing it really was true: 'Fuck ME!'

I took Anita by a charm-braceleted wrist – each charm with a different story behind it - and waltzed her around the still-closed front office. She didn't resist despite her surprise, and distaste for the forbidden word which the dramatic critic Kenneth Tynan had recently dared to utter on BBC television.

'Whatever you're so happy about,' she protested mildly, 'there's noah need for that kind of language.'

How far I couldn't expect to go in journalism had been made clear early in my first week with the *Hunts Post*, 'the county newspaper for Huntingdonshire', four and a half years earlier.

I was calling on a Methodist minister named the Reverend Brian Brown to collect news of his church's recent activities, my heart already in my boots. Surprisingly, the Reverend was only a few years my senior and sporting a fashionable Tony Curtis haircut. He kindly asked all about me, soon discovering I'd arrived at the county paper for Huntingdonshire straight from school.

One question was whether I hoped to get to Fleet Street when my traineeship with the *Hunts Post* ended, three long years from now. When I said I did, he gave me a pitying look he must normally have reserved for conducting funerals.

'I'd forget about that if I were you,' he said. 'Nowadays, no Fleet Street paper is going to look at somebody without a university degree.'

This was 1961, when only around three percent of British school leavers went on to university. My down-at-heel private school in Ryde, Isle of Wight, sent most of its brightest and best to Warsash Navigational College, the Forestry Commission, or the National Provincial Bank. But a thin trickle reached the country's handful of, mostly Victorian, universities, belittlingly known as 'redbricks'; and every few years, some prodigy would attain the thousand-year-old glory of Oxford or Cambridge. The names of this select company, at long intervals on the school's honours boards (I particularly recall K.P. Please and W.M. McLachlan) resounded down the decades like warrior kings' in the Norse sagas.

That I should try even for a redbrick had not occurred to any of my teachers, to either of my divorced but still warring parents nor – it goes without saying – to me. How could it with my father on the brink of bankruptcy at the end of Britain's second-longest seaside pier?

In 10 years under his management, Ryde Pier Pavilion had seemingly been coerced into every role possible for a giant domed structure of slatted wood, half-a-mile out at sea. It had been in turn a roller-skating rink, a penny-in-the-slot arcade, a silver-service restaurant, and a rock 'n' roll joint, all without any profit visible to the naked eye. Its latest reinvention, as a self-service cafeteria by day and a dance hall by night (with Nick Olsen at the Compton Melotone electric organ), showed little sign of breaking the cycle.

On the face of it, making money with the Pavilion did not look difficult. Every summer in those days, vast numbers of holidaymakers came to the Isle of Wight, crossing the Solent by ferry to disembark at Ryde's abnormally long pier. There being no other source of food or amusement at the pierhead, my father had an exclusive first opportunity to fleece them.

But with Clive Norman there were two major obstacles to success at the fleecing game. Firstly, having served as a Royal Air Force officer in the Second World War, he considered running a pier pavilion beneath him and despised the overwhelmingly working-class clientele and the things he was obliged to do for them – like judging knobbly knee contests or leading off the dancing of the Gay Gordons – with an intensity he barely troubled to conceal.

Secondly, the Pavilion's labyrinthine premises included a pub named The First and Last because it could serve your first drink when arriving on the Isle of Wight and your last before departing. For Clive, unfortunately, there never seemed to be a last and he'd long since graduated from just a man who 'liked his beer' to full-blown alcoholic, although at that time almost no one in Britain used the word.

He was therefore more often to be found boozing in his own bar than supervising his large, itinerant workforce, the majority of which were robbing him blind. I knew by heart those lengthy monologues to total strangers about life with 57 Squadron at Upper Heyford and the riotous evenings in the officers' mess that relieved the strain of their last mission: '…. everyone would get completely piddled, even the padre. They'd dip your bare feet in black paint, then lift you up to put your footprints on the ceiling. On mess-nights, you *knew* you were going to ruin an expensive dress-shirt…'

A decade after the War's end, he still used RAF slang, like 'Roger', 'Wilco', 'prang' and 'line-shooter', called doctors 'medics' and young girls 'popsies' and, like the Dambusters' leader, Guy Gibson, owned a Labrador with a name commonly given to black dogs in the 1950s but abhorrent and unprintable today.

Even at the height of summer and the Pavilion's proletarian revels, he retained the persona of an officer and gentleman in his tweed jacket with leather elbow patches, unstiffened shirt collars and trousers as billowy as prewar 'Oxford bags'. The heroic image was completed by his close-cut dark hair in a deep widow's peak (cause by tight-fitting flying helmets, he said) and the near-angelic good looks that ought to have taken him so much further.

The Pavilion had been built in the 1880s as a theatre for concert-parties and minstrel shows, and still had its stage and two dressing-rooms connected by a narrow backstage passage. There a bundle of fly-fishing rods from Hardy's of Pall Mall rolled up in green canvas stood in the seaweed-smelling twilight, awaiting the happy day when he could get off the pier, put knobbly knees and Gay Gordons behind him and return to the life of genteel country pursuits they had so rudely interrupted.

Meantime, he took care that no breath of vulgar showmanship should ever taint his dealings with his public. Around the Pavilion's pink and grey frontage, powerful loudspeakers informed the crowds pouring from the ferries of amenities they might otherwise miss in their lemming-rush to dry land. He made these broadcasts personally, in a melancholy boom that gave 'hot or cold meals, tea, coffee and light refreshments' all the allure of casualty lists after the Battle of the Somme.

At school I was considered thoroughly disreputable since he had me working for him on summer term weekends as well as through the holidays, collecting dirty crockery in the cafeteria and tending bar in the First and Last when I should have been attending Founder's Day church services or taking part in inter-house athletics.

My school uniform and equipment were in horrible disrepair, for I could never bring myself to add to the burden of the fees ('Eighteen guineas a term,' as he often reminded me) by demanding a new cap or PT clothes. On one soul-shrivelling occasion, the headmaster pulled me out of the lineup for the annual panoramic photograph of pupils and staff because mine was the only blazer among 200 without a badge on its breast pocket.

I took a crumb of comfort from being not quite the school's shabbiest boy; in the class above mine there was another whom I thought a fraction more decayed-looking.

Classmates often asked if I actually lived at the end of the pier – a natural assumption since I went there every day, passing through its turnstiles and using its tramway without payment. But it was only Clive who made his home in the Pavilion, sharing one of its former dressing-rooms with the woman who used to be the skating teacher at our roller-rink. It was supposed to be a secret, although obvious to all his staff and pier-employees at both ends, from the tram conductors to the men who slid the wooden gangways on and off the ferries.

My own domestic situation on shore was almost as unconventional, for I lived with his widowed mother, my Grandma Norman, who sold seaside rock from a kiosk at the pier gates and, in contrast with his seaborne enterprises, made an almighty success of it.

But to Grandma Norman, the Kiosk (on which her presence naturally conferred a capital K) was more than a business, it was an obsession. Winter and summer, seven days a week, she opened it at eight each morning and didn't close until nine at night or later. Tall and handsome in a gipsy-ish way, her pink nylon overall always left unbuttoned to reveal a Jaeger twinset and cameo brooch, she looked as out of place as Clive in the seaside hurly-burly – but for her, unlike him, it was an asset. 'Mrs Norman, the rock lady' was the most famous figure on Ryde Esplanade. The outsize personality that had once been entirely concentrated on me was now shared among taxi drivers and deckchair attendants, the endearments in a burbly West Country accent that had once been mine alone served out to each of her customers with their cigarettes or sweets:

'Ten Weights, dear? … A quarter of Murraymints, love? … Two candyfloss, my duck? A box of Black Magic, duck? … Quarter-pound or a half?'

She never went anywhere but to and from the Kiosk, spending each 13-hour day there without need of television or radio. Other than at its three serving windows, her only socialising took place in a screened-off recess where she had a tiny sink, a gas ring and a deck chair nestling among the piled confectionery boxes in which she took an afternoon rest, still intensely aware of what her all-female staff, varying in number from one to four, were doing at the windows. 'Maria!' her voice would float out, extravagantly rolling the 'r'. 'Count the change back to the customer like I showed you, love.'

Back there she entertained the various sales reps for cigarettes, ice cream and the rock of which she sold 16 tons per summer, not only in sticks in various sizes but in the guise of kippers, apples, bananas and false teeth. There, too, on the one-burner gas ring she did her only cooking for me - enormous fried-bready breakfasts whose aroma wafted onto the Esplanade. Even then, she'd be constantly darting out to serve her early morning regulars; to her inquiry 'And what can I get you, my duck?' the reply was sometimes a wistful 'Bacon and egg, please.'

This was the only time in the day when I could eat without guilt. My lunch and tea I had in the Pavilion cafeteria where Clive had not only invented hyperinflation two decades ahead of its time but pioneered the stingy concept of 'portion control'.

Cheese and biscuits, for instance, were a triangle of Dairylea spread, a microscopic blob of butter and three Jacob's cream crackers. One afternoon, in my adolescent ravenousness, I took my plate back to the counter and asked for an extra one. It was an offence of Oliver Twist proportion; with the disillusionment in his hazel-brown eyes that cut me deeper than his worst anger, he explained that every cracker I so thoughtlessly 'wolfed down' meant his losing a halfpenny in profit.

The last of the Kiosk's staff would have gone home by 6.30, leaving Grandma Norman alone there, when she was always happiest. Not for at least another two hours would she 'cash up' - always a gratifying experience – then put on a Burberry raincoat, purchased in 1918, over her pink overall and push a wheeled basket the short distance around the corner to Five Castle Street, where we lived.

Castle Street was a sunless lane mostly consisting of goods-entrances to Esplanade cafes and ice cream parlours. Number Five had once been a pub whose name no one now remembered; a narrow three-storey building of sour yellow brick with a blistered dark brown front door, our quarters were on its first and second floors and the ground floor served as storerooms for the Kiosk's stock.

Since it would already be around 9.30, she would go straight to bed, though not yet to sleep. The wheeled basket contained a couple of pint bottles of Guinness and among the shoe trees at the bottom of her wardrobe lurked a bottle of Booth's gin and several small ones of Schweppes tonic water. She would spend the next hour or so sipping Guinness or gin and tonic in utter contentment, crunching cheese biscuits from an economy-size bag and reading a historical novel by Jean Plaidy or Margaret Irwin.

Five Castle Street had been my escape from boarding at Ryde School, which I'd been doing since my parents' break-up with the hopelessness of a convict on Devil's Island. At the time, all that had mattered was no longer being cold and hungry, beaten on any and every pretext and under constant attack for not having the right shoes. Grandma Norman called it 'a safe haven' – even though she herself had no need of such a thing - but the truth was that she regarded the Kiosk as her home and Castle Street merely as a place to sleep.

It bothered her not at all that the flat had neither bathroom nor hot running water and the only toilet was a doorless recess on the far side of the rear ground-floor room (which once must have been the pub's saloon bar). True Victorian that she was, she believed that too many hot baths weakened you and that a cold water 'wash-down' from a basin and jug once a week or so did the job just as well. And instead of that long trek downstairs, there was what she called 'the po' or 'the Edgar Allan', supplemented by a dreadful chair arrangement known as 'the commode'.

That and all other fixtures and fittings had been supplied by Miss Ball, a dusty little woman with wild frizzy hair and an educated accent, whose 'antique' shop, a few doors away, sold fruit and vegetables on the side. Rather than have to think about it, Grandma Norman took everything Miss Ball offered, even the stuffed hoopoe under a glass dome, the used nasal irrigation set and the four petrified wooden flower tubs.

Nowadays, the building as it was then would certainly be declared unfit for human habitation. The cellar was structurally dangerous, so permanently blocked off, and the ground floor, where the rock was stored, oozed with damp. Stray cats came in through the cellar and haunted the almost ceiling-high cardboard cartons of sugarified kippers and false teeth, adding the mouldy reek of their pee to the age-old mildew and grime.

I could never invite friends there or even say where I lived, if not the Pier Pavilion. When I started going out with girls, my worst nightmare was that one of them might see my top floor bedroom with its view of the pier slantwise; its bedside table (from Miss Ball) a slab of orange wood, rocky on two unmatching pairs of antelope-horns.

I looked so awful in my dilapidated, badgeless blazer that after school, for my walk down Ryde's plunging hills to the sea front, I avoided busy Union Street and instead crept along parallel, unfrequented Union Lane, past the Mead Lawn Tennis Club, so enviably cool-looking and blissfully unconcerned with holidaymakers, boarding houses, beaches and donkey rides. When I arrived outside

Five Castle Street, I used to look carefully both ways like a Resistance fighter in Nazi-occupied France until I was sure no one would see me slip through its blistered brown front door.

The late 1950s are remembered as an era of teenage rebellion but there wasn't a drop of it in me. I believed in Clive and the way he did things with all my heart. Each Whitsun, the summer season's official start, hope revived in me that this would be the one when the Pavilion made his fortune at last. It took me years to realise that with him in charge, all the sunshine and gullible crowds in the world would have been to no avail.

As I'd always done, I clung to Grandma Norman's portrayal of him as a paragon of nobility – which his performance as a husband had not diminished – and a hard worker of Herculean proportion. 'And he's *so* worried financially,' she would observe sadly yet again, although I felt sure she must be slipping him some of the profits on the Kiosk's annual 16 tons of rock.

The chief manifestation of that nobility and hard work, of course, was his total enslavement to her: he sent salad lunches down from the Pavilion by tram every day for her and her helpers and, despite his myriad preoccupations at the pierhead, was always on call to replenish the Kiosk's stock and do odd jobs there or at the flat.

Often, his care went much further. 'He put a belladonna poultice on my back last night,' I remember her telling me, sitting up in bed with her gin and tonic from the wardrobe. 'And he took my shoes off for me and put my slippers on. He was so gentle ... he's like a *woman*!' At the time, this did not seem at all unhealthy, just one more reminder of the impossibility of ever measuring up to him.

Five Castle Street was also home to my two-year-old sister, Tracey, who'd been in the custody of my mother, Irene, since the divorce but was turned over to Clive and Grandma Norman shortly after my liberation from boarding school. She'd been born when Clive had already absconded with the roller-skating teacher and he'd initially tried denying paternity even though, throughout all his infidelities, Irene had never so much looked at another man. But all that was forgotten when he saw Tracey, for she was the image of him in every way - every way that I wasn't.

She was, indeed, a gorgeous child with a mass of tight golden curls and a smile that made strangers rhapsodise over her in the street. Neither her father nor grandmother being in a position to provide steady childcare, she was looked after by a series of women seconded from the Pavilion's kitchen staff. Each evening, she was put down in Grandma Norman's single bed, then awoken at Guinness-and-gin time and given fizzy pop and crisps, the genesis of a lifelong struggle with her weight.

Grandma Norman referred to her as 'Baby' in the Victorian manner – 'Hush, you'll wake Baby' – sang her ancient nursery songs like 'Nellie Bly caught a fly' and apostrophised her ecstatically in the third person: 'She's her nan's little bit of all right … her nan's little bit of fluff … her nan's little bit o' cobbly cheese … there's not a flaw in her … not a *flaw* in her.' While this was going on, I could only watch sheepishly, conscious of all the flaws there were in me.

I had got into the habit of saying my prayers at boarding school, where it was the only sure protection against bullies and 'homos'. Now, aged 13, I prayed that Tracey would grow up to be as big a success as her brother was a failure.

Both Clive and Grandma Norman talked incessantly about the past, especially the wondrous time known as 'before the War'. Born at its height as I had been, I saw it as a great grey wall, shutting off all the colour and excitement of 'history' back through Queen Victoria, the Crimean War, the French Revolution, Cavaliers and Roundheads, knights in armour, Ancient Britons …I wished I'd been alive in many previous ages but above all the 'Naughty [Eighteen] Nineties' or 'the Roaring Twenties', whose frivolity and fun were at the furthest possible extreme from this drab postwar world-without-end.

Time always passes more slowly for the young but for me, in my absolute certainty of having nothing whatever to look forward to, it had a viscous feel, as if it might soon congeal into a complete stop. The approaching end of the Fifties and dawn of a new decade seemed to promise nothing beyond a six in place of a five.

Neither of them took any interest in my schoolwork, which I understood completely: what relevance could it have to struggling with a pier pavilion or shifting rock? Nonetheless in 1959, when I was 16, I managed to pass the General Certificate of Education in six subjects at Ordinary Level and went into the sixth form to do Advanced Level English and French. It wasn't called studying those subjects but 'reading' them - the university expression, suggesting I was already as good as there.

The school ceased to regard me as a delinquent; I was made

a prefect, took the lead in Shaw's *Arms and the Man* and got into the rugby First Fifteen. Even my chronic shabbiness was slightly alleviated by a Rael-Brook drip-dry shirt in pale grey, acceptable to the uniform code, that I could wash every night and wear the next day.

During this time, Grandma Norman moved from her flat above the derelict pub at Five Castle Street to a slightly larger but equally squalid one above a derelict café at number Two. Ever enterprising, she turned the ground floor into a fish and chip shop, run for her by a young man named, if you can believe it, Mr Oxford. 'Where there's muck, there's money,' I remember her saying with a rosy wink over her bedtime Guinness.

The reek of frying batter inevitably rose to the flat and impregnated my clothes. In the sixth form there were only three of us doing A-Level English with the headmaster himself. One day when we were deep into King Lear's storm scene, he suddenly sat upright like an alerted meerkat, sniffed the air and said, 'Has someone been eating *chips* in here?'

I passed both A-Levels and at the end of my last term, in July 1961, was awarded both the English and Sixth Form prizes. The head's final report spoke glowingly of my 'responsiveness' and ended: 'If circumstances were other than they are, he might now be beginning a university course.' That the school might have thought it worth trying to make circumstances other than they were – for instance by steering me to one of the Isle of Wight County Council's generous and widely-bestowed grants for tuition and accommodation – naturally never crossed my mind.

Throughout my school career to the fifth form, I'd believed my sole talent to be drawing, especially caricaturing, and had always said my ambition was to become a cartoonist. Oddly enough, a possible alternative was first suggested by the teacher who most disapproved of me and my background, the elderly, bushy-browed geography master Mr Symonds, nicknamed 'Sinbad'. Our homework had been an essay on the Scottish Central Lowlands, to which I'd added a detail gleaned from my wistful study of menswear advertisements - that the silk-producing town of Paisley was 'noted for its startling ties'.

Sinbad tossed my exercise book back to me, slightly moderating his usual look of distaste, and said, 'Have you ever thought of being a journalist?'

The prospect was far from attractive. Like William Boot in Evelyn Waugh's *Scoop*, everything I knew about newspaper life had come from films – the incessant pressure and panic, the ranting editors and sackings on the spot. All the journalists I'd heard of had exotic names like Hannen Swaffer or Chapman Pincher or Sefton Delmer or Donald Zec that made them seem born to the profession. By contrast, Philip Norman, which I hated as much as every other bit of myself, sounded irredeemably weak and unconvincing.

With a sixth former's intellectual pretensions, I thought I'd like to be a dramatic critic like *The Observer's* Kenneth Tynan with his razor-edged prose and fearless use of taboo words like 'sex' and 'constipation'. But no doubt he had walked into his job after a glittering career at Oxford or Cambridge.

The only source of information for someone at my level was a booklet entitled *A Career in Journalism* furnished by the Island's education authority, which informed me I would need to learn shorthand and typing, be physically fit and have 'an understanding wife' because of the irregular hours. Its only illustration was a black-and-white photograph of a telephone box with a thin-faced, trench-coated, trilby-hatted man inside, dictating a story from the supposed scene of a fire. Nothing could have looked more utterly devoid of glamour.

Nonetheless, I wrote letters offering my services to the weekly *Isle of Wight County Press*, whose archaic front page consisted only of advertisements, and the *Portsmouth Evening News*, in which Clive had been a page lead in 1954 after drunkenly smashing up the mirror-lined bar of the Starboard Club in Seaview.

Both regretted they had no vacancies.

*　　*　　*

As things turned out, I was to be given my start on the mainland some 200 miles away and owe it partly to Brussels sprouts and partly face cream.

The divorce judge had ordered Clive to pay Irene £5 per week maintenance (as well as to keeping me at Ryde School when he'd been all for the state sector) but the payments had quickly lapsed. Realising the futility of pursuing him and with no resources of her own, she'd had no alternative but to find a job.

Before our move to the Island, Clive had managed an 18th century coaching inn named the Cross Keys in St Neots, Huntingdonshire, Britain's smallest county after Rutland. In reality, Irene had done most of the managing while he was out shooting or fishing the nearby River Ouse. Now she contacted the brewery which owned the Cross Keys on the off chance that his old job might be vacant and, by an extraordinary coincidence, it was.

One of Clive's parting shots had been that at her age (42) no other man was going to look at her. But while running the Cross Keys she'd met a farmer called Gerald Davison who had 2,000 acres, mostly of Brussels sprouts, around the nearby village of Southoe and drove a two-tone Ford Zodiac, the first British car seriously to resemble an American one. ('Thank you, God,' I'd breathed in my prayers in Ryde School's boarding house. 'A *rich man*.')

She'd subsequently joined the Elizabeth Arden company as a beautician, a job for which she had a natural talent. Obligingly, Elizabeth Arden assigned her to a circuit of its treatment salons in roughly the same area as Gerald Davison, rotating between Peterborough, Norwich and King's Lynn. The constant travelling involved was why she'd handed back Tracey to Clive and Grandma Norman.

At Glass's department store in Peterborough, she made up the face of a Mrs Sharman whose husband owned a string of weekly papers throughout western East Anglia. In the course of one such treatment, it emerged that his *Huntingdonshire* (traditionally shortened to 'Hunts') *Post*, was soon to have an opening for an 'editorial trainee'. Such was Irene's skill at minimising crows' feet and waxing off superfluous hair that Mrs Sharman offered to mention me to him.

She kept her promise and, in the nick of time before leaving school, I was interviewed by the *Hunts Post's* editor, F. J. Johnson, a ferocious-looking man with livid red cheeks and a drooping black moustache, who snarled rather than spoke. He made it clear that the interview was purely a formality, and I was being offered the job, now designated an 'apprenticeship'. I would be given a six-month trial at three guineas (£3.30p) per week and, if satisfactory, indentured for three years, at their end taking the Proficiency Certificate of the National Council for the Training of Journalists.

'You'll have a chance to do a bit of sub-editing … bit of feature-writing,' snarled Mr Johnson. I nodded eagerly despite having no idea what he meant. 'You'll also be expected to do things like fetching the chief reporter's cigarettes and making the office tea.' He smiled, perhaps recollecting his own apprenticeship but resembling the Devil gloating over souls in Purgatory. 'It doesn't do any harm...'

A week before I was due to start, Irene came to Ryde to drive me up to Gerald Davison's farm, where I was to stay. Her reunions with Clive could be tense, for she was forthright in her criticisms of Tracey's care and took every opportunity to rub in how far she now was from the life she'd led with him; the drinking and blatant womanising and finely-calculated humiliations and beatings-up.

This time, what was essentially the hand-over of me went quite smoothly; she didn't make too much of her new navy-blue Harvey Nichols suit with matching two-tone shoes, and even managed to be polite to his mistress. In his pierhead pub, the First and Last, on the night before my departure, seven or eight Tavern ales reduced him to tears and he took £50 from the till and stuffed it into my breast pocket, as if in apology for that missing blazer-badge.

We left on the 8.30 ferry. Grandma Norman had to be in the Kiosk of course, but he emerged from his 'secret' backstage love-nest in the Pavilion to wave me off from its long wooden front steps. Looking back at the upraised arm, the widow's peak and pale, ballooning trousers, I felt a sudden quiver in my throat.

'I think he was still drunk when he woke up,' my mother said, not totally without affection.

So it came about that, aged 18, I was a *Hunts Post* reporter, interviewing a woman named Grace Hicks, who had been deemed newsworthy for reaching the age of 92.

I was good at listening to old ladies after all those years of practice with Grandma Norman and returned to my desk to compose 800 words portraying my rather unremarkable, sweet-sucking subject as a 'serene' and 'gracious' personage whose stored-up wisdom in the ways of the world 'I, a product of the jet age, secretly envied.'

The ferocious aspect and articulation of my new editor, F. J. Johnson, was matched by extreme violence of movement; every morning, he stamped up the stairs to his office like a man trying to put out a forest-fire by himself and slammed the door with a force that rattled windows.

I had watched him storm into the reporters' room and snatch

what I now knew to call my 'copy' from his in-tray, creasing the pages as if he held a personal grudge against them.

A few minutes later, he threw the door open again and gave me a glare verging on the homicidal. 'Your first name,' he snarled. 'Do you spell it with one "l" or two?'

'One,' I replied faintly. I thought he must be writing to Mr Sharman, the paper's owner, to say I'd already shown myself to be hopeless and there was no point in continuing my six-month trial.

Dave Wakefield, the reporter who'd been detailed to show me the ropes, had the desk behind mine. 'Why do you think Mr Johnson wanted to know that?' I asked him.

'He probably wants to give you a byline,' Wakefield said.

'What's a byline?' I asked. In all seriousness.

'You know... when it says, "writes Bill Bloggs" or something.'

Sure enough in the next Thursday's paper, there were my words on the front page, headed 'Serene and gracious at 92', filling the whole left-hand column, and underneath in bold type:

PHILIP NORMAN

He'd given me a byline – and an addiction that heroin couldn't have matched.

*   *   *

2

Says Philip Norman

I served my apprenticeship in the ancient county town of Huntingdon – best known for its connections with Oliver Cromwell – mostly in a state of yearning hopelessness, totally believing what that nice young Methodist minister had told me about never getting to Fleet Street without a university degree.

Paralysing boredom, too, since the *Hunts Post* didn't do news but information, chiefly about village community events that were the same in every village. Page after page was crammed with one-paragraph reports of jumble sales, whist-drives and Parish Council meetings in Brampton, Buckden, Kimbolton, Spaldwick, Offord Darcy, Offord Cluny, Holywell, Great Gidding, Little Gidding, Hemingford Grey or Hemingford Abbots, supplied by a network of amateur correspondents in handwritten copy, often a wild scrawl reminiscent of Jack the Ripper's taunting letters to Scotland Yard. This was known as 'District' and the staff reporters spent most of their time deciphering and typing it so that the printers could read it.

'Surely,' I used to think, 'in the three years I'm here, there's got to be at least *one* murder.' There wasn't.

To the east, Huntingdonshire turned into the Fens, that vast agricultural plain, criss-crossed with water-filled dykes, rife with legends of ghosts and witchcraft and said to be the incest capital of Britain. Certainly, there were villages where everybody seemed to have some feature in common, like protruding teeth or red hair. But the Fenland libido did not stop there; local magistrates courts frequently dealt with (unreportable) cases of 'gross indecency' involving horses, calves, even chickens.

The awesomely flat expanse was traversed by several railway main lines, their traffic-crossings often lacking gates or warning bells and, in the remoter areas, no more than crude wooden ramps. One Saturday morning, when only F.J. Johnson, Dave Wakefield and I were at the office, some actual news came in: a Land Rover carrying six farmworkers including two young boys, crossing the Norwich main line in early morning fog, had been hit by an express train.

Wakefield was immediately dispatched to the scene in the office Morris 1000, taking me along. The police and fire brigade were already there and told us no one had survived. The crushed Land Rover had been removed, but a deep gash in the planks showed the force with which the train had ploughed into it and on the wet grass beside the line the bodies still lay under a tarpaulin.

'Poor Philip ... he's been blooded,' snarled Mr Johnson compassionately at the sight of my face when we returned. 'You'd better go and have a double Scotch on expenses.'

The following week, it happened that Wakefield and I were driving over that same Fen to see a man who'd amassed multiple rosettes in horse-ploughing competitions. Once again there was fog, and we came to a railway line with another wood-ramp crossing. We waited a few minutes and then, still hearing only thick, damp silence, decided to risk it.

Halfway across, I looked to my left and saw a silhouette as high as a house loom out of the fog only a few feet away. Wakefield had the presence of mind to put his foot down hard and the train rattled heedlessly past behind us.

As office junior, my particular charge was 'Huntingdon calls', a weary Monday and Tuesday morning trudge around the town and its satellite Godmanchester (pronounced 'Gumster') chronicling the past week's social activities of churches, chapels, societies and committees with their never-changing cast of chairmen, treasurers, and servers of refreshments. Each name printed, no matter how many times before, meant a copy of the paper sold.

With me I carried two types of questionnaire, one printed in green the other with a black border, to be completed with my assistance by households where there had been a wedding or a death. No great surprises here either: brides invariably walked down the aisle in ballerina-length dresses of broderie anglaise, carrying bouquets of freesias, lilies-of-the-valley and maidenhair fern, the deceased went to their graves to the strains of *Love Divine* (sometimes misremembered as 'Love's Divine') or *The Day Thou Gavest Lord Is Ended*. Often, I would arrive at the house of mourning while the wake was going on and be offered a glass of sherry and a piece of cake – on one occasion, rather nice Victoria sponge made by the corpse a few days previously.

All local newspaper journalists can quote from a rich store of obscene misprints and unintended double-entendres, but I still maintain that the *Hunts Post's* were in a class of their own. And in those days before there was a *Private Eye* to reprint them, staff and readers alike simply pretended they weren't there. It reminded me of the *Arabian Nights* story where a bridegroom accidentally breaks wind just as he enters the bridal chamber and the servant women in attendance try to cover it up by rattling their ornaments.

There was for example the *Post's* report on the retirement of a much-loved district nurse whose grateful patients were said to have subscribed to buy her 'an electric cock'. There was the centenarian who received a congratulatory telegram from 'Her Majesty the Queer'. There was the obituary of a woman who'd done floral arrangements for high social occasions like the Farmers' Ball and the Young Conservatives' Ball, which reflected that 'some of the most important balls in the county will miss her touch.'

The runaway winner appeared in one of my local news paragraphs, concerning a female youth leader from Kettering, Northants, who'd spent a week on attachment at Huntingdon's youth club. I had written that at the end of her visit, she'd hosted a lunch at which she thanked the Borough Councillors who'd sponsored it. 'Thanked' appeared in the paper as 'whanked', that suggestion of an old-school elocution teacher somehow making it even worse. But as usual, among readers and staff alike, the only reaction was a loud rattling of ornaments.

My one consolation amid all the drudgery were the bylines the ferocious F.J. Johnson continued to give me – although never telling me so in advance. These were now usually for reviews of amateur dramatic productions at a column and a half's length, of which I once did three in the same week. Aged women continued to be a rich source: my interview with soon-to-be 100 Miss Albinia Briggs filled most of the front page under Mr Johnson's ingenuous headline 'She's grand and she's gay – and what a memory!'

He made me part of the story with a bold type introduction saying the *Post's* birthday greeting had been 'delivered by *Hunts Post* reporter Philip Norman' and that 'eighteen-year-old Norman came back to write this appreciation of a lady who was an octogenarian when he was born.' A less-than-nobody all my life, I suddenly found myself a somebody, even if only in Britain's smallest county after Rutland.

Innocent that I was, it took me some time to realise how unpopular I was making myself. The ethos of the *Hunts Post* reporters' room was to always do as little as possible, and for its lowly apprentice to be seeking extra work like this and receiving such recognition was considered in the worst possible taste.

After the tall, melancholy-looking Dave Wakefield and his Jack-the-lad crony, Jim Nightingale, had typed up their court-sitting or Council committee meeting, they would play cards with the ruggedly handsome sports editor, John Clark. They knew a wide variety of games and the slap of the cards was punctuated by their cries of 'Solo!' 'Stick!', 'Twist!', 'Misere Ouvert!', 'And one for his nob!' or 'Stop the Bus!'

On Wednesdays, F.J. Johnson went to Sharman Newspapers' printing works in Peterborough, 30 miles away, to put the paper to bed, accompanied by the chief reporter, Clive Brown, a chubby, humorous, courteous man (whose cigarettes I never had to fetch as he didn't smoke). Usually only Wakefield, Nightingale and me were left in the reporters' room, and they and John Clark would clear a space and play football with a lump of compressed paper and Sellotape, using the open doorway to Clive Brown's room as a goal.

At first, nostalgic for the camaraderie of my school sixth form, I tried to become one of the lads; I learned to play Solo and Stop the Bus, took the unpopular role of goalie in the office football games and was rather pleased to be given the nickname of 'Norm'.

But as my addiction grew, I would defect from the goalmouth to stay at my desk, working on my next potentially byline-worthy piece (a laborious process as the typewriter I'd been assigned had no letter 'e' and I had to ink them in.) Then, Jim Nightingale would roughly push desk and me together back against the wall and do his best to hit me with the ricocheting 'ball'.

Somehow Nightingale always knew when I was chasing a byline and took obvious pleasure in forcing me back to Huntingdon news by telling me in his cooing undertone that there'd been a death in the Walks East or the Godmanchester Philatelic Society was planning a coach trip to Walton-on-the-Naze. And he and the others lost no opportunity to remind me of my first duty as office junior. Just when I thought I'd found the mot juste would come their gleeful chorus of 'Tea, Norm!'

I managed never to crack, no matter how hard that sticky paper wodge caught me on the side of the head. I made their tea and held my tongue and followed up on Godmanchester Philatelic Society's coach trip and lived only for Tuesday nights when I met the packet of galley proofs off the bus from Peterborough, wondering whether this week I'd find a 'writes Philip Norman', a 'says Philip Norman' or, most rarely and desirably, a 'by Philip Norman'.

Gerald Davison, now beyond any doubt my mother's boyfriend, differed greatly from the usual concept of a farmer, being tall and distinguished-looking with an aquiline profile and an upper-class accent. When they'd first met, she was 43 to his 33, but in the late 50s such age differences were much less noticeable and she hadn't troubled to mention it. At that point, when I was thanking God for sending her a rich man, Mr Davison (as I naturally had to call him) seemed to me a dashing, even fashionable figure, the first non-teenager I'd ever seen wearing tapered trousers.

He'd since turned out to be an eccentric beyond even my already wide experience. Much of this stemmed from his un-agrarian fondness for words, many of them his own invention; for instance, he would make up a name like 'Pooce' and give it to every one of his farm workers, then numbering about eight. On Fridays, when they lined up in his kitchen for their pay packets, he'd simply keep repeating 'Here you are, Pooce' and the right one would always step forward.

The most famous story among many told locally about him involved the Brussels sprouts, of which he cultivated 1,800 acres and in which he took immense pride. Early one morning during the autumn sprout-harvest, he decided to check on how work was progressing. It was beautiful weather and he drove his two-tone Ford Zodiac to the field, and around the edge of it, wearing only a pair of maroon wool bathing trunks, very holey around the crotch, and suede desert boots, topped off by his old school tie (Uppingham) and an outsize cigar.

His sprout-pickers were women from the Fens, casual employees who'd never seen him before so naturally were unaware of the tangled black body hair growing just as thickly on his back as his front. When one of them saw him approach, two-tone Zodiac and Old Uppinghamian tie notwithstanding, she thought he was an escaped gorilla and called the St Neots police.

His home, Southoe Manor Farm, lay just off the old Great North

Road and down a long, raised track with a sprout field on one side of it and one of marrows on the other. The cluster of farm buildings at the end included a concrete hangar where he'd once kept his own private plane, now used as a grain silo.

The house, in which he lived alone, was a long, low-lying grey stone building of indeterminate period, full of reminders of a more manorial past. You went through the kitchen (water still drawn by a pump) into a long-redundant servants' wing with its own yard; beyond that were ruined hothouses, vegetable and herb patches even a pigsty. There was an immense garden with an ivy-covered walk giving onto a wide lawn, then long grass with some patches of asphalt which had once been a tennis-court. In the clock-towered front drive was an empty stable leading to a tack room with every bridle and bit still in place and a calendar for 1946 on one wall.

The present domestic staff consisted of an ancient woman from Southoe village named Mrs Gray, nicknamed 'Gravy', who'd been housekeeper since Mr Davison's father's time, and an equally ancient man known only as Pestel, who walked two miles to the farm each morning just to stoke the Esse kitchen range and light the log fires in winter. Needless to say, after living with Grandma Norman, I found all this blissfully normal as well as luxurious beyond imagining.

Mr Davison, too, was in recovery from a difficult marriage, hence the immediate empathy between my mother and him at the golf club sucking-pig-supper where they met. His wife, Kay, known by him as 'Mrs McNab' or 'Madame Patti', had had numerous affairs with other farmers in the district and had only recently left him to live in London, In the smaller of the farmhouse's two sitting rooms was an expensive radiogram, a radio-cum-gramophone in a lacquered wooden cabinet, but with a jagged hole where the turntable had been. Mrs McNab/ Madame Patti had sawn it out and taken it with her as a source of ready cash.

Mr Davison's advent had none of the drawn-out awkwardness around my father's inamorata; from the start, he treated me with hectic joviality, calling me variously 'Pip,' 'Pipston', 'Pippin','Philip-Philippino', 'old boy', 'old chappie' or (in exaggerated public school) 'old fell-eaw'; while my sister, Tracey, whose godfather he'd become, was 'T', 'Triddles' or 'Triss'.

He and my mother did not exactly live together, for she kept her job with Elizabeth Arden, rotating between their Peterborough, Norwich and Kings Lynn salons and usually spending only weekends at the farm. Nor did they sleep together so far as I know, for he stayed in the little room with the narrow single bed he'd occupied since he was a small boy, and she took over the former master bedroom along the corridor.

But each gave the other something more important to them both at that moment. When she was at the farm, she cooked for him and mothered him - rather more than she ever had me in fact – while he gave her the cocktail party-attending, race going life she'd always wanted and I had for her.

If Mr Davison's manor house failed to live up to the name, the homes of the neigbouring farmers, who were all his friends, never did; each one was majestically Elizabethan or elegantly Georgian, tastefully furnished – and with every part of it in use. These other farmers, unlike Mr Davison, were happily married and highly sociable, always going in a group to Newmarket and the other race meetings they attended throughout the year.

They welcomed my mother – and me – into their circle, expecting Mr Davison to bring us to their frequent lavish parties as a matter of course. There I found myself talking to men who wore leather-elbowed jackets and smoked briar pipes just like my father's – but in their case legitimately – and discovered the untruth of his frequent declaration that there'd been no nice food since 'before the War.'

Tracey and I were usually at Southoe for Christmas and on Boxing Day we'd be taken to a buffet supper given by a couple named Ken and Joan Furbank, whose gorgeous manor house, with peacocks on the lawn, was at Diddington, a village some four miles from Mr Davison - although they considered themselves his next-door neighbours. Supper was a stupendous feast: whole hams and joints of beef, multicoloured salads with 'dressing' rather than Heinz salad cream, French cheeses, trifles smothered with whipped cream, and Joan Furbank's home-made meringues, crowding a candelabra-ed table which, to my eyes, seemed to stretch to infinity.

The first time we were there, I overheard my mother chaffing someone who'd arrived a little late: 'I bet Roly's hungry … yes, Roly's *always* hungry…' Surely, I thought, all this is much too special just to eat when you're *hungry*.

I was at the farm throughout the arctic winter of 1962 when freakishly persistent snowfall paralysed the whole country for months. Manor Farm had no central heating, all the pipes froze and every morning as I walked through Southoe village to catch the Huntingdon bus, the milk bottles left at front gates wore curly topknots of solid cream. The weather brought me my one and only perk from the *Hunts Post*, a supply of Haliborange tablets to keep up my resistance that I used to eat like sweets.

In those conditions, birds could find little to eat, and Mr Davison's Brussels sprouts, just coming up under the snow, made a banquet for thousands of wood pigeons. So famished were they that the usual deterrents of banging bird-scarers and flickering tinfoil ceased to have any effect. The next-door farmer, Jack Pigg (yes, truly) left an old car at the side of his sprout field, hoping it might fool the pigeons into thinking there were people around. But people being around made no difference either.

The sight of the gorging grey multitudes replaced Mr Davison's hectic jollity with barely coherent frenzy. Whenever the two of us walked up the icy track towards his woods (yes, he also had woods), he would scoop up a ravaged sprout, tenderly brush the snow off and murmur 'It's all pecked! *Pecked*!' like a grieving parent, then leap up, windmill his arms and shriek 'Hoy-yoy-yoy-YOY!' without putting up a single bird.

In the *Post's* local chit-chat column, Hearsays, I wrote a paragraph about the 'Southoe man' who was trying to defend his crop with 'cries calculated to blanch a pigeon's soul.'

Although resigned to never reaching a national newspaper, I was masochistically fascinated by those who had. I never missed Granada Television's *What The Papers Say* which, despite being transmitted (live) from that mysterious entity 'The North', was presented by metropolitan stars like the *Daily Mail's* acerbic Bernard Levin. I longed to be Levin, savaging every other newspaper, and every politician – sometimes in Latin - rather than covering Huntingdon's Road Safety Committee. I looked him up and, of course, he'd been to the London School of Economics like America's President John F. Kennedy.

One week, rather than Levin or James Cameron or Michael Frayn, the presenter was announced as 'Harold Evans, editor of the *Northern Echo*.' It was a paper I'd never heard of, clearly not a national yet something more than those serving a specific city or town like the *Birmingham Mail* or the *Peterborough Evening Telegraph*. This Harold Evans wore studious-looking glasses and a rather old-fashioned body-swathing double-breasted suit and spoke in an urgent yet precise accent only just identifiable as northern.

He was the sole non-Fleet Street figure to appear on the programme, initially as an obvious try-out but then as regularly as Levin or Frayn and always like a powerful draught from more moral northern climes. Where his fellow presenters were cynical and clever-clever, he was sincere and passionate; while they merely poked fun at the press's grotesqueries, he treated them as wrongs to be righted.

Life on the *Hunts Post* did not become any more pleasant with time. F.J. Johnson, in his choleric way, and Clive Brown, the chief reporter, both approved of me - which was the most important thing - but otherwise, like George Orwell as a police inspector in Burma under the British Raj, I grew 'conscious for the first time of being hated by large numbers of people.'

My fellow reporters continued to deplore my neglect of making their tea in my pursuit of bylines, and what I admit was the variable quality of the brew. One day, I found all their unemptied cups lined up on my desk in a silent, congealing protest. And among my Huntingdon 'news' contacts, my barely-concealed boredom with their social lives was starting to cause comment. John Clark told me with obvious satisfaction that Mrs Tattman of Ambury Hill, from whom I collected a list of tombola winners every Monday, thought me 'a bumptious fancypants.'

Early in 1963, I decided I could stand no more of any of them, nor of the smallest English county after Rutland and would have to find another job even though only two-thirds through my indentures.

By then, my fantasies centred on a glossy monthly magazine named *Town*. It had formerly been *Man About Town*, the house journal of the menswear industry, but had lately passed into independent ownership and widened its remit to everything exciting that suddenly seemed to be happening in London. Each issue I collected from W.H. Smith in Huntingdon High Street brought yet more agonising proof of what I was missing.

Despite its name-change, *Town* retained a strong male fashion bias and for me, in my worn-every-day sports jacket, old school trousers and unweatherproof Dolcis shoes, that was its primary interest. Like a pigeon on Mr Davison's Brussels sprouts, I gourmandised its spreads of shortie raincoats, thick-striped shirts, trousers with sloping cuffs and patch pockets, suede waistcoats, elastic-sided Chelsea boots and 'slubbed' silk ties.

Only when thoroughly sated by shortie raincoats would I turn to editorial content bearing no resemblance to the drab little British magazines I'd grown up with, like *Everybody's* and *John Bull*. *Town's* articles were phenomenally long and of such concentrated fashionability that I often found them incomprehensible. Its photographs, nearly all black and white, were enormous and cropped in unorthodox ways, sometimes showing only half of someone's face or just legs and Chelsea-booted feet.

Its masthead told me that the editor was Nicholas Tomalin, someone of whom I'd never heard but whose name – to my eyes – suggested an archetypal product of Oxford or Cambridge who'd look down on the *Hunts Post* from the greatest possible height. Nonetheless, with a 20-year-old's insouciance, I wrote to him, asking for a job on *Town* in any capacity whatsoever. Much to my surprise, he wrote back saying that it had no vacancies, but offering to see me anyway. His very signature - both casual and learned looking - seemed to me a mark of his infinitely superior caste.

Town's offices were not in Fleet Street or anywhere near it; they were in Edgware Road, where long ago, before she had the Kiosk, Grandma Norman used to take me to look at shop windows full of old swords and armour.

Nicholas Tomalin was about 30, with slightly peaked dark hair and close-set, penetrating eyes. To my disappointment, his clothes seemed little influenced by his magazine's fashion pages; just a faintly-checked shirt, its collar not even button-down, and dark tweedy trousers. His office was small and cramped and shared with an absent colleague, but I was impressed to see a jacket matching his trousers on a hanger behind the door. Where I came from, men hung their jackets over shoulder-misshapening chair backs.

I had brought along the pick of my bylined Hunts Post cuttings, displayed in transparent envelopes inside a black plastic binder I thought of – seriously - as my only friend. There were several specimens of the pop music column to which F.J. Johnson had gloweringly agreed and which I'd named DISCourse. Tomalin turned the plastic pages, at one point giving a slight smile. I wondered if he was reading the DISCourse beginning 'The wind of change doth begin to blow among Huntingdonshire groups ...'

Finally, he handed the binder back. 'Well,' he said, 'all this looks quite bright and original.'

He didn't ask whether I'd been to university, just how much the

Post was paying me (a little over £6 per week by then) and where I was living. Since that would have been too complicated to answer, I just said 'With my mother.'

'Oh well, it's not so bad if you're living with Mum,' Tomalin said. 'I started on ten.'

When I asked if he thought I had any chance of ever rising above *Hunts Post* level, he looked at me with his close-set eyes and nodded. 'I think you're going to make it.'

I knew there was no opening for me on *Town*, but Tomalin suddenly offered a ray of hope. He said its management was shortly to launch a news magazine called *Topic*, modelled on America's *Time* and *Newsweek*, and then he'd be editor-in-chief of both titles. 'Would you be interested in working for *Topic*?' he asked. 'You'd be a librarian-cum-researcher, but with the possibility of moving on to do reporting.'

I said I would be interested (the understatement of the Millennium) and he said to leave it with him.

Back in Huntingdon I waited and waited but there was no word from Tomalin. Then when the next month's *Town* came out, his name had disappeared from its masthead and the editor was given as Clive Irving.

I wrote to Clive Irving, explaining how things had been left with his predecessor; he replied in a typed letter of a single line that *Topic* had no more vacancies for researchers, followed by a perfunctory 'so sorry.'

His signature had the same look as Tomalin's: casually learned. 'Bloody Oxford and Cambridge again,' I thought.

* * *

3

Which college, Sir?

Early in 1963 my father finally managed to get off the end of Ryde Pier, selling the remainder of his lease with British Railways' Southern Region to a businessman from the mainland. I met the Pier Pavilion's new showman only once and didn't catch his name; my impression was of lank black hair, a loud checked jacket and a bony face on which second thoughts could not have been more plainly written.

His tenure would be brief, for in 1966 the Pavilion was demolished except for its iron legs, which remained stubbornly rooted in the chalk seabed – and still do to this day.

Clive was not quite done with entrepreneurism on the Isle of Wight. After offloading the Pavilion, he spent some months running Grandma Norman's fish and chip shop, an ignominy to which he'd always sworn never to be reduced. Unfortunately for him, where there was muck there wasn't money: that summer brought the first potato famine in Britain for 100 years and chips became all but extinct. He tried fish and parsnips, fish and turnip, even fish and mangelwurzel, but none caught on and that autumn he left the Island forever.

With him went the woman who'd shared his illicit quarters at the pierhead since 1956: a mattress on the floor of the former dressing-room, and the backstage passage, with unscreened washbasin and WC (also used in summertime by the various electronic organists he engaged to play for dancing).

When she had first appeared on our skating-rink with her white boots and mesmerisingly short skirt, I had been about six but, like everyone else, had called her 'Joan'. After he'd run away with her and they'd returned together to their draughty domed love-nest, she had become 'Miss Salsbury', symbolising the unquestioning respect he demanded for her from his employees - and, of course, me.

One day towards the end of his time on the pier, he took me aside, looking grave, and said 'I think you're old enough to start calling Miss Salsbury "Joan."'

Despite having done just that as a six-year-old, I felt privileged. That is, until I found out he had already notified his staff that they shouldn't go on calling her 'Miss Salsbury' either because she was now Mrs Norman. I'd had no idea he was thinking of marrying her, and subsequently never found out when or where it had happened. Asking him directly would have been a waste of time, for I knew the answer already. It would be the same as when, aged 10, I'd pleaded with him to come home to my mother and me: a toneless 'Mind your own business, Philip.'

During the weary knobbly knee-judging summers on the pier, he'd often spoken longingly of idyllic holidays 'before the War' in Hungerford, Berkshire, and fly fishing on the River Kennet. Now he had the only stroke of luck I can ever remember. For just a few hundred pounds, he bought a row of three cottages in Hungerford High Street whose owner automatically became a 'freeman' of the town. The ancient privileges that came with it included fishing rights on the Kennet, by then one of Britain's most sought-after trout-waters. So the Hardy rods, stored backstage at the Pavilion for so long, could be unrolled from their green canvas at last.

Rather than amalgamate the three cottages, he chose to start living on dry land with Joan in the left-hand and most modern of the row, which was pebbledash-fronted, with leaded windows. The middle one was used chiefly to house Grandma Norman's enormous half-tester brass bed with seven-foot headposts, which had been in storage in London for the 10 years that she'd been on the Island. The last, the only one with a thatched roof, had a sitting tenant, a frail old lady named Miss Smith whom Clive left *in situ* with no alteration in her peppercorn rent and to whom he was always charming and helpful, even when she requested him to wash her front step with her used bathwater.

Yet even here, so far from the sea and its indignities, his old life haunted him in a particularly galling form. Hungerford High Street after dark was mostly wrapped in the sleep of centuries, barely a light showing. But directly opposite the cottage where he'd chosen to live was a fish and chip shop, hugely busy with potatoes plentiful again that stayed open late and was a popular rendezvous for bikers.

His business now was fruit machines, sited in pubs in and around Hungerford, often disfiguring historic anglers' inns that were supposedly dear to his heart. They'd made fortunes for other people with their unlimited jackpots but no sooner did Clive go in for them than the government changed the rules, limiting payouts to five shillings (25p). Rather than becoming Berkshire's Mister Big, he resembled an overworked doctor, always on call to repair some machine with a name like 'Las Vegas' or 'It's MAD Money'.

Meanwhile, Joan, who had always had an arty, folksy side – 'clever fingers', she called it – opened a hairdressing salon named Lady Fayre. Hungerford at that time was not nearly as chic as it later became and the salon answered a need, soon employing two or three assistants, even taking on a trainee. Its premises were in another beautiful, centuries-old building near the Eddington river bridge, yet somehow the atmosphere of Ryde Pier Pavilion seemed to reconstitute itself there: a sort of damp desperation.

As my stepmother, albeit not – and never – gazetted as such, Joan seemed no different from the Miss Salsbury she had previously been, showing me neither affection nor hostility; showing me nothing in fact. Her sharp-featured face still wore its faintly rueful look, as if acknowledging she'd smashed up my world without regretting it. In her presence, I still felt awkward and clodhoppping as well as acutely conscious of the sexual spell she'd cast over my father; it caused me horrible embarrassment, for instance, whenever I heard him call her 'Joanie'.

He, on his side, demanded my total acceptance of her despite having shown how little my acceptance mattered with their clandestine marriage. Indeed, where I was concerned, he put her on a pedestal my unlucky mother had never known - although I gathered he was prone to knocking her about just as much when he'd been drinking.

In their tiny cottage sitting room, the smaller of the two armchairs (purple knitting always left on one arm) was not just where she liked to sit, but something sacred, inviolable. If ever I chanced to trespass on this chintz-covered Ark of the Covenant, he would look at me with the disappointed hazel eyes that had always made me wither inside and say it 'wasn't fair'.

I still tried to live up to his ideals of manhood, chiefly by drinking as much as he did – or pretending to - on our endless rounds of the pubs harbouring his machines and at the cottage later into the small hours. Nothing arouses a boozer's ire like someone not wanting to booze along with them. If ever I asked for plain ginger ale without whisky or said I was tired and wanted to go to bed, he'd mutter that

I was 'milky' or 'a prig'; his code for saying I was like my mother with an undercurrent of old suspicion that I might be gay.

Despite the cloud of incipient bankruptcy always hanging over him, his largesse could be spectacular: for my 21st birthday he gave me £200 to buy a secondhand Morris Mini-Minor in ivory white. But once out of his sight, I was clearly out of mind. He never asked me a single thing about my job on the *Hunts Post*, nor commented on the cuttings I sent him.

It took some while longer to prise Grandma Norman out of the Kiosk, even though neither of her precious sons was now on the Island. Her firstborn, my namesake Uncle Phil - who made Clive look positively normal - had died of a stroke in 1960, his wife, deservedly known as 'poor Lorna', and my cousin Dina having made their escape two years previously, with a police escort to the ferry to protect them from him.

In fact, Grandma Norman had refused to join Clive in Berkshire unless he found her a replacement for the Kiosk, allowing that it might not sell 16 tons of rock a year. That proved impossible in Hungerford but something turned up in Lambourn, a 40-minute drive over the Downs where racehorses exercised, yet still just inside the Berkshire boundary.

For sale on the main road through the village was a little sidelong house with the ghost of a shop window, that had once been a grocer's. A more solid reminder could be seen on its end wall, a blue and orange enamel sign in which was embedded an outsize thermometer. 'Lyons Tea,' it read, 'Degrees Better.'

There were many top racing stables in the district and the streets and many pubs thronged with jockeys, apprentices and stable lads. It was a rowdy place whose atmosphere on Friday and Saturday nights was less West Country than Wild West.

Nonetheless, Grandma Norman decided on the little sideways house with the outsize exterior thermometer and paid the full asking-price for it. Clive did up the shop and living quarters to the small extent she demanded and in six weeks she was back behind a counter in her pink nylon overall, selling packets of tea and tins of Brasso to boy-sized men in riding breeches and flat caps, calling all of them 'love' and 'my duck' and 'duck'.

My sister Tracey, now aged nine, went to live with her, as in Ryde, and started at a convent school in Newbury. Undomesticated though Grandma Norman had become after years at the Kiosk, she made a brave stab at looking after a nine-year-old but found many of the demands beyond her.

At school, Tracey was studying the evolution of tadpoles, a number of which she kept in a glass tank at Lambourn. During the holidays, when she went to stay at Gerald Davison's, her grandmother reluctantly agreed to look after the tadpoles. When it came to feeding them, Grandma Norman vaguely recalled Tracey saying that at one stage they turned carnivorous, so she tipped some left-over stew into the tank.

The bathroom at Southoe Manor Farm, surprisingly, had a dark blue bath and basin and pale blue tiled walls like a bit of 1930s Hollywood mislaid among the fields of Brussels sprouts. It was there as I lay in the blue bath that my transistor radio played an odd new pop single whose bleating harmonica, stop-start beat and rather droney vocal duet seemed to hover on the edge of comedy.

On the BBC's old Light Programme, even music presenters (no vulgar deejays then) spoke like Shakespearian actors.'"Love Me Do",' this one enunciated. 'By the *Beatles*.' I couldn't but share his amusement at the preposterous name.

Amazing to recall, these newcomers with their outlandish fringes and round-collared suits at first seemed as ill-favoured as their name was suicidally ill-chosen. Their first significant press coverage came during their debut national tour when they tried to gatecrash a dance being held by Carlisle's Young Conservative Association. However, their real offence that night had been to wear black leather jackets which, only 17 years after the War's end, still awoke memories of Hitler's SS.

In common with nearly everyone over 20, my *Hunts Post* colleagues dismissed them as a passing fad like every other 'beat group' except Cliff Richard's Shadows. Dave Wakefield, a rabid Dixieland jazz fan, called them 'loud' and 'scruffy' while John Clark derided the lyric of the follow-up single that took them to number one, *Please Please Me*. 'Come on, come on, come on? Load of bollocks, isn't it!'

Everything changed after their second album, *With The Beatles*, its cover showing four polo-necked faces half in shadow like soulful art students or denizens of the Parisian Left Bank. With that, pop music ceased to be working class and for gullible teenagers only; even the stern manageress of the *Post's* small-ads department learned to tell John Lennon from Paul McCartney, and conceded that all four had 'sensitive faces.' Newspapers stopped putting 'pop' inside quotation marks like something they preferred not to handle without rubber gloves.

When the Rolling Stones made the once-outrageous Beatle cut look like 'short back and sides', the length of young men's hair became the burning topic of the day. My own was nowhere near Mick Jagger level - both my forehead and collar clearly visible - yet even the amiable Clive Brown took to pointing a finger at me and, like a joke sergeant-major, barking 'Haircut!'

My slightly lengthened sideburns put me under such pressure from my mother and Mr Davison that I foolishly let her take them off with hot wax, the way she did her clients' leg and facial hair. The waxing was agony and when they grew back, it was in separate little tufts.

By now, my off-diary work included a page for younger readers to which I gave the cringe-worthy name Youthwise. *The Hunts Post* changed from its ancient, obscenity-prone flatbed printing press to a new process called web offset, which could reproduce illustrations without the trouble and expense of engraving metal. I started drawing cartoons for Youthwise and designed a heading of guitar-playing figures for my DISCourse column, naturally with a generous byline.

As Beatlemania spread from Britain across Europe, the *Hunts Post* suddenly remembered it was supposed to be training me for the Proficiency Certificate of the National Council for the Training of Journalists. To take this before the end of my indentures, I would have to follow the Council's prescribed three-year course in one year and hope to scrape through its exams in law, local government and newspaper practice.

This, finally, exposed me to further education: Fridays on 'day-release' at Peterborough Technical College, attending lectures with fellow trainees from papers like the *Ely Standard*, the *Spalding Journal*, the *Stamford Mercury* and the *Kings Lynn News and Advertiser*, in addition to taking correspondence courses in essential law for journalists and newspaper practice (i.e., what was meant by terms like 'overmatter', 'em', 'en' and 'flong'.)

At least I could make the 60-mile round trip in my ivory-white Mini, my transistor radio on its rear window ledge. As I drove back one foggy Friday evening in November, the Hollies' *Stay* suddenly cut off and a voice with a strange hollowness about it said, 'We have just heard that President Kennedy has been shot...'

I took the greater part of the exam with my classmates in a church hall in Stamford, Lincolnshire, but the paper on local government in a room by myself at Peterborough Tech. As I'd followed only a third of that course, the National Council For The Training of Journalists had agreed that my tutor could set me some questions based on what I'd learned so far. I was one of the few members of his class to have paid attention, so he simply gave me my latest three essays to do again, even letting me use a typewriter. I rattled them out almost verbatim and got 98 percent.

Nonetheless, being me, I thought I must have failed the overall exam. When we all turned up at the Tech for our results, the principal beckoned me aside; I assumed he wanted to break it to me gently how poor mine had been, but he said I'd got the highest mark in the country and would receive a prize for outstanding results.

It was a book token for 30 shillings (£1.50), presented by the editor of the *Slough Observer*. I wrote and told Clive about it, enclosing the little front-page story about me that F.J. Johnson put into the Hunts Post, but received no reply.

*   *   *

My almost obligatory next step, only 16 miles to the south-east, was the evening *Cambridge Daily News*. It had recently been rebranded the *Cambridge News* and turned into a modern-looking tabloid; it had a new editor, Keith Whetstone, aged only 33 and said by F.J. Johnson to be 'a very dynamic young man.' With my Proficiency Test result and black binder full of bylines, I pretty much walked in.

At my leaving party from the *Hunts Post*, Mr Johnson presented me with a ballpoint pen and said I had been 'an ornament to the staff' – a judgement with which perhaps not all its readers, like Mrs Tattman of Ambury Hill, would have agreed.

The *Cambridge News* occupied a modern glass-fronted building on Newmarket Road and it felt like real progress to be there, climbing up and down contemporary staircases and hearing teleprinters chatter out the national and international news the paper carried on its front page. The massive downside was being IN Cambridge rather than AT Cambridge. Each day, I had the university all around me - the stacks of bicycles everywhere, the castellated walls of honey-coloured stone, the medieval archways into beautiful gardens, the punts swarming on the River Cam, the glimpses through leaded casements into softly-lit libraries – yet could be no part of any of it.

Worse, I would sometimes be mistaken for an undergraduate. It happened most painfully when I visited Arthur Shepherd, the lovely menswear shop in Trinity Street to buy a pair of the cavalry twill trousers with plain, sloping cuffs I'd hungered for since they'd been in a *Town* magazine fashion-spread.

They cost six guineas but as I reached for my wallet, the assistant opened a ledger and asked, 'Which college, Sir?' In those pre-credit card days, the name of any Cambridge seat of learning was a sufficient guarantor and he was about to put the trousers on the slate.

Despite the *Cambridge News's* superior working conditions (including the first sandwich-vending machine I ever saw) it was not a happy place. Keith Whetstone, its 'dynamic' young editor, made one appearance at the Newsdesk early each day, smoking a curly-stemmed pipe, but was seldom visible otherwise. The news editor, Eddie Duller, had a puggy face, glasses and bog-brush hair, rather like my late persecutor Jim Nightingale, and regarded all his reporters as incorrigible skivers whatever their level of productivity. As for his news-editing skills, the office saying had it right: 'Outlook over Cambridge – Duller.'

With weary resignation, I heard from my new colleagues about the broad, sunlit highway from the university to Fleet Street; how every year the nationals sent teams to recruit the brightest stars of the student newspaper *Varsity* and *Granta* magazine (of which, I discovered, not to my great surprise, Nicholas Tomalin had been editor.) Classy new undergraduate publications were always springing up, like *New Cambridge*, modelled on the *New Statesman*, with contributors clearly marked for fame like Clive James and Germaine Greer.

Just as clearly, they were not destined for the tabloid *Daily Mirror* or *Daily Sketch* but the 'quality' Sunday broadsheets. I had once thought the *Observer* the most hopelessly desirable of these, thanks to Kenneth Tynan's play-reviews, but no longer.

A couple of years earlier, the Canadian press baron Roy Thomson had purchased the stuffiest of them, *The Sunday Times*, and effected a complete transformation. The paper now buzzed with innovations like a separate Review section which paid fortunes to serialise the memoirs of politicians, and an 'investigative' unit called Insight which had revealed the full seamy depths of the Profumo Scandal. Thomson's latest coup had been to sign up the Queen's brother-in-law Lord Snowdon, a photographer before he married Princess Margaret, to undertake special assignments for the paper and act as its 'creative consultant'.

Less sure footed, it seemed, was Thomson's introduction of a 'colour supplement', a glossy version of newsprint supplements commonplace all over North America. The first issue contained a photograph of a new young fashion model named Jean Shrimpton by a new young photographer named David Bailey which caused such outrage among the *Sunday Times's* traditional readership that it published an apology the next week. The supplement had failed to attract significant advertising and was losing so much money that Fleet Street commentators dubbed it 'Thomson's Folly', but its proprietor insisted it would be persevered with.

One Sunday, leafing through the *Sunday Times's* newly-energised pages, I spotted a familiar name: an entire half-page, headed 'Atticus', was signed Nicholas Tomalin. It seemed to be a gossip column but, rather than bitty paragraphs, was entirely about old canal towpaths, of which it was passionately but amusedly in favour. 'Atticus' was written in Latin letters with the 'u' looking like a 'v'. Oh, that blend of the light-hearted and erudite only Cambridge could give!

Another familiar name came up during a rare social interaction between our pipe-puffing editor, Keith Whetstone, and a group of reporters including me. On a nearby desk lay a handout from Granada TV about *What The Papers Say* and a photograph of Harold Evans – still the only 'provincial' editor to present the programme – studying a front page skeptically through his round spectacles.

'Yes, he's making quite a name for himself,' Whetstone admitted, clearly not much relishing the idea of another 'dynamic' young editor. 'People are saying that if he doesn't slow down, he'll burn himself out.'

It soon became clear that, just as surely as I wasn't going to Fleet Street, I wasn't going anywhere on the *Cambridge News*. The two jobs on the paper I coveted, theatre or film critic, had long been held by much older men who showed no inclination to move.

I managed to start up my DISCourse column again and do comic drawings for it, which led to requests for cartoons from the Women's

Page and Books editors and, occasionally, even the news pages. As an extension of DISCourse, I interviewed the now rather out-of-date Billy Fury backstage at the ABC cinema (he wore thick pancake makeup and was shaking with nerves); Manfred Mann and Unit Four Plus Two in their dressing-room at the Corn Exchange, and the Cambridge-based parents of the man who'd played the saxophone solo on Georgie Fame's first hit single, *Yeah Yeah*.

Occasionally, if the regular University Correspondent was away, I'd have to report a debate at the Union where, several more times, I was asked the name of my college.

I had a ground-floor bedsit in a depressing house in Rustat Road, far from the city centre and mostly occupied by foreign students below Cambridge level. In the room next to mine was a jovial Zambian named Richard Leakey with whom I became friendly enough to confess my frustration at the *Cambridge News*. He suggested I might do better in Lusaka, if not on one of its newspapers then as a government information officer, and I gave it serious consideration.

A few months earlier, I'd started going out with a young woman from the Cambridgeshire 'County set', the realm of foxhunting and Young Conservatives and double-barrelled surnames, whose family lived in a country house large enough to be called a grange. When I spent weekends there, I didn't, of course, bunk with her, but was given a little book-lined room that felt just like one 'in college'. Sometimes I'd pretend it really was.

In Cambridge, she attended The Academy, a secretarial school for daughters of the County whose students constantly benefited from the university's huge male majority, particularly during the annual May Week of lavish college balls. During the preceding week, it held its own 'May Ball' to which suitable young men from the better colleges were invited, so giving every Academian a choice of potential escorts to the real things.

I attended the one in May, 1965, and found it so oppressive that I wandered away from the scenes of revelry and loitered beside an open window. The Academy overlooked the Cam on one of its narrowest stretches and directly opposite, only about 30 feet away, was Magdalene College, ablaze with light and looking stunning.

One of its leaded casements was open and I could see right into a student bedroom whose male occupant was there in bed. After a moment, he got up and closed his window, then lay down again, pulling the covers up to his chin. Whoever he was and whatever he was studying, I would have given my soul to change places with him.

Ironically, I owed my liberation from such torments to the young County woman – or, rather, to her mother, who had the very opposite of liberty in mind for me.

England's County sets in 1965 functioned little differently from in 1865 and a daughter who reached the age of 20, as this one recently had, without acquiring a fiancé was considered a social failure. Although a young Guards officer would have been preferable, I had been selected for the role and was expected to step into it at any moment; a fact well-known to everyone in her circle but me. When I discovered champagne was already waiting in the fridge for the moment when I popped the question, I decided my only option was flight.

In those days, job opportunities for provincial journalists were listed in the grandiosely named *World's Press News*, a mere half-page of unenticing small-ads like 'Romford Recorder requires general reporter, courts, councils, good note [i.e. shorthand] essential. Above union rate for right man.' But the first time I looked there, concerned only with finding something as far as possible from the champagne in the fridge, what should I read but:

Reporter/drama critic wanted, Northern Despatch.
Apply, Arnold Hadwin, Editor, Priestgate, Darlington, Co Durham

Jack Amos, the *Cambridge News's* chief sub, filled me in on the *Northern Despatch* – although I was going to apply anyway. 'It's the *Northern Echo's* evening stablemate. You *know* ... the *Northern Echo*. Edited by Harold Evans, who does *What The Papers Say* on TV.'

'But isn't the *Northern Echo* an evening?' I asked.

'No – big, *big* morning, the *Echo*. Circulates all through County Durham, Teesside, Tyneside and Northumberland, as far south as York and almost up to Scotland *The Despatch* is just for Darlington. Nice town though,' he added encouragingly.

The train journey to Darlington took me for the first time into the real North, as opposed to half way house Huntingdonshire, recognisable when all the brickwork I could see through my window started turning dark red. On reaching my destination, the first thing

I saw was a plinth with a life-sized replica of Locomotion Number 1, the steam engine that pulled the world's first passenger train, from Darlington to Stockton-on-Tees in the 1820s.

The *Northern Despatch's* – and *Northern Echo's* - headquarters was a redbrick building occupying a whole block of central Darlington. You entered through a high-ceilinged front office like a bank but the only way to the editorial departments was a narrow, winding staircase with a stained-glass window at its first turning.

The *Despatch's* editor, Arnold Hadwin, was a small, wiry man who looked as if he might once have been an Olympic sprinter. He talked to me standing at a big window outside which the North stretched far and wide and red-bricked in the smoggy sunshine.

My result in the Proficiency Test evidently still carried great weight.

'Well, I should very much like to have you, Mr Norman,' he said after a few minutes, 'provided we can come to terms.'

'I was going to ask for £25 a week,' I said. Mr Hadwin winced and replied that it was 'out of the question'. £21 almost was, but for the top boy in the country, not quite. It still felt like a fortune.

That July, I drove the almost 200 miles back to Darlington in my underpowered white Mini with big Jaguars flashing their headlights officiously behind me in the fast lane; progressively more intimidated as I reached Northamptonhire, then Nottinghamshire then Yorkshire and saw steadily multiplying factory chimneys and rows of giant cooling towers.

The evening of my first day on the *Northern Despatch*, I was sent to review the cabaret at the Fiesta Club, almost next door to Bank Top station and Locomotion Number One. The main attraction was an obscure singer named Gerry Dorsey, soon to be renamed Engelbert Humperdinck and become internationally famous, at one moment outselling the Beatles.

For his first song, *Dancing In The Street*, the Fiesta's ropey house band started too slowly and as he turned to them and hissed 'A little bit faster,' I thought 'What the hell have I *done*!'

*   *   *

4

If it was only a threepenny
bus fare, you should have walked

After the well-appointed *Cambridge News*, the *Despatch's* reporters' room had come as a severe shock with its undersized desks, ramshackle shared typewriters and huge grubby white plastic tub full of used carbon-paper. So much so that on my very first morning I'd bought the latest *World's Press News* and started looking for another job, much to my new colleagues' amusement.

Then something totally unexpected happened. For the first time in three and a half years in journalism, I found myself having fun.

On my first weekend, in Darlington, which I expected to be bleakly solitary, my fellow Despatch reporter, David Watts, invited me to a dance on Sedgefield racecourse to hear a band named the Truth that his friend, Guy Simpson, was helping to publicise. I met a nice girl called Gail and when Guy introduced the Truth as 'the North-East's greatest band after the Animals', I cheered them to the rafters and danced with Gail to their almost equally good version of *We Gotta Get Out of This Place*, singing along and waving my arms.

Dave Watts and I had come from Darlington in Guy's car and after the dance he went far out of his way to drop Gail home, then he and Dave waited uncomplainingly while I said goodnight to her in the darkened front porch of her house.

My first two major jobs for the *Despatch*, in their different ways, were great fun. Each of them took me to the cathedral city of Durham, twenty miles north of Darlington, which the paper would sometimes stretch a point and include in its area.

The first was to describe the annual Miners' Gala (pronounced 'Gaila') when coalminers from the pits that still flourished all over County Durham marched through the hilly streets with the ornate banners of their 'Lodges' and the pavements became a rolling, clinking carpet of empty Newcastle Brown Ale bottles. The rally that followed provided my first real-life sight of the Labour Prime

Minister, Harold Wilson, then only a year in power, whose address in that much-parodied nasal accent seemed less political speech than stand-up comedy routine.

The second, at Durham's Calouste Gulbenkian Museum, was to witness the unwrapping of an Egyptian mummy which X-Rays had shown to have spent 2,000 years in its casket with an artificial forearm, one of the first-ever prosthetics. I had a front row seat at the 'operation'; as its resiny bandages were carefully peeled away, the mummy's ribcage looked like a chicken after all the best bits had been eaten. Not much else was happening in the *Northern Despatch's* world on either day and both of my purely descriptive and, frankly, rather rambling pieces, to my amazement, ran as front-page splashes.

My Newsroom colleagues showed me as never before the home that journalism afforded to eccentrics and misfits. Wiry, hyperactive Mick Stacey had until recently been a schoolteacher; frizzy-haired, MG-driving Bill Minns soon switched to selling antiques; chain-smoking, coughing Waldo Skipsey passed around nude photographs of his surprisingly pretty young wife; brooding John Butler, who always wore two jackets on top of two jumpers – the legacy of being shipwrecked in the Atlantic during the War – could speak six languages including Serbo-Croat.

The chief sub-editor, Cyril Fawcett, was a small, shock-haired man in a permanent state of despair, usually attributable to the chief reporter, Dick Tarelli, who, despite his surname, was County Durham born and bred. Tarelli's consuming preoccupation was the daily gossip column, Under The Town Clock, to which we reporters were expected to supply paragraphs; almost every morning began with his anguished cry of 'There's noah *Clock*!'

Promptly at noon, the critical time for an evening paper, he disappeared to the bar at Darlington Conservative Club, not returning until well after three. The fresh scent of beer on his breath reminded me of my father, as did his raging ineffectuality.

Tarelli's only real power point was vetting our expenses claims, which he did like a boozy Ebenezer Scrooge dealing with multiple Bob Cratchits. Once when I charged three old pennies for a bus fare, he crossed it out with a flourish. 'If it was only a threepenny fare,' he said, 'you should've walked.'

In off-duty hours, I went around with the brawny but soft-spoken

Dave Watts and Guy Simpson, who had a Beatle fringe and slightly resembled the hot young Liverpudlian comedian Jimmy Tarbuck. Guy worked in the Darlington office of the *Middlesborough Evening Gazette*, so strictly speaking was 'the opposition.' However, he'd started as a copy boy on the *Despatch* and knew all its secrets (for instance, that a former, cricket-mad editor had appointed Dick Tarelli chief reporter solely because of Tarelli's prowess as a fast bowler.)

It was a huge relief to have found kindred spirits with whom to discuss the Beatles' second film, *Help!*, Paul McCartney's debut as a solo vocalist on its soundtrack album with *Yesterday*, and how Tom Jones could have been so misguided as to follow *It's Not Unusual* with that embarrassingly coy *What's New Pussycat?* Neither Dave nor Guy seemed to think me the weirdo and misfit I'd felt in Huntingdon and Cambridge, nor bear me any ill-will for getting bylines - which, anyway, were freely distributed on the *Despatch*. I realised that what I'd always heard was true: people in the North really were nicer than in the South.

Wherever we were, the talk soon turned to the man who had put the *Northern Echo* and Darlington on the map. Although neither Dave nor Guy worked with him, they were always full of 'Harry' Evans's doings, his latest appearance on *What The Papers Say* or the crusades he regularly launched with the *Echo*. Most of them concerned environmental abuses for which the region's huge industrial interests had never been challenged before, and had eye-catching tag-lines like 'Let's Speak Out For Clean Air' or 'Lorry Menace'.

But the North-East alone couldn't contain his crusading spirit. The *Echo* was currently seeking a posthumous pardon for Timothy Evans, who had been hanged for the murder of his wife and baby daughter in 1950, when they'd actually been victims of the serial killer John Reginald Halliday Christie. Harry's 'Man On Our Conscience' campaign had already prompted questions in Parliament and reinvigorated the spasmodic national debate about capital punishment.

To begin with, I saw him only in the early evening when the *Echo* took over the *Despatch's* reporters' room and sub-editors' table. Then, it seemed, the squalid, sleepy little domain Dick Tarelli ruled over by day expanded to twice its size and become dramatically low-lit and expectant like a theatre with the curtain about to rise.

The desk-bound presenter of *What The Papers Say* in real life wore no glasses and was in perpetual, frenetic motion, a slight figure with an unexpected suntan, in a dark blue suit that set him far apart from his shirtsleeved, mostly older subordinates. If his office door were left open, he might be visible hurtling around the room like a silent squash ball, for he had a chair fitted with high-speed castors that allowed him to move from telephone to bookshelves to editorial conference with the minimum delay.

I had found a nice bedsit in leafy Coniscliffe Road, at the top of a steep iron staircase, overlooking a small public park. But it was basically just a place to sleep. Most evenings would find me with Dave and Guy at Club La Bamba, the ritzier of Darlington's two clubs, where top music acts like Georgie Fame and the Migil Five regularly appeared and reporters didn't have to be members. The rule was that men had to wear 'a light-coloured shirt' which meant the grubbiest white drip-dry would get you in but the most expensive charcoal grey silk from Turnbull & Asser wouldn't.

As the *Despatch's* drama critic, I had decided that Darlington's rather listless Civic Theatre and local amateur dramatics weren't nearly enough for me and, with Arnold Hadwin's ready agreement, made my circulation area almost as wide as the *Echo's*. The furthest I went was Sunderland, 27 miles away, to review a production of Shakespeare's *Coriolanus*. Dave Watts came with me; he edited the paper's motoring page, so we made the journey in a giant BMW he was road testing.

The *Despatch* had a weekly tabloid-sized insert called Teenage Special, despite a continuing dearth of evidence that any teenager ever looked at it. In its employ, I saw the Rolling Stones perform at the ABC cinema, Stockton, just before the storm broke over their 'obscene' new single, *Satisfaction*. Afterwards, I interviewed Mick Jagger on a chilly back staircase; he wore a white fisherman's-knit sweater and swigged from a Pepsi-Cola bottle with elaborate tilts, the quintessence of rebellion.

From all I had read about the Stones, I expected snarling Neanderthals, but the other four were perfectly polite, each in turn signing the same page of my notebook for my sister, Tracey. Then Charlie Watts drew a border around the signatures and added 'the Rolling Stones' in case anybody didn't realise who they were.

On top of all that, plus the quotidian duties of magistrates' courts, inquests, and 'Clock Notes', I wrote a weekly column of personal opinion called As I Please (cribbed from the one George Orwell did for Tribune magazine in the 1940s) and reviewed films, books and cabaret. I wrote about anything that caught my fancy, from the giant Victorian tea-caddies I saw in an old-fashioned grocer's to the filled rolls – known in the North as 'butties' – at our favourite pub, thereby scoring an indefinite free supply from its grateful landlord.

The trouble was that I wanted to be read, not just in Darlington and its immediate environs but in Billingham and Northallerton and Bishop Auckland and Chester-le-Street and Alnwick and Whitley Bay, southward as far as York and northward almost to the Scottish borders. I didn't want to be on the *Northern Despatch* but the *Northern Echo*.

I took to hanging around the office during its *Echo* hours, just to see and feel that magical Harry Evans effect. One evening, I was walking there from my bedsit and had just reached the grocers with the outsize tea-caddies when a big Ford Consul drew up beside me, a window was wound down and a voice called 'I take it we're going to the same place. Hop in.'

Behind the wheel sat Harry. I was amazed that he recognised the gawper in the passage outside his office and that such a celebrity could be so informal.

'Come on,' he repeated. 'Hop in'. It was only a further five minutes to the office and it wasn't until the Consul made a wide turning-circle into his parking-space that I managed to volunteer something:

'Very good lock this car's got.'

Echo journalists normally held themselves aloof from *Despatch* ones. But later that evening, the Darlington staff's heavily-freckled star reporter, Mike Corner, reminisced to me about Harry's inspirational leadership during the Arctic winter of 1963 when the North had suffered far worse than the South - worse even than Gerald Davison's Brussels sprouts - and how his *Echo* rescue teams had fought their way to snowed-in Durham pit villages with supplies of sandwiches and hot coffee.

'I'd go through Hell for him,' said Corner, a suspicion of tears shining under freckled eyelids. 'So would everyone on this paper. We'd all go through Hell for him.'

Since the *Echo* also carried national news, being around it at night kept me in touch with events in London. There was something illicit, almost indecent, about reading tomorrow morning's stories on smudgy galley proofs: about the Wilson government's efforts to stop our former Southern Africa territory of Rhodesia from unilaterally declaring independence, or the BBC's launch of a second television channel, BBC Two, which its minuscule audience were having to watch as if through a heavy blizzard.

Down in London, too, major changes were taking place in my own profession, albeit at the stratospheric level from which, I accepted, my degree-less state must forever exclude me.

The Sunday Times's colour magazine, once derided as 'Thomson's Folly', had turned into a huge success, bulging with advertisements for products illustrating how far Britain had come from its postwar austerity – After Eight wafer-thin mints, White Horse whisky, Scandinavian hi-fi units, fluffy white Kosset carpets – and featuring cookery recipes using quantities of butter and double cream which, a few years earlier, would have been considered downright criminal.

It was generally referred to as a colour 'supplement' but, in truth, seemed more like a stand-alone magazine of a kind never seen in Britain before - except, very slightly, in *Town*. Its photographic essays by potent new names like David Bailey and Terence Donovan (not to mention the Queen's brother-in-law, Lord Snowdon) competed with legendary American titles like Life and Look; its fashion-coverage made *Vogue* or *Harper's Bazaar* seem dull and old-fashioned by comparison.

Now there were fresh jibes about colour-supplement living, meaning one could turn its pages without a beat from hedonistic images of Jaguar cars and Courvoisier brandy to heartbreaking ones of child victims in the Vietnam War. Nonetheless, two other former 'heavy' broadsheets, the *Observer* and *Daily Telegraph*, had started magazines of their own, albeit on a less opulent scale. And the lately-ennobled Lord Thomson of Fleet could consider his creation, as he'd famously said of his television interests, 'a licence to print money.'

One weekend in my pleasant Darlington bedsit, I read something in the *Sunday Times Magazine* that altered my whole conception of journalism and writing.

It was an interview with P.J. Proby, an American singer transplanted to Britain who wore his hair in an 18th century pigtail and whose trousers regularly split up the crotch in mid-performance, possibly having been designed to do so, to the frenzied delight of his (very) young female followers. The byline was Francis Wyndham, of whom I'd never heard. The colour portrait by David Bailey of Proby in a baby blue jumpsuit took up most of the opening double-page spread.

Rather than obeying the ironbound journalistic formula 'who, what, where, when', it had the narrative style and structure of a short story. The tone was like none I'd ever seen applied to pop music, utterly deadpan and objective, indeed consisting mainly of quotes in which the singer spoke, and misspoke, for himself. It was both satiric and empathetic; you understood that here was a ridiculous narcissist taking pop fakery to a new level, and slightly creepy withal, yet you still rather warmed to him.

Some lines were incomprehensible to me, for instance the phrase 'ineffably camp' applied to Proby's stage act and an observation that in profile he had 'a fleeting look of Mary McCarthy'. But the overall effect was revelatory; I knew I could do it that way too, if I tried, and from then on dreamed of a byline over such a piece in the *Sunday Times Magazine* even though I knew very well it could never happen.

Back on my humble level. the first step to getting onto the *Northern Echo* was getting *into* the *Northern Echo*. Since I had no idea whether Harry Evans had noticed any of the stuff I was turning out in such quantity for the *Despatch*, I would have to write something on spec' for the *Echo*, aimed at catching his eye.

This meant ingratiating myself with the features editor whose name, I learned from Dave Watts, was David Spark. However, to my surprise, no such individual was to be found on the power corridor leading to Harry's office.

Then one day, Dave pointed out a tall, thin, brown and seamlessly bald man passing the reporters' room's glass partition in the strangest manner: he'd take two or three loping steps, give a really long, high skip, take a couple more steps then do it again – three skips even on that short stretch. 'You were wanting Spark,' Dave said. 'Well, there he goes.'

Tracking him to a remote office in the lower part of the building, I found someone very unlike the almost demented euphoria of his walk. David Spark was agonisingly shy, only with the greatest reluctance admitting to his role as features editor with special responsibility for the leader page where Harry Evans editorials currently demanded justice for Timothy Evans.

My offer to write some short humorous pieces with my own

cartoon illustrations seemed to generate no spark of enthusiasm, but I left with an impression that he'd said yes.

I took each piece to him as I wrote and drew it. Spark glanced through them without comment except to say that one didn't work and I should pick another subject. In the end, there were five. Had he any idea when he might use them, I asked. No, he hadn't.

I heard nothing subsequently and concluded that the pieces and drawings had been nowhere near good enough for Harry Evans's *Northern Echo*. I'd already come further in journalism than anyone without a degree could expect, and ought to be grateful for that. Whenever David Spark's hairless silhouette went high-skipping past the reporters' room, I looked the other way in embarrassment.

One morning, Dave Watts slapped a copy of that morning's *Echo* down in front of me, saying, 'Get a load of this.' The contents-panel announced that today Philip Norman would be starting 'a new foot-of-the-page column'. I turned to the leader page and the piece all along the bottom - known as the basement - was headed *Philip Norman Looks At Life – 1*.

It was the one about buying my first pair of elastic-sided Chelsea boots with a schoolfriend named Gerald Littler. The shop didn't have them in my size, but I wanted them so much that, insanely, I settled for a size smaller. My struggle to get the left boot onto my foot involved not only Gerald but a helpful salesman wielding a small white shoehorn. At one point, I stuck it behind my heel and gave a heave, and it snapped like a wishbone. It turned out to be ivory, a cherished possession for 25 years.

The next time I passed Harry's office, the door suddenly opened and he pulled me inside almost as if abducting me. Then - as always in the future – I was strangely bashful about looking directly at him. I registered only eyes with unusually thick lashes and the precise northern diction that was actually posh Mancunian

'That piece about the shoehorn,' he said, 'is *Byzantinely* funny.'

It was praise almost too rarified to take in. I vaguely pictured my little adventure with the Chelsea boot being infiltrated by jewelled turbans and veiled dancing girls.

'I loved the line about the manager being like a senior wrangler in shoe sales,' he went on. (I'd remembered the term from Cambridge University because it sounded so like the Wild West.) 'And I want more of your cartoons. You've got a lovely line.'

I didn't just glow; I was positively radioactive. No one in newspapers – in my whole life – had ever said things like that to me.

Now, suddenly, the only childhood ambition I'd ever had came true; I was a proper cartoonist, quite legitimately waiting around the *Echo* every evening to find inspiration in the stories going to press. Harry himself would often suggest a topic or tone down a caption he thought went a little too far. And the next morning, there it would be on the front page.

Meanwhile, *Philip Norman Looks at Life* was running every week on the *Echo's* leader page in addition to all my work for the *Despatch*. Harry continued lavish in his praise of my 'Byzantine' humour, but had some criticisms, too, although the pieces always appeared without interference.

'You can be a bit obscure sometimes, you know,' he told me after reading number 4, headed 'Crescendo for the Lead Guitarist'. 'For instance, what's this word here?'

'It's "Yicch," I said. 'An expression of disgust.'

'You see ... that's just what I mean. Sometimes the champagne turns into cooking sherry. From you, I want only the champagne.'

One night, after approving a cartoon about the further delay to the building of the Durham Motorway, he casually took my breath away on a still grander scale. 'Stan Hurwitz is leaving John North. I've been thinking you might be just the person to take over from him.'

John North was the *Echo's* pseudonymous gossip-columnist, but one very different from 'Jack Darneton', the alleged signatory of the *Despatch's* Under the Town Clock. Rather than Darneton's niggardly quarter-page, John North occupied almost the whole of the one opposite the *Echo's* leader page and, instead of Darneton's scrappy group-written paras, it dealt with a single subject each day in an idiosyncratic first-person singular. The anonymity imposed on its author was more than compensated by its prestige and influence and freewill.

The prospect was dazzling: to be rescued from magistrates' courts and council committees and Dick Tarelli and write just one piece a day largely of my own choosing, even be part of Harry's morning editorial conference. Then he seemed to back-pedal a little. 'I'm not quite sure yet I want you to do it. There are a few other hats in the ring.'

Two nights later, he called me to tell me he'd decided to give John North to a man named Bill Cain he was bringing in from outside. 'Bill's really good,' he said, flatteringly suggesting he felt a need to justify his choice. 'I can show you his cuttings if you like.'

Just the same, I was to move from the *Despatch* to the *Echo*, his prerogative as editor-in-chief of both. A vacancy had also come up in its Newcastle office and it was mine for the asking.

'In Newcastle, you'll be with Tom Little, who's our music critic, and Nick Scurr, our second-string covering Newcastle United,' he told me. 'Tom can be a bit of a tartar at times, but you'll love Nick. Everyone does.'

I had my leaving party at the King's Head hotel. Arnold Hadwin very generously came along and, despite my shameful lack of loyalty, wished me the best of luck. All evening, I kept hearing the same about my two colleagues-to-be: that Tom Little could be a bugger ('could be', of course, understood to mean 'was') but I was sure to love dear old Nick Scurr.

Several of the *Echo's* branch offices were in larger. more important places than sleepy little Darlington, but nowhere was this disparity greater than in the one for which I was bound. Newcastle was the regional capital with its historic seaport and shipbuilding industries and, not least, the size and diversity of its media. Ranged against the *Northern Echo's* three-person staff were an indigenous morning, evening and Sunday (all owned by the acquisitive Lord Thomson), plus correspondents for every national, the Press Association news agency, innumerable freelances, a major outpost of the BBC and the headquarters of the new Tyne-Tees commercial TV company

As I drove into the city over its elegant Tyne Bridge and saw the other bridges up- and down-river and the panorama of new skyscrapers and giant construction cranes, I already felt totally overwhelmed.

The *Northern Echo's* office was in Eldon Square, a little pocket of Georgian elegance just around the corner from Grey's Monument. There I joined the supposedly impossible Tom Little and supposedly adorable Nick Scurr and found that in my case the opposite was true. Little, a rubicund, impatient man in his late 50s, initially lived up to his reputation, piling ridiculous amounts of work onto me to see how much I could take. But once that proved satisfactory, he treated me almost like a son. And the slightly younger Scurr, lean, good-looking and genial, couldn't stand me.

Here at the epicentre of the vast Tyneside conurbation, life proved surprisingly relaxed. The reporting of Newcastle's teeming commercial, jurisprudential and local governmental life we mostly left to Lord Thomson's *Morning Journal*, *Evening Chronicle* and *Sunday Sun*, simply sending the *Echo* rewrites of their major stories.

Tom Little occupied himself with his classical music concerts and reviews and a Friday column called A View From Tyneside, and Scurr with covering Newcastle United. Between them they made a substantial freelance income from 'linage': phoning stories to the nationals and Northern Stock Exchange prices to the Exchange Telegraph service, making use of my copy without asking me, let alone cutting me in. That was fine since it left all the 'specials', as Little called feature pieces, to me. Bylines therefore abounded.

I soon came to love 'N'cassel' for a warm, enveloping individuality that - I realise now – answered my yearning for security and to belong somewhere. I loved the cobbled hills with names like Bigg Market, Cloth Market and Groat Market that plunged to the Tyne; the sheer and seemingly endless flight of steps called Dog Leap Stairs; the Long Bar that was the world's longest; the Carricks teashops where I almost lived on Welsh rarebits with poached eggs; even the yellow Atlantean double-decker buses with their flat fronts and absence of interior steps.

Not quite everything was wonderful: my new bedsit in Jesmond, the student area, had a grimness reminiscent of living with Grandma Noman – no washbasin, just a pail of water kept under a wooden 'washing-stand' that could have come from Miss Ball.

But in the evenings, I was always out, reviewing plays at the Theatre Royal or the Flora Robson Playhouse or meeting up with Dave Watts and Guy Simpson to catch the latest big music name at the most famous of all the North East's clubs, La Dolce Vita. Last thing, I'd go to the office to put in a call to the central police station exemplifying how things were in 1965, even in an avowedly 'tough' city like Newcastle. Nine out of ten times when I asked the duty sergeant if anything was happening, he replied in that curiously soothing Geordie accent, 'Noah, it's been very quiet.'

Although Harry Evans was now thirty miles away, I felt his eye always on me. A stream of memos, known on the paper as 'Harry Herograms', reassured me I was giving him champagne, not cooking sherry: 'I thought your piece on Jack de Manio was excellent this morning....' 'Very witty essay on the orangutang paying the charity cheque into the Yorkshire Bank'... 'I must say you are settling down very well in Newcastle and justifying the high hopes I had for you ...' His scrawled italic *HE* seemed to be in flight, as if fitted with the same high-speed castors as his office chair.

My self-confidence so increased that I began to think of myself as his favourite on the *Echo's* staff, despite knowing from Dave Watts that others were frequent recipients of his praise, like the brilliant chief sub, Frank Peters, and the scoop-getting Luke Casey in the Stockton office.

Peppery Tom Little might have been expected to resent an editor so much younger than himself, but the very opposite was the case. 'He gives young kids like you their heads and gets tremendous results out of them. He's like a great orchestral conductor ... he makes people play better than they really can. And most importantly, he'll always back his staff to the hilt.'

I learned this for myself after reviewing a performance of *Oklahoma* by the Newcastle and District Amateur Dramatic Society who were big enough to hire the Theatre Royal for their productions. Doubtless to help meet the large overhead, 'souvenir' programmes cost a thumping half a crown (15p), and the audience chattered distractingly throughout, both of which phenomena I sharply noted.

The society's 'Honorary Business Manager' wrote a letter of complaint to Harry, who sent me a carbon copy of his reply: 'I see nothing wrong in our critic expressing the view that your programmes were too expensive nor in his criticism of a bad-mannered audience.' Freckly Mike Corner had spoken truth: 'You'd go through Hell for him.'

During my time in Newcastle, there were two big national stories. Harold Wilson's government failed to stop Rhodesia's Unilateral Declaration of Independence (UDI). And Kenneth Tynan, no longer my hero as a drama critic but Literary Manager of the new National Theatre, became the first person on British television to break the taboo of a word that had existed and been widely used since Chaucer's era or before. He did it in a purely abstract way, remarking that very few people these days would be surprised to hear the word 'fuck'. The resulting uproar, including four separate motions of condemnation in the House of Commons, showed how wrong he was.

In December 1965, the Beatles passed through Newcastle on what would be their last ever British tour and Dave Watts and I managed to talk our way into their presence backstage at the City Hall. Newly created MBEs by the Queen and fresh from their triumph at New York's Shea Stadium, they might reasonably have ignored two such nonentities. But John and Ringo talked to us as if we were their oldest friends and Paul threw me his violin bass - which, Heaven be praised, I caught – to prove how lightweight it was.

That same week, I was at the Royal Station Hotel interviewing the famous clairvoyant Maurice Woodruffe in a group including half a dozen of 'the enemy' from the three Thomson papers. The Newcastle Journal man's request for a demonstration of Woodruffe's powers was curtly refused. But when he saw me, without even asking my name, he said 'You... listen! You're going to write a book and a play and I want you to get on with it.'

I'd never had the least thought of doing either thing and I turned the implausible concept over in my mind for days afterwards. The excitement receded a little when I read a story about Woodruffe which for once didn't attest to his uncanny second sight.

The paper in which his prophesies appeared, the *Daily Sketch*, had been taken over by the *Daily Mail* and he'd written to his new editor asking what his future was going to be under the new setup.

Early in 1966 came catastrophe: it was announced that Harry Evans was leaving the *Echo* to join the *Sunday Times* in London.

There had long been talk of how many nationals wanted him, particularly the *Manchester Guardian*, the august daily of his hometown, recently made country-wide and renamed *The Guardian*. But finally, an irresistible offer had come from Lord Thomson's hugely glamorous and innovative creation, to be 'chief assistant' to its editor, Denis Hamilton.

To me, it seemed a stroke of bad luck on a par with those which had always dogged my father. I'd only just found the first person ever to make me think anything of myself; now I was to lose him.

It was an equally heavy blow for everyone on the paper he'd led with such distinction and dash for the past four years. Some sympathy was even felt for the *Echo's* unpopular management in the task of filling his superpowered shoes. They didn't even try, picking someone already on the staff, oddly with the same surname but no other resemblance to him. It was to be the industrial editor, Don Evans, whom in Darlington I'd never met or even seen.

I listened despondently as Tom Little told Nick Scurr the gossip about what awaited Harry at the *Sunday Times*. 'Apparently his first job is going to be reorganising the sports pages. But that "chief assistant to the Editor" is a giveaway. Mark my words, he'll be taking over the reins from Denis Hamilton before you know it.'

For a dizzying moment, I'd thought that, once established at the *Sunday Times*, he might call me down to join him, but then Little added: 'He's promised to give Don Evans a chance by not starting to poach *Echo* people.'

The North East gave him a huge send-off, with a fulsome tribute in every rival paper and interviews on both BBC regional and Tyne-Tees Television. In each of them, saying how much the region had come to mean to him, he brushed a tear from the corner of one eye.

After his departure, it was as if all the air had been let out of life. Don Evans turned out to be a nice man and an indulgent editor who carried on using my cartoons and let me start a pop column called Disc and That. But no one now was making me play better than I really could.

About three weeks later, a letter for me arrived at the office; a creamy envelope with **THE SUNDAY TIMES** embossed on the flap. As I unfolded the sheet of crested paper, I saw it didn't come from Fleet Street but 'Thomson House, 200 Gray's Inn Road, London WC1', and pictured cutting-edge journalism being practised among Dickensian cloisters and bewigged barristers.

The urgent italic signature *HE* had been replaced by an equally urgent *Harry,* but it was only a request for a story about overworked young hospital doctors I'd had in the *Echo* that he evidently needed for some kind of background research.

I sent off the cutting by return but heard nothing further from him.

It was Dave Watts who told me about the announcement in an edition of the *Sunday Times Magazine* I had somehow missed: that it was to hold a series of talent competitions, for young writers, photographers, cartoonists and fashion designers. Entrants must be under 23 on March 31, 1966. My 23rd birthday was on April 13.

The details of each competition appeared separately Sunday by Sunday accompanied by an entry form with big black stars around it and I had to wait impatiently for two weeks to discover what entrants to the writers' one were required to write about.

It seemed more journalistic than literary: 'a profile of anyone living', to a maximum length of 2,000 words. The judges would be Godfrey Smith, the editor of the *Magazine*, J.W. Lambert, the literary editor of the newspaper, and the novelist Andrew Sinclair. The winner would be named Young Writer of the Year and receive a prize of £250 and a foreign assignment for the *Magazine*.

There were daunting aspects to entering, aside from the utter impossibility of winning in a world so full of people my age with Oxford or Cambridge degrees. This was the first time I'd seen the word 'profile' apply to a piece of writing, and 2,000 words were an unknown quantity to a newspaper reporter accustomed to measuring material in inches who'd never written anything longer than about 800 words. But the 'anyone living' as a subject was easy.

That same afternoon, while half-watching an old gangster film on television, I began scribbling what I hoped could be termed a profile of Grandma Norman using everything she'd told me about herself over the years, mostly while I was lying beside her in the half-tester brass bed with seven foot headposts, for so long the safest place I knew.

I could hear the burbly West Country voice that so often broke into chuckles, telling me about her girlhood in Somerset when her father used to give her her own little glass of every drink served to him; about her marriage to the 'master mariner' William Norman when she was 18 and he was 40 and his death by German torpedo in the Irish Sea in the last year of the Great War; about their last outing together to buy him the Burberry raincoat she still wore; about the terrible migraines she suffered in those years – which she pronounced 'm'grains' like some healthful breakfast cereal or obscure Scottish clan – when 'I was in such pain that I wouldn't have cared if the whole of the German Army in their spiky hats had marched past the end of my bed with *fixed bayonets*.'

I remembered all about her emigration to America as a young widow with four children; (two from Grandpa Norman's first marriage as well as Clive and Uncle Phil); about their Atlantic crossing on a liner that at breakfast gave you 'as many prunes as you could eat for 10 cents'; about living with her sister, Gwen, in Seattle a city so hilly that the Model T Fords, known as Tin Lizzies, could only get up them in reverse; about her time in Chelsea's artists colony during the

Twenties, that era I loved so much; about the General Strike when Oxford and Cambridge students, having all the fun even then, came up to London to drive the buses and took you anywhere you wanted for sixpence; about working as a traveller for the Waverley Book Company so as to be able to send Phil and Clive to private school, and the several men who'd wanted to marry her (including a painter from New Zealand whose grandmother had been 'a cannibal'); all rejected 'because I wasn't having anyone ordering my boys around', despite the power of good it might have done them both.

On from there, through the grey wall of the War into the becalmed 1950s, joining my father on the Isle of Wight, selling 16 tons of rock a year from the Kiosk, filling the early morning Esplanade with the smell of fried bread, drinking Guinness and gin in bed at Five Castle Street, eventually relocating to the little shop in Lambourn, and turning it into a Kiosk without rock, calling everyone along the way 'love' and 'my duck' and never regarding her two 'boys' as other than perfect (whatever the evidence to the contrary), it all poured onto the page with barely a pause while Humphrey Bogart and Edward G. Robinson, I think it was, shot machine guns at each other on the black-and-white screen.

In studying the *Magazine*, I'd noticed how many of its articles, and picture-captions too, had an urgent, staccato quality thanks to the use of semicolons rather than full stops. I tried to give my Grandma Norman piece that same kind of rhythm, spraying semicolons around with the abandon of the gangsters' tommy-guns.

I typed a fair copy on special white bond paper and counted and re-counted it neurotically to make sure I hadn't gone over 2,000 words. I showed it only to Dave Watts, who said he liked it, and to Tom Little, who didn't seem to all that much. 'But do we understand what makes the old lady tick?' he asked, filling me with such doubt that I almost didn't send it in. But at the Post Office, as I slipped the yellow 'Recorded Delivery' receipt into my wallet, it felt somehow momentous.

I entered the Cartoonists Contest, too, for which no subject was specified, but only because Dave insisted I should. The first Gerald Scarfe cartoons had just started to appear – spiky caricatures of a venom unknown since Gillray and Rowlandson in the 18th century. Lord Snowdon, Princess Margaret's photographer husband, for instance, was depicted as a leering leprechaun with a telephoto lens like a giant phallus rearing from his crotch and a badge saying, 'By Royal Appointment'. My thumbnail drawings in the *Echo* seemed the feeblest of doodles by comparison.

Early in May, I received a mysterious postcard with a view of London's Soho Square and handwriting so terrible, I could decipher only odd phrases: 'I am glad we preferred literature to journalism ...You have a funny, quirky eye and it is a novelist's one ... I am already an admirer of your style...' It was signed, so I thought, 'Arden Sinclair'. I'd forgotten that one of the Writers Contest judges was a novelist named Andrew Sinclair.

Then I dreamed I'd won it, which seemed a sure sign that I hadn't.

Three days later, a second letter arrived with **THE SUNDAY TIMES** on its creamy envelope, this one signed 'Godfrey Smith, Magazine editor'.

*   *   *

5

It's a lovely life down here

The feeling of receiving such news was so close to pure terror that I found all kinds of excuses to delay phoning his colleague, Mrs Susan Raven, so they could find out something about me before making the announcement.

Even when I'd flagellated myself for stupidity half a dozen times and a line came free at the *Northern Echo* office, allowing Anita to connect me with the *Sunday Times's* number, TERMINUS 1234, its very ring – more like an urgent musical note - almost made me hang up in panic.

Mrs Susan Raven had the kind of clipped upper-class voice I remembered from many a bossy vicar's wife when I was on the *Hunts Post*. However, there was nothing of those ecclesiastical Gorgons in the way she thanked me for getting in touch and congratulated me on winning the competition.

'I thought the piece you wrote was an absolute hoot,' she said. 'So-o funny about your granny drinking the gin in bed.'

In the first interview I'd ever given rather than inflicted, I explained that I came from Newcastle but had grown up on the Isle of Wight, that I'd written my winning entry while watching an old gangster film on television and that I'd also entered for the Cartoonists Contest. To me, it sounded horribly lame, but she seemed to be noting everything down, with punctuating murmurs of 'Fine... fine...'

'And have you decided what to do with your £250 prize?' she asked.

'I thought I might buy a new suit,' was all I could manage.

'Fine ... *fine*,' she said fortissimo, as if opening a church bazaar or disciplining a delinquent choirboy. 'We'll be running your piece in the Magazine. ... that's what we hope, anyway. And Godfrey, our editor, would very much like to meet you.'

I didn't say I was sorry, but I was far too busy at present, and an appointment was made for the afternoon of Thursday the following week.

'Fine … *fine*. And we'll be happy to pay your train fare. First-class of course.' Then a form of goodbye I'd never heard before: 'By-*yee*!'

A couple of day later, I had a phone call from someone who introduced himself as Chris, followed by a surname he had to repeat three times: 'Angeloglou… *Angeloglou* … A.N.G.E.L.O.G.L.O.U.'

'I'm the picture editor at the *Sunday Times Mag*,' he eventually went on to explain. 'Part of your competition prize is a foreign assignment for us and we've been thinking it might be fun to pair you up with the winner of the Photography Contest. Is there anywhere in the world you're dying to go?'

I said there wasn't anywhere in particular, although the real answer was 'everywhere.'

'Oh, well, leave it with us to have a think about,' said Chris whatever his name was.

Grays Inn Road was only 15 minutes by taxi from King's Cross, where the trains from Newcastle came in. At that end, there were no Dickensian cloisters or bewigged barristers, just small hotels, often with Welsh names, dingy-looking pubs and small blocks of balconied 1930s flats.

After about half a mile, on a slightly downhill stretch and on a slight curve number 200, or Thomson House, finally came into view. It was worth waiting for: six floors of slanted windows, each one atop a panel of shiny copper. Along the pavement outside, half the black cab population of London seemed to be arriving or departing or waiting with their meters running.

You entered through double glass doors and over a black mat as thick as a carpet with the THE SUNDAY TIMES across it in white. The spacious front lobby was lined on both sides by squashy black leather sofas with stainless steel frames. On a dais to the right, two uniformed commissionaires stood behind a telephone-littered desk, below a wall of hugely blown-up black-and-white photographs from recent issues of the paper. One of these, showing a group of grimy-faced street children somewhere foreign, was credited to 'Snowdon'. Even in Newcastle it had been big news when the Queen's brother-in-law announced that his work for the *Sunday Times* would democratically dispense with the 'Lord'.

After a minimal wait on one of the black leather sofas, Mrs

Susan Raven arrived to collect me. The vicar's wife of our phone conversation turned out to be small and trim, with black hair bobbed in the new Mary Quant style, wearing grey wool dress breaking just on the knee and black patent high heels.

Up a short flight of steps was a bank of lifts with pink doors. We got out at the fourth floor and Mrs Raven ushered me into the presence of Godfrey Smith. His Christian name and the elegant italic signature on his letter, had suggested someone tall and willowy, but he was an enormously fat man with straggly greying hair, sideburns like earmuffs and the face of an overfed cherub on a Renaissance ceiling.

'Aha!' he said. 'Our prizewinner! This is the very greatest of pleasures!' His voice, although booming, was precise and mellifluous; like his signature, it seemed to belong to a slimmer man.

His office was quite small and narrow, but luxuriously red-carpeted. What struck me immediately was its lack of any visible editorial activity. The desk at its far end was bare, the black worktop that extended its whole length equally virginal but for a set of *Sunday Times Magazine* back-issues in navy blue binders, The only sign that anything ever happened here was the unusual number of low-slung armless black leather chairs.

'Now,' Godfrey Smith said, 'first things first. Can I offer you the tiniest tincture of vino?' He opened a small refrigerator below the worktop, something I'd never seen in an editor's office. 'Here's a very respectable Chablis. Or perhaps you'd prefer Dopf Perle d'Alsace, which combines the virtues of hock and Moselle?'

'Chablis, please.' In truth, I would happily have drunk lighter fuel.

He poured about half the bottle into a glass for me, the other half into one for himself and raised it. 'Your very good health, dear boy – and once again, many congratulations.'

While I savoured the huge novelty of drinking wine in mid-afternoon, he told me about the Writers Contest's three runners-up. 'One was a Cambridge student, writing about Horace Bachelor - you know, the football pools forecaster.' (So, I'd beaten a *Cambridge student*!) 'It was extremely cleverly done, all in Bachelor's own words that we can drop straight into type. Another was a 16-year-old girl, writing about her father. She's absolutely wild … clothes from charity shops … huge holes in her tights…'

The memory caused an almighty guffaw, or rather succession of them, which convulsed his whole ample frame, put the buttons down the bulging front of his yellow shirt under still greater strain and became a drawn-out coughing fit that turned the jumbo cherub face an almost worrying shade of scarlet.

Recovering himself at last, he took a draught of wine and looked at me with a smile. 'Well, now – what are your plans?'

I knew what he meant and replied without hesitation. 'I want to work for the *Sunday Times*.'

He was clearly expecting this; in fact, the matter had been settled already thanks to a higher power than a cartload of Oxbridge degrees.

'Harry Evans has told us what a bright lad you are, and I've been given carte-blanche by our editor-in-chief, C.D. Hamilton, to take you on.'

I could only sit there, staring into my glass, wondering when I was going to wake up.

'As a rule, we don't employ staff writers on the *Magazine*,' he went on. 'We largely rely on freelancers. But perhaps you could spend, say, six months with us and then go onto the paper ...another six months with the Newsroom, another six with Insight and so on until you find your niche.'

He said I must also meet his features editor, Peter Crookston, and while this 'really super bloke' was being sent for, I talked about the inspirational figure Harry had been on the *Northern Echo* and how bereft the whole North-East had been since his departure.

'Well, he's certainly making his mark at Thomson House,' Godfrey Smith said. 'And he is very charmingly direct. I remember that at the meeting where he outlined his plans for the new sports pages, he began by saying "I could be wrong about all of this."' How typically Harry, I thought – deaf to the faintness of the praise - and how much they must already think of him here.

Peter Crookston came in without knocking and sat down in the low leather chair just inside the door. He was about thirty and strikingly handsome, a little like Brian Poole, the leader of the Tremeloes, but my whole attention focused on his trousers, an outsize check until lately worn only by circus clowns and Rupert Bear. When we were introduced, he said 'Congra'ulations' with what seemed a faint Tyneside accent

'So what I'd suggest,' Godfrey Smith resumed, 'is that you start on the *Magazine* for six months at the NUJ minimum and if we still like each other after that, you'll be offered a staff appointment.'

The union minimum for London, I knew, was around £26 per week, and on the *Northern Echo* I was already getting close to £24. I brought this up, hating myself for ruining the roseate atmosphere. He looked at Peter Crookston, who suggested 'Thirty?' That and his very pleasant manner – and taste in trousers – suggested I already had an ally here.

'How much notice do you have to give your present paper, dear boy?'

'A month,' I said.

'So, you could come in July?'

I said I could.

'Excellent, excellent. Sheila, my secretary, will drop you a line to that effect. And now I know Harry Evans is most anxious to see you.'

Mrs Susan Raven led me up the stairs to the fifth floor, from which came the familiar clatter of a newspaper composing room but much louder than any I'd ever heard. Halfway up, we met a man in a biscuit-coloured suit coming down with a page proof flapping negligently in one hand. His perfect en brosse hair and beautiful, wary face somewhat recalled Elsa Lanchester in The Bride of Frankenstein

'Mark,' she said, 'This is Philip Norman, who's just won our Writers' Contest. Philip – as I suppose I can call you now – this is Mark Boxer, who runs the paper's Review front.'

'Let me know if you have any ideas,' he said and, without waiting for an answer, continued on his elegant way.

Harry was in a spacious corner office, shirtsleeved at a long wooden lectern covered with layouts, presumably his new sports pages. He looked just the same except for a slightly longer-pointed shirt-collar, and already knew about everything that had happened with Godfrey Smith.

'I know you put in a word for me,' I stammered, 'and I'm so grateful, Mr Evans.'

'Oh, for pity's sake, call me Harry.'

Everyone on the *Echo* had of course, but only a select few to his face. 'I'd find that a bit difficult,' I said.

'Come off it.' He gave me a pretend dig in the ribs. 'I'm glad you held out for more money. Will you have a cup of tea with me?'

The tea arrived, not in newspaper office mugs but on a tray with a flowered bone-china pot, matching delicate cups, sugar-tongs and a strainer. As he poured for us both, I mentioned Godfrey Smith's idea that I should spend six months on the *Magazine*, then move on to the Newsroom and Insight.

'I should have thought Atticus was more up your street.' Oh, and when he said it, that half-page of free-ranging, ironic commentary, topped by its pediment-like ATTICVS, so long the exclusive preserve of ex Oxford or Cambridge, suddenly felt like my birthright.

To encourage this line of thought, I gushed about what a fan of Atticus I'd always been, especially when Nicholas Tomalin wrote it, and mentioned I'd once met him and was hoping to do so again.

'Nick's in Vietnam,' Harry said.

Before he could elaborate, a group of other newspaper high-ups came in and claimed his attention, among them a big, shambling man smoking a pipe with a curved stem who addressed him as 'Hawwy'.

'You'll find it's a lovely life here,' he called after me.

I rejoined Mrs Susan Raven, who took me down to the third floor and a small window in a corridor wall where a longish queue of people waited, all holding identical sheets of pink paper. Each of them pushed their pink slip through the window and received a wad of big blue £5 notes. When her turn came, Mrs Susan Raven produced such a slip, pushed it in, then handed me four for my first-class return train fare.

Now we must get you photographed,' she said. 'I'm going to take you up to our Roof Studio which, as you probably know, was designed by Lord Snowdon. I beg his pardon – *Snowdon*.'

The winding stairs to the roof showed off the knee-length of her grey wool dress to great advantage and I wondered if my long-nurtured fantasy of being seduced by an older woman might finally be on its way.

I tried to pay attention as she told me she'd been an extra unofficial judge of the Writers' Competition. 'Godfrey called me in and asked me for my candidate and I said, "There's no doubt in my mind it should be Philip Norman." As soon as I started reading your piece, I thought "He's pastiching our style in the *Magazine*, he's taking us off." One could tell by all the semicolons.'

In the Roof Studio, I was put into a kind of grotto of black fabric and photographed by an almost completely hairless man with widely protruding ears, using one of the new Nikon cameras so often shown in *Sunday Times Magazine* advertisements. I was used to seeing people photographed for newspapers with just a couple of clicks and a thank you, but he used up an entire roll of film, continually changing position and talking to me in a low, soothing voice like a vet to a nervous hamster.

Before we left, I was allowed a peep into the main studio-space designed by Lor…by Snowdon. It had a vaulted glass ceiling, a pine floor and a pair of armless, legless and headless torsos, one white, the other bright red. On a pedestal stood a Victorian slot-machine, the kind where you shot a ball around a spiral onto a row of cups. So much of the Victoriana commonplace and oppressive throughout my Fifties childhood was now the height of designer chic, but none more than this.

At one time, Ryde Pier Pavilion had contained dozens of such machines, along with many other more complicated kinds worth ten times its present hugely inflated price. But when my father switched the Pavilion from penny arcade to silver-service restaurant, he'd sold them all off for a few pounds as scrap metal.

A week later, another creamy missive with Godfrey Smith's slim man's signature proved it hadn't all been a mirage. I was to join the *Sunday Times Magazine* as a writer for six months 'on a retainer of £30 per week'. He repeated the notion of my then spending six-month periods in different departments of the newspaper, like the Newsroom and Insight.

Accustomed to a salary as I was, the word 'retainer' had a worryingly impermanent sound not quite dispelled by that wondrous '£30'. And from the moment it had first been mooted, I'd known I didn't want to be passed around the paper like a parcel. Having made it to the *Magazine* I meant to stay there.

I'd never managed to impress either of my parents and doubted whether even my getting to the *Sunday Times* would affect the status quo of 23 years; however, the *Northern Echo* owed me a week's holiday and, so blinding was my euphoria, I paid a visit to each in turn and the partners to whom I now took second place by several hundred miles.

At Southoe Manor Farm, the main point of interest for my mother was 'When do you get the moolah?' (Although I couldn't forget how none of this could have come to pass without her Elizabeth Arden treatment room.)

It was lovely Joan Furbank, the 'next-door neighbour' from Diddington, four miles away, who gave me the big hug, saying she knew I'd go places when I wrote in the *Hunts Post* about the pigeons ravaging Gerald Davison's Brussels sprouts and his cries of anguish during the snowbound winter of '62.

Mr Davison said, 'Well *done*, old boy!' but he said that all the time when I hadn't done anything. However, he loved the idea that I'd be working for a man called Godfrey and, in his usual manner, twisted the name into as many different shapes as a piece of chewing-gum, reciting them aloud even alone in the cab of his combine-harvester: 'Gottfried ... God-preserve-us ... Gott in Himmel ... Godfrey Evans ... Godfrey Davis ... Godfrey Wynn ... Godfrey, Seaman and Farrell.'

With my father in Hungerford, my news seemed to weigh little against the thanklessness of operating fruit machines with jackpots reduced to five-shillings. He showed no curiosity about what I'd written - even though it was about his mother and mentioned him – nor did it give me licence to sit in the armchair consecrated to my stepmother, Joan.

Whenever either of them referred to my new job, which wasn't often, they said it was with 'The Times'. I kept explaining it was the *Sunday Times* and that the two papers were entirely separate, but to no effect.

I had brought my one carbon copy of the piece, on dun-coloured *Northern Echo* copy paper, for Grandma Norman to read. This she did in the back room of the little sideways grocer's shop in Lambourn, pausing now and again to answer the 'ting' of the shop bell.

When she'd finished, she took off her glasses and gazed into the cold fireplace without speaking for so long, I had to ask her what she thought of it.

'You always were a little boy who listened,' she said.

Then she took my hand, closing her eyes and saying, 'Phil...' in the faraway voice that had always portended something very serious.

'When I'm gone, I want you to *have* that old brass bed of mine that's at your daddy's.'

The *Magazine's* announcement of the competition-result, in mid-June, was no mere by-the-way, but filled two columns of its lovely chaste typeface, headed 'New Faces', with a mugshot of me, taken from the Roof Studio session, and of Diana Winsor, who'd been placed second.

Clipped prose, exactly conveying the voice of Mrs Susan Raven, said the three judges' verdict had been unanimous, that J. W.

Lambert, the newspaper's literary editor, had been reminded of 'a smiling Joyce Cary' (of whom I'd never heard, so didn't realise it wasn't a woman), that the novelist Andrew Sinclair had found me 'funny, quirky and full of illuminating non-sequiturs' (which was almost as far above my head) and that Godfrey Smith had exceeded the official first prize by giving me a job.

I spent my last weeks on the *Northern Echo* basking in the glory of a career-leap almost on the level of Harry Evans's to the same place, three months earlier. Just as he'd done, I appeared on BBC North's and Tyne-Tees' early evening news programmes, saying (quite truly) how much I'd loved being in the North East – although both my interviewers seemed more interested in hearing about Grandma Norman.

At Council committee meetings and inquests, tough stringers from the *Express* and the *Sun* who'd once barely noticed me now treated me with respect, even reverence; the numerous opposition from Lord Thomson's *Newcastle Journal* and *Evening Chronicle* almost fought for the privilege of buying me a coffee at Pumphrey's in Grainger Market.

Diary stories about my award appeared in the *Hunts Post* and *Cambridge News*, both of which had so carefully concealed from me that a journalist could have fun. The *Northern Despatch's* Under The Town Clock also carried one, headed 'Good for you Philip', a testament to the generous spirit of Arnold Hadwin, who'd given me my first foothold up here when I was in flight from Cambridgeshire's county set.

I received two letters from London publishers, one signed Gillon Aitken (even more of a gender puzzle than Joyce Cary) from Hodder & Stoughton; the other signed Anthony Blond of Anthony Blond Ltd. Both expressed not just willingness but scarcely-controllable impatience to consider any work of fiction I might write.

There were congratulatory letters, too, from people on whom I'd been unaware of leaving any impression, like David Orehams from the *Newmarket Journal*, a day-release classmate at Peterborough Tech, and Canon Alexander Morris, the incumbent at All Saints Church in Huntingdon, the latter so very nice, I regretted all the times I'd rung his doorbell in pursuit of whist-drive results, mutinously uttering 'Balls to the Canon'.

The greatest accolade was to be invited by my bureau chief, Tom Little – that 'bastard' who never was – to his house in Gosforth to have dinner (cold salmon and whisky) and meet his surprisingly blue-stocking American wife. Amid all the flattery being heaped on me, only he sounded a note of warning. 'You'll be going into the *Sunday Times* with your head held high,' he said. 'But you'll have to keep it high.'

One evening, walking up Newcastle's cobbled Bigg Market in bright sunshine I thought back to sunny evenings on Ryde Pier in the 1950s when my life seemed to stretch ahead, weekdays and weekends alike, without a single thing to look forward to.

But *now*…

Godfrey Smith had said my prizewinner's cheque would reach me 'in a few days', but it still hadn't arrived and I was becoming impatient to buy the new suit the *Magazine's* readership expected of me. Then I heard from his secretary, Sheila McNeile, that there was to be a ceremony at which all the winners in the under-23 talent contest's various categories – photography, fashion-designing and cartooning as well as writing – would be presented with their awards, 'Oscars-style'.

Was there no end to the glamour and excitement?

The pink lift doors had almost shut when they were re-opened from outside to let in a man in a dark blue suit with the head of a satyr. So total was the resemblance, I half-expected the hand that pressed the button for the sixth floor to be a cloven hoof. Something told me this was Anthony Blond, one of the publishers from whom I'd received wooing letters. He gave me a smile, from which tusks all but sprouted, but neither of us spoke.

A large crowd with some splashes of brilliant colour was already assembled under the Roof Studio's vaulted glass. Waiters in dinner jackets circulated with champagne-bottles wrapped in white napkins and waitresses in black dresses with silver platters of nibbles. The little Victorian slot-machine, my fellow refugees from the end of the pier, looked down from its plinth as if thinking - like me - how times had changed.

Mrs Susan Raven, wearing a green floral minidress with a white collar and pale pink shoes with lipstick to match, took me round, determined I should meet everyone in the room – or, rather, that everyone should meet me. I seemed to hear nothing but my own name: 'This is Philip Norman … the winner of our Writers' Contest…

Have you met Philip Norman? … wonderful piece about his grandmother… It's Philip Norman … Oh, so *you're* Philip Norman…'

I met my two runners-up, 16-year-old Linda Gillespie, whose tights were as hilariously full of holes as Godfrey Smith had said, and Robert Lacey from Selwyn College Cambridge, whose subject had been Horace Bachelor and his guaranteed system for winning a fortune on the football pools. We discovered that, when standing in for the *Cambridge News's* university correspondent, I'd heard Robert speak at the Union as R.W.D. Lacey. He even knew an acquaintance of my former County girlfriend named Virginia Walmisley-Dresser.

I met the winner of the Photography Contest, Quentin Jacobsen, a Londoner with a blond Beatle fringe and a gold front tooth, wearing one of the Edwardian-style striped blazers that had made the same sudden leap into fashionability as Victorian slot machines. He said that he, too, had been rung up by the man named Angeloglou with the suggestion that we should team up on a foreign assignment.

I met the Fashion Contest's joint winners, picking up on their accents with with pleasure; they were friends named Anne and Lynn, both students at Newcastle College of Art. Nearby stood a dressmaker's form displaying Anne's winning entry, a waisted coat with thick vermilion and gold stripes and gilt buttons down its front. Still palpably in a daze, she told me Godfrey Smith had liked the coat so much that he'd bought it for his wife.

I met the *Sunday Times's* literary editor, J. W. Lambert, a handsome grey-haired man, whom my piece had reminded of 'a smiling Joyce Cary' and who asked me if I'd like to do 'the odd book review' when I started my new job. I met a man in noticeable black slip-ons and white socks with a faint peninsula of hair on his forehead whose name, Derek Jewell, I'd often seen above the newspaper's jazz column but who turned out to have a much more important role as deputy editor of the *Magazine*.

Climactically, I met Gerald Scarfe, tall, good-looking and polo-necked, with a shy, polite manner, in every way the opposite extreme from his caricatured monstrosities. He told me he'd been a judge in the Cartoonists Contest but none of the entrants had been good enough to deserve the prize. I didn't mention having been among them.

In what seemed only a few seconds but must have been about an hour-and-a-half, the crowd fell back into a semicircle and Godfrey

Smith called me forward to receive the slip of paper representing more money than I'd ever dreamed of having. It had been rather disappointing not to see Harry Evans, but he was there in my new editor's graceful – indeed, slim man's – speech:

Harry told me "You've got to take him on because you'll never find a harder worker ... and he looks like Byron.'" That came as much as a surprise as my 'Byzantine' humour as a *Northern Echo* columnist.

In another seeming second or two, Godfrey was shepherding the party's principal guests across the road to the *Sunday Times* pub, the Blue Lion – a name which, for me, partook in its glamour; up north, one only ever saw Red Lions. After buying champagne for everyone, he came shouldering through the crush – he had the shoulders for it – and told me, 'We can't let the evening end here, dear boy, so we're going on to Chez Victor.'

I had no idea what or where this was, so Gerald Scarfe gave me a lift in his silver E-Type Jaguar, his stunning red-haired girlfriend seated on my lap. The E-Type's long nose lunged through almost empty grey streets. To our left, I could see the new Post Office Tower, both telephonic marvel and entertainment with the revolving restaurant at its summit. In the hot dusk it seemed to shimmer and glitter like a mirage

We reassembled on what felt like the edge of Soho, in a red-fronted restaurant with a sign on its door that read 'Le Patron Mange Ici'. Godfrey Smith was evidently well-known here; a whole section had been reserved for us, half a dozen tables with pink cloths were ready, several waiters were uncorking bottles of white wine and an unsmiling man, 'Victor' presumably, was enthusiastically 'dear boy'ed by him.

The rest of the evening passed in a golden glow in which I hardly knew what I drank or ate or said. I sat at a table with Godfrey and a very tall, bearded man he introduced as 'Michael, our art director,' a term completely incomprehensible to me. Mrs Susan Raven sat at the table to our left, opposite a woman wearing a dress that seemed made from fresh Spring flowers, the rest of her not so much.

The bearded Michael had little to say; the only thing I heard from him all evening was 'I'm going to have escargots.' I expected Godfrey to eat as well as look and behave like Friar Tuck, but his entrée was a white fillet of something without noticeable sauce; a slim man's dish even.

Almost everything I said seemed to set off his explosive guffaw and flattery continued to rain on me from everyone else, but Michael and the woman dressed in fresh flowers. At one moment when I thought I was being particularly fascinating, she leaned forward and said in a nasal voice, 'Oh, don't talk such balls … I suppose I can say that now you're joining us.'

Just after midnight, Godfrey was presented with an immense bill, which he merely signed, and the party broke up amid more congratulations to me. At Quentin Jacobsen's suggestion, the two of us paired off with the fashion prizewinners, Anne and Lynn, and he led us into Soho, to a discotheque called Le Kilt on a ground floor with a long window looking into the street.

As Anne and I were dancing to the Mamas and the Papas' *Monday Monday*, she shouted, 'What's Meriel McCooey like?'

'Who?' I shouted back.

'That woman sitting across from you … don't tell us you didn't recognise her. She's their fashion editor. Wasn't that dress amazin'?'

Afterwards, the four of us drove around in a taxi with both its windows pulled right down and the scent of blossom from – I supposed – Hyde Park blowing in.

'Where is this?' I asked Quentin.

'This?' he said, amused by my ignorance. 'It's Bayswater Road.' The way I was feeling, I could have kissed it.

The *Magazine* had booked me into the Great Northern Hotel, right beside King's Cross. My train back to Newcastle the next morning was packed and I spent most of the journey standing in a noisy junction between two carriages, thinking about last night and how much I'd like to have it all over again.

Which I would – in a multiplicity of forms – many, many times.

* * *

Part Two

* * *

6

By catheter, do you mean spinnaker?

I started on the *Sunday Times Magazine* at the end of July, 1966. It happened to be the week that England beat West Germany in the football World Cup final at Wembley Stadium, taking the nation's morale to a high it hadn't known since the end of the Second World War (which, by a sweet coincidence, had had the same combatants and outcome).

It also happened to be the zenith of Swinging London when – largely at the urging of America's *Time* magazine – hundreds of thousands of young people were pouring across the Atlantic to Europe's newly-dubbed 'style capital,' expecting to bump into the Beatles or Twiggy or David Hockney or Julie Christie around every corner. But for the present I would be living far from the swinging hotspots of Carnaby Street and the King's Road, having billeted myself with my mother's parents, Grandma and Grandad Bassill, at their terrace house in Lynette Avenue, Clapham South.

Before Grandma Norman ran the Kiosk, she, too, had lived in Clapham, on the north-eastern side of its expansive Common known as the Old Town. After all the time I'd spent with her, and Grandma and Grandad Bassill on the south side, Clapham to me was far more London than any of the monuments or museums across the river to which one went on a number 88 bus.

My grandfather, Frank Augustus Bassill, had been a cameraman for the Pathe newsreel through the long pre-television ages when the only filmed news was shown at cinemas with the trailers and ice-cream ads. In the First World War, he had been one of only five 'official cinematographers' on the Western Front; in the Second, he'd gone with Winston Churchill on the battleship Prince of Wales to film Churchill's first meeting with President Franklin D. Roosevelt off Newfoundland.

He'd circled the world on Royal Tours and covered every major British sporting event from the Test Match to the Grand National more times than he could count. All without the newsreel's vast audience ever knowing his name, for its cameramen were always anonymous, however historic their footage.

My tiny, vivacious, quick-tempered grandma, Agnes (the couple were known as 'Ag and Gus') came from true Cockney stock, brought up in Lambeth, her father for many years the stage-manager at Gatti's music-hall in Westminster Bridge Road. She was one of eight children of whom four others, her sisters Lou, Alice and Flo, and her brother, Alf, had lived into old age. She spoke in the refined Cockney so perfectly rendered in H.G. Wells's *The History of Mr Polly* which, for instance, turned her surviving brother's name into 'Elf'.

Grandad was so quiet and reserved, it was hard to hear any particular accent; he came from Earls Colne in Essex. but consorting with prime ministers, sometimes even Royalty, in his work had made him 'classless' decades before it became essence of everything new and young and fashionable.

Soon after his retirement from Pathe in the early 1950s, gangrene had developed in his left leg, the delayed result of wartime intestinal surgery, and it had been amputated at the thigh. He'd just learned to walk with a prosthetic limb when the gangrene was found to have spread to his right leg and that also had to go.

In the palmy newsreel days, he'd been able to take Ag on cruises to Madeira, once even to Royal Ascot in a picture hat and a dress, my mother remembered, of 'triangular beige lace'. Now she looked after him devotedly without seeking any help from the State in the form of district nurses or home helps.

Her unremitting hard labour and Grandad's enforced immobility (and, no doubt, residual pain) might have been expected to make 63 Lynette Avenue a sombre place, but their little back kitchen-cum-living-room had for years been a haven of cheerful normality for me with its overhead strip light and vase of plastic flowers and napkin rings and the ballerina tea cosy. enveloping a defunct cigarette lighter with a wooden stand like a lighthouse.

On the mantelpiece there had always stood a large, framed photograph of my mother and father during the War, Clive in RAF uniform, peaked cap dashingly aslant, hands in pockets, pipe clenched in his magnetic dimpled smile. Since the divorce, a small snapshot of Grandad wedged in the frame had loyally obliterated his face.

That was my fiery little Ag all over, but her support of my mother had been more than merely symbolic: despite having Grandad to cope with, she'd looked after Tracey as a baby for several months while 'Renie' was looking for a job, never making the slightest heavy weather of it.

Grandad spent most of each day sitting in a wheelchair at the big kitchen table but she made sure there was always something to divert him … continuous hands of Patience in the morning …', a cup of tea with Mrs Dale' (the radio soap Mrs Dale's Diary) at four o'clock …a game of shove-halfpenny before their high tea at six.

Because of his age, his two artificial legs were only about 18 inches high with rockers instead of feet to lessen the risk of his toppling backwards. Sometimes, if the weather was good, she would put on his rockers and he'd use two sticks to get himself into the tiny back garden, overlooked on every side, where his white-haired, child-height figure would spend an hour or so, gamely digging with a trowel.

They were not demonstrative with me, still less with each other; Grandad called Ag 'Mum' and she referred to him as 'Dad' no matter whom she was speaking to. I never saw them kiss, but nor did I ever hear a harsh or hurtful word pass between them.

I arrived early on the Sunday before my first week on the Magazine. I wasn't going to miss Sunday lunch, always a delicious roast cooked by Ag in the little back scullery, with Marmite added to the gravy. As usual, we started with the glass of sweet Vermouth she termed 'a Martini', then Grandad poured me a light ale in the silver tankard his Pathe colleagues had given him on his retirement (which is on my desk as I write this.)

After lunch, he had a nap by himself in the front sitting-room with the outsize glass cocktail cabinet, left over from more social days, and the 'Magicoal' electric fire. Then Ag wheeled him back, put on his short legs with rockers and fetched the shove-halfpenny board, and he and I played several games with his head only a little higher than the table edge.

He was so unchangingly modest and low-key, it only now occurred to me that I was kind of following in his footsteps. According to my mother, Ag had been a little miffed by my writing about Grandma

Norman in the *Sunday Times* competition when 'Dad had such an interesting life.' But he never mentioned it and, in almost subliminal ways, communicated that he was proud of me.

Of necessity, Ag and Gus occupied the ground floor only, sleeping in what had formerly been a rather dark dining room. The first floor was let to an Irish couple named Nancy and John, who had three small children. Nancy was a hospital nurse – a useful kind of person to have around under the circumstances – and John worked as a cellarman at the new Hilton Hotel in Park Lane. He would often bring home a bottle of whisky or gin for Ag, which she refused to believe he might have acquired by any other than totally honest means.

From the first floor, a long, straight staircase ascended to two small connecting back bedrooms, the first pink, the second dark green. Nobody else being in the house, both of them were at my disposal. I hung my clothes in the green room's fitted wardrobe, above a row of Grandad's discarded full-length artificial legs including one still wearing a brown mudguard shoe and a maroon sock.

Then I got into the pink room's lumpy single bed, next to a white chest-of-drawers with a sepia photograph of him at Wembley during the 1920s, operating a box-shaped camera on a tripod and wearing a top hat.

But it was a long time before I could sleep.

The next morning, I faced a tricky Tube journey, starting from Clapham South on the windy Northern Line – my long-familiar carrier to and from both grandmas – then changing onto the faster, impersonal Central Line to Chancery Lane, the stop nearest the *Sunday Times*.

Chancery Lane station was, I found, not in Chancery Lane but on the T- junction where Grays Inn Road met High Holborn. The first thing I saw on emerging was the row of faux-Elizabethan shopfronts shown on packets of Old Holborn pipe tobacco, innumerable ounces or half-ounces of which I'd once served out while helping Grandma Norman at the Kiosk.

From this end, Grays Inn Road had all the Dickensian archways and cloisters one could wish. I waved down a taxi and asked for Thomson House but after only a couple of hundred yards, the wonderful copper-fronted edifice came into sight.

In my excitement, I'd set out much too early and it was still only just after nine. I paced the surrounding narrow streets for about 40 minutes before crossing that beautiful black mat and approaching the two commissionaires on their dais. I gave my name, mentioned the *Magazine* and – this being when IDs and security checks were unthought of – was waved through to the pink-doored lifts.

Even now, the *Magazine's* section of the fourth floor was deserted. A telephone started ringing and, from long-ingrained Newsroom habit, I answered it. On the line was a woman whose name I didn't catch, with a query about the recipe in yesterday's edition. 'Did it really mean use two pints of double cream?' she said in a strangely faint and faltering voice.

'I'm afraid I couldn't tell you,' I said. 'You see, I've only just …'

'It can't have meant two *pints*. I made it for my family for dinner last night and now none of us can stop being sick.' Then the line went dead, for a reason not hard to guess.

It was past 10.30 when my new colleagues started arriving: first a man in an electric blue suit with an expression of savage disdain I later found out was his normal one; then a couple of the 'dolly birds' I understood to be unique to London, white-lipped and silver-eyeshadowed in bare-legged minidresses like foreshortened shirts. All of them ignored me.

Finally at 11.15, Godfrey Smith himself appeared, wearing a brown suit under severe stress at every point, his straggly hair still wet at the back from a bath or shower it was impossible not to visualise in all its abundant, lathered nudity. 'Ah!' he boomed. 'Our prizewinner! Welome!' He was the only person from whom I was to hear that word.

He showed me to a small-ish grey steel desk about half way down the concourse with a bulky green Olympia typewriter on it. Across the way, a tall young woman with points of hair swinging beside her face like Sandie Shaw, and somewhat similar bone structure, was settling into a niche largely constructed of thick reference books. Godfrey introduced her as 'Brenda Jones, our very accomplished and charming sub-editor.'

'A lady sub,' I murmured, to my retrospective shame, and she responded with a long-suffering smile.

It turned out that the *Magazine* had an assignment ready and waiting for me. Godfrey took me back into his narrow, red-carpeted office – whose desk still lacked any sign of editorial activity – and asked if I'd heard of Francis Chichester.

I had, although with total indifference until now. Chichester was a London map dealer and long-distance yachtsman who'd made news a couple of years ago by winning the Transatlantic Single-Handed Race despite having recently beaten supposedly terminal lung cancer. Now aged 64 he was to attempt the first solo circumnavigation of the world since Joshua Slocum's in 1895, racing against the times of high-speed clipper sailing ships with cargoes of cotton or tea like the celebrated Cutty Sark. But whereas Slocum's voyage had taken three years, Chichester aimed to do it in around seven months with a stop-off halfway in Australia.

I had been wondering what Harry Evans had been up to since revamping the *Sunday Times's* sports pages and now Godfrey enlightened me; at his impetus, the paper was part-sponsoring Chichester's voyage in return for weekly reports of its progress. The *Magazine* would be running an interview with the lone mariner and a colour spread on his boat, Gipsy Moth IV, to coincide with his departure on August 27th.

'Harry and I felt you were the ideal candidate, dear boy, since you come from the Isle of Wight, so presumably know all about sailing.'

It was the moment to have confessed that I'd never been a part of the Island's large and mostly upper-crust sailing community; that the son of an end-of-pier showman could never think of using the summer for mere recreation; that despite growing up half a mile out to sea, I'd never once set foot in a sailboat, and couldn't even swim. But I wasn't going to refuse an assignment for which Harry Evans had picked me.

'I believe you're to meet Chichester tomorrow and go out in the Gipsy Rose, or whatever,' Godfrey said. 'Peter Crookston will give you all the info. Bon voyage, skipper!' And he gave another of his giant guffaws that almost parted his suit at the seams.

Peter Crookston's office was along a corridor off the main concourse and he, too, had only just come in, as had a secretary who might have stepped straight from the pages of *Vogue*. Once again, his trousers were impressive, pale green hipsters, though I noticed his matching shirt was a mass of creases at the back.

He didn't welcome me but in his pleasant Geordie-sounding way, gave me all the info: that evening I was to drive down to a marina on the Hampshire coast named Bucklers Hard with a photographer named Ian Yeomans, and we were to spend the next day with Chichester on Gipsy Moth IV's shakedown cruise around the Solent.

The *Vogue*-like secretary then took me to the *Magazine's* business manager, Bruce Jeffcott – a gravely polite man, almost as new to the place as I was – to learn how to draw advance expenses for travel, hotels and the like. This was done by means of a pink form on which you wrote the nature of the assignment and how much you wanted, and which could be countersigned not only by Jeffcott, Godfrey or Peter Crookston but any other of the *Magazine's* several assistant or associate editors.

At Bruce Jeffcott's suggestion, I requested £50 and he signed a form before I filled it in. I took it down to the third floor – remembering the way from my previous visit with Mrs Susan Raven - where I joined the queue of other pink form-bearers at the cashier's window and had ten blue £5 notes unquestioningly shovelled out to me. It felt like winning on a fruit machine in the days, so lamented by my father, when jackpots were unlimited.

From there I found my own way to the Library – or Morgue, as it used to be known in every newspaper office – to collect all possible information on Francis Chichester, Joshua Slocum and clipper ships, in those days consisting of fat brown envelopes full of cuttings dating back half a century and more.

Although on the same floor as Cashiers, the Morgue was in a different world where modern strip-lit corridors gave way to dark Victorian woodwork, heavy brass doorknobs and lavatorial-looking white tiles. For Thomson House's sumptuous, copper-faced exterior was just a façade, grafted onto what had been the rear of the pre-glamour *Sunday Times's* original building. The true front entrance, where the printers clocked in, faced a cobbled lane and the carpark of the Post Office's Mount Pleasant headquarters.

That day happened to be an unusually quiet one on the *Magazine* with several of its leading figures, including Mrs Raven, away on holiday. I was left to myself to read the Francis Chichester cuttings and skim through his autobiography, *The Lonely Sea and the Sky*.

Just to the right of my new desk was a grey steel cupboard which, I found, was full of *Sunday Times* headed stationery and large, luxurious stiff-backed notebooks, to which one could help oneself. On the *Northern Echo*, you weren't allowed a new notebook without producing your old one to prove its every possible space had been filled.

I took two of those and a stack of creamy bond notepaper and envelopes, which I immediately put to use by typing boastful notes to Dave Watts, Guy Simpson and Tom Little to prove (as much to myself as them) that I really and truly was here.

The Lonely Sea and the Sky was dedicated to Chichester's wife, Sheila, no seafarer herself but nevertheless a stalwart supporter of all his previous long-distance voyages and, by his account, the sole reason he was in a condition to attempt this ultimate one. For she'd refused to accept his lung cancer was terminal, and put him on a regimen of her own, combining vegetarianism and prayer, that had effected a complete cure. That was a promising line for my piece now that mysticism was all the rage and Indian sitars were even turning up on Rolling Stones records.

I also learned that before taking to the sea, Chichester had been an aviator, undertaking equally solitary, high-risk adventures in de Haviland Gipsy Moth biplanes, hence the naming of his boat Gipsy Moth IV.

Crumbling sepia cuttings from 1929 recorded his departure on what was intended to be the first solo flight around the world. It had come to a premature end while taking off from an airfield in Japan, when he'd looked down to wave at the cheering crowds and flown straight into telephone wires which hurled his plane back onto the ground like a stone from a catapult. His first thought on realising he had survived, he wrote, was 'thankfulness that I hadn't been made a eunuch.'

'Was glad he hadn't been castrated,' I jotted in one of those lovely new notebooks.

Ian Yeomans turned out to be the almost hairless man with right-angled ears who'd taken my picture in the Roof Studio a month earlier. Uniquely among the *Magazine's* photographers, he was kept in-house for more routine jobs like this.

He seemed not to mind being teamed with a such a provincial novice and it was a pleasant journey down to the Hampshire coast in his car, I was aglow at being on my first assignment for a national, with £50 in my wallet and the right to say, 'I'm from the *Sunday Times Magazine*.' I could hardly wait.

Despite being based on the roof of Thomson House, Ian was well acquainted with all the *Magazine's* principal figures so I quizzed him about the three I knew so far, starting with Mrs Susan Raven, on whom I still had vague sexual designs.

'Ah, dear Susan,' he said with a reminiscent chuckle. 'She used to be married to Simon Raven. It was only to get the name, really, because we all know which way *he* swings. don't we?'

I nodded sagely, despite never having heard of Simon Raven, then a novelist of some standing and a well-known 'bohemian' as the euphemism had it before people said 'gay'.

'It's in one of his books, I forget which … how he was at some ball at Cambridge, dancing with this little girl from Newnham, who had his flies undone before he knew what was happening.'

Godfrey Smith, I learned. was known as 'God'; self-evidently not the traditional wrathful deity with a beard like a set of organ-pipes, flinging forked lighting around, but one of the jollier pagan kind, cavorting with scantily-clad nymphs, laurel wreath askew, and downing cups of wine.

And I'd been right: Peter Crookston did come from Tyneside, indeed had once been picture editor on the Newcastle Journal, so was a natural kindred spirit for me.

'Peter's like God's favourite son,' Ian said. 'When he found Joan Hunter-Dunn, from the Betjeman poem, for the "Where Are They Now?" issue, the morning it appeared, God had a bottle of champagne delivered to him.'

It turned out that God had only recently taken over the *Magazine*, having previously run the paper's Special Projects department, overseeing all its top feature writers like David Leitch and Pauline Peters.

'Who was editor before him?'

'It was Mark Boxer. Haven't you met Mark yet?' I recalled the exquisite figure like a male Bride of Frankenstein I'd passed on the stairs with Mrs Raven that first wondrous day inside Thomson House.

'Last year, he went off amid a huge fanfare to edit a new Thomson glossy called London Life all about its swinging scene. But the whole thing was a terrible fiasco and he's been trying to get the *Magazine* back ever since.'

'Doesn't that make God feel rather insecure?'

Ian gave me a pitying glance. 'You've seen him … does he *look* insecure?'

Bucklers Hard – a name which caused us both equal amusement – was a harbour on the Beaulieu River close to the New Forest, whose native wild ponies wandered freely over its grassy approaches. The river mouth was only a few hundred yards away and beyond it, the Solent and the Isle of Wight at a point unfamiliar to me. It felt strange to realise that, since my departure from Ryde pierhead five years earlier, my career had come in an almost complete circle.

We'd been booked to stay overnight at the Master Builder Hotel (which, of course, meant *boat*builder) close to the water's edge, where we found we were to share a twin-bedded room. This passed off without awkwardness even when Ian got into bed wearing only a white T-shirt saying DOWN WITH THE SUNDAY TELEGRAPH.

The next morning – flawlessly sunny yet again – we met Francis and Sheila Chichester on the path to the marina. He was a little nutbrown man with white sideburns, wearing a dark blue baseball cap, not a common headgear then, and looking altogether too frail and bony to combat the world's fiercest oceans; she was a much more substantial figure in a cherry-red trouser suit and a headscarf. While he was softly spoken and reticent, she was neither; when I held out my hand to shake hers, she put a press release about herself into it.

We walked down together, passing a foal ('the colour of liqueur honey' I inwardly noted) elegantly sprawled on the grass. 'If only one could take *that* on board,' Chichester said wistfully, at which his wife gave him what Grandma Norman would have called 'an old-fashioned look.'

And there at the end of a little jetty was Gipsy Moth IV, as I now knew a 38-foot ketch (i.e, two-masted) with a cold-moulded hull and a kind of elevated rudder at the stern denoting its revolutionary self-steering gear. As well as the last word in small-boat navigational aids, it was one of the first examples of the multiple sponsorship that would later become familiar on Formula One racing cars and football players' shirts. Around twenty different brands were piggybacking on the voyage, from Marconi, who'd supplied the radio equipment, to Whitbread's beer, who'd supplied draught bitter in a newfangled pressurised metal keg that would keep it in prime condition throughout the epic voyage.

Chichester himself was a walking advertisement, his baseball cap displaying the logo of the International Wool Secretariat; Gipsy Moth's lockers piled with sweaters and cardigans of 'pure, new wool', as the ubiquitous slogan went. It was so typical of the Sixties to have made even wool seem suddenly novel and exciting.

Sheila Chichester showed us over the pristine silver and white superstructure, whose every plank and rope and centimetre of sail was brand new. Below deck, we viewed the steering-gear Chichester could operate from his bunk, if necessary; the specially designed gimballed chair that would maintain equilibrium even amid Cape Horn's 40-foot waves; and the keg of Whitbread's bitter,

She described how she'd planned all his stores and the meals, dominated by nut cutlets and nut roasts, he'd be preparing for himself; the only area lacking her supervision was his toolbox. 'Before every voyage,' she told us, 'I'm simply *longing* to sort out his screws.' I heard a muffled snort from Ian Yeomans, somewhere behind me, but managed not to react.

There were to be four of us on Gipsy Moth's shakedown cruise, Chichester, Ian, myself and a PR from the International Wool Secretariat, a rugged young Australian obviously familiar with boating in these parts. I hadn't expected to need a coat, but he warned that the Solent could be chilly even on a day like this, and fetched me an old US army combat jacket from his car.

So, my first ever experience of sailing was aboard what would be the 20th century's most celebrated small boat, around the same stretch of sea I'd gazed out at all through my childhood, with its string of water-girt 19th century forts, its passing liners and tankers, its far-off yacht races like hundreds of white shavings from the Moon.

At one point, we passed the end of Ryde Pier, close enough to see its ironbound wooden piles and the barnacled stone staircases down to open platforms where a small boy who hadn't been taught to swim often used to stray without anyone knowing where he was or how easily he could slide off their green-slimy surface into the water.

The Australian PR proved a useful crew member to Chichester but I was completely useless, baffled by his shouts of 'pick up that sheet!' and 'watch out for the boom!' which consequently dealt me several sharp blows to the back of the head. Ian Yeomans, meanwhile, seemed to be everywhere with his two Nikons, hanging perilously over the side or shinning up and down the mainmast; even Chichester called him 'very intrepid'.

It was around six when we passed from a now choppy, grey Solent, back into the Beaulieu River estuary. Suddenly there was a grinding, sludgy kind of noise from below and Gipsy Moth IV came to a complete stop. The sailor soon to challenge the oceans of the world had run onto a sandbar in one of Britain's most tranquil waterways. I couldn't help thinking of the aviator in an earlier Gipsy Moth, too busy waving at people on the ground to notice telegraph-wires ahead.

All Chichester's efforts to unstick the keel proved futile, so a shabby old grey launch had to come out from Bucklers Hard to tow him free. As I watched it approach through a pair of brand-new binoculars (supplied by the Zeiss company) I realised Mrs Chichester was standing in the bows.

I had been about to ask Chichester what made a man want to spend more than six months all alone at sea, but when the expression on her face came fully into focus the question seemed to answer itself.

I was used to daily paper deadlines and, helped by the smooth action of my green giant typewriter, I'd completed the Chichester profile by noon the next day. I left the top copy with Godfrey's secretary, Sheila, and handed the carbon to Peter Crookston as he came through the swing doors from the corridor where his office was, wearing a wonderful shirt of broad purple and black stripes.

'Finished already?' he said in surprise and gave me an awkward little pat on the shoulder. 'You're not on the *Northern Echo* now, you know.'

By the end of the afternoon, there had been no response from either recipient so, as Peter seemed to be my immediate superior, I went and asked him if it was all right. 'It's fine,' he said in a tone clearly conveying that it wasn't. Then his *Vogue*-model secretary told him Margaret Drabble was on the phone for him and he turned away to more important matters.

I returned to my desk in a kind of trance of despair. Although I still had to hear from Godfrey Smith, I had no doubt his reaction would be the same. I'd had the opportunity of a lifetime and blown it. Better not to have got this far than to fail so instantly and miserably.

Just before five, Godfrey finally emerged from his office and came towards me, holding my copy but, ominously, without his usual indulgent smile. 'I've shown this to Harry Evans,' he began, reminding me who it was I'd *really* failed. '… Harry thinks it's a super piece and he'd like it for the paper's Review Front this Sunday. So

I've agreed we'll just run Ian Yeomans's pictures of the boat in the *Magazine* – which I believe are excellent. Very good work, dear boy.'

In a fifth floor office noticeably larger and grander than before, Harry greeted me with that smile of his, implying there was no limit to my audacity.

'Very nice,' he said – how ineffably sweet that 'nice' after 'fine'. 'I love your line about the foal the colour of liqueur honey. I've told Godfrey I'll have to borrow you for a couple of days to go over one or two little points.'

For the next 48 hours we were almost equal colleagues as those one or two little points were addressed. 'I think we're going to have to lose Sheila's quote about sorting out Francis's screws,' Harry said. 'I know all's pure to the pure, but *Sunday Times* readers unfortunately aren't …and when you say "catheter", do you mean "spinnaker"?'

The section about running aground underwent slight rejigging. As he pointed out, we couldn't suggest the intrepid adventurer the *Sunday Times* had signed up was accident-prone. I found a quote from Chichester I hadn't used – that getting to know every new boat entailed at least one balls-up and he was glad to have it over with before Gipsy Moth set sail in earnest. Harry pounced on this and made it the ending.

On the Thursday, the two of us went to a meeting with Chichester at his rather classy map shop in St James's, followed by lunch at an anonymous hotel in Euston (Harry clearly not having the same relationship with food as Godfrey). Chichester seemed to have forgiven or forgotten my performance under sail and gave me a signed copy of a small book his company published called Chichester's 50-Mile Map of London. The lunch was most interesting for its revelation in passing that Harry was 38.

On Friday, the proofs were sent for approval, not to Chichester but to his wife. I expected her to veto the bit about him flying into the telephone wires, but the message that came back via a secretary was only 'Mrs Chichester asks that you don't used the word "castrated".'

And on Sunday, there it really was on the front of the *Sunday Times's* Review section, filling the ocean of space usually devoted to the memoirs of former cabinet ministers; headed **THE LONER** in black Ultra Bodoni, illustrated by a blown-up Ian Yeomans headshot of Chichester in his baseball cap (so giving an almighty plug to 'pure, new wool') and with the strapline *Philip Norman profiles a singular man*.

In the office on Monday, I expected some kind of reprise of winning the Writers Contest. Little did I guess that on the *Magazine* it was the rule to ignore everything in the paper, just as it was on the paper to ignore everything in the *Magazine*. The only compliment was a back-handed one from the business manager, Bruce Jeffcott, likewise a newcomer to *Sunday Times* politics: 'I picked up the Review section yesterday and there was your name. "Hello," I thought, "I know *him*..."'

When I saw Peter Crookston, in yet another glorious shirt, I couldn't resist asking smugly whether he'd seen the piece. 'I did,' he said in his mild way, but no congratulations followed. 'I only wish you'd waited and talked to me about it first because your intro was completely wrong.'

I thought of answering 'Harry Evans didn't think so,' but fought it down. Why go on annoying someone whose Tyneside background, never mind his shirts, dictated that we should be blood brothers? And, after mentally re-running the intro four or five times, I felt he might have a point.

Afterwards, Harry offered me the job of talking to Chichester by wireless (the Marconi kind, that is) and turning his adventures afloat into weekly reports for the paper's news pages. It would have involved shuttling back and forth to the transmitter in Plymouth when I didn't want to lose a moment in Swinging London – and probably meant never returning to the *Magazine* - so I managed to get out of it and a Newsdesk secretary with a yachting background was seconded instead.

But the writer who could put 'catheter' when he meant 'spinnaker' wasn't yet done with world-circumnavigating lone sailors.

* * *

7

What you can accomplish with a crochet hook

On the Friday evening of my first week with the *Magazine* there was a champagne party in the main concourse where I'd been found a desk. It was a belated farewell to Ivor Lewis, who'd already handed over as business manager to Bruce Jeffcott and become editor of the Thomson Organisation's new evening paper at Hemel Hempstead in Hertfordshire. I toasted him enthusiastically even though I'd hardly spoken to him and couldn't imagine why anyone should want to be in Hemel Hempstead instead of here.

On the following Monday evening, there was another, identical gathering except that we drank Veuve Clicquot rather than Pol Roger. This one was to celebrate the *Sunday Times's* sales having reached 1.5 million, an unprecedented number for a Sunday 'heavy' which the *Magazine* considered solely due to itself.

These were legitimate causes for celebration, but often it would be for no particular reason that at about this time slim white boxes appeared, fluted glasses were set out on a desk top and Godfrey Smith emerged from his office, clapping his hands for all work to cease like Mr Fezziwig with his apprentices in *A Christmas Carol*. As I soon discovered, what he called 'fizz', and summoned up at every possible juncture, was the essential lubricant of working for Godfrey.

No one had ever shown me around the office, formally introduced me to my colleagues or explained the workings of a production process completely new to me. However, since my desk was right at the centre of things, I soon pieced it together for myself.

My most important discovery was the meaning and profound significance of the term art director. As such, Michael Rand completely controlled the *Magazine's* visuals: he alone chose its photographers and illustrators, dictated its covers, its typefaces, the layout of its pages and the running order of its contents, so that the whole wondrously innovative, uber-chic Sunday morning spectacular was, in effect, an expression of one man's personality.

In human terms, that personality was more elusive owing to his uncanny resemblance to the bushy-bearded Victorian sailor on the Player's cigarette packet. Voluminous facial hair hadn't yet become fashionable, and never would in this particular shape which smacked more of the Fifties than the Sixties he captured so brilliantly in graphics.

Beards are always thought to be hiding something but Rand's seemed to hide everything. He was a man of few words, non-existent body language and unfathomable thought processes. Whatsoever was put forward for the *Magazine*, even by Godfrey himself, faced the crucial test of whether 'Michael liked it'. If he did, it would run for pages at the front, looking gorgeous; if he didn't, it was relegated to the back with the chess problem and 'Mephisto' crossword. Yet either way, that Player's Navy Cut profile remained impassive and inscrutable.

To the right of my desk was the narrow screened-off area where galleys of type and photostats of photographs were pasted onto layout sheets with their headlines before being passed, or not, by Michael Rand in his large, glass-partitioned office across the way. Hence, I came into daily contact with a black-haired youth about my age in a monogrammed white shirt, whose bony face was a mask of raw acne. His name was David King and he bore the confusing title art editor.

I was no stranger the word 'fuck' but had never heard it used in public as relentlessly as he did in all its forms, always at the top of a cawing near-falsetto voice. It was mostly aimed at the quiet young women who worked on layouts with him, but it over-punctuated his bare and spotty-faced rudeness to everyone and about everything. His behaviour was tolerated, it appeared, because he was Michael's special protégé, to the extent of an almost equivalent job title. Although I was only a few feet away, he ignored me completely apart from the occasional contemptuous side glance.

Other than at champagne party time, Godfrey tended to stay in his office, his presence signified by periodic shouts of laughter which I used to hope might have been caused by something I'd written. From time to time, a finished layout was taken into him, to be signed with a slim man's 'G.S' in red ink and the date in Latin numerals. Otherwise, he would be lounging behind his unencumbered desk, reading a newspaper and smoking a cigar.

Every week or so, the advertising manager, Donald Barrett, an almost farcically pinstriped man, would come in to see him, but it was only ever a social call. Ad agencies clamoured to pay the *Magazine's* whacking rate of £3,000 per colour page, the more so since sales had hit 1.5 million. Those whose clients did not meet its particular code of luxury and fashionability - like package holidays or frozen peas – were rejected.

The dynamism Godfrey lacked was supplied by his deputy editor, Derek Jewell, a man of enormous warmth and many enthusiasms. I can see him now, almost dancing down the concourse in his usual black slip-ons and white socks, hailing male colleagues as 'sweetie', which Swinging London now allowed straight men to do. And savouring the startlingly beautiful name of David King's patient colleague in the layout department: 'Gilvrie Misstear! Can anyone really be called Gilvrie Misstear? The Gilvrie Misstear Story! My Life with Gilvrie Misstear! Gilvrie Misstear and Me!'

Boundlessly energetic, he wrote extensively for the *Magazine* on top of his 'Jazz/Pop' column in the paper. It was he who dealt with the layouts of Ian Yeomans's Gipsy Moth IV photographs for the issue before Francis Chichester's departure on August 27TH. The opening panoramic shot from Gipsy Moth's bows made the Solent look as threatening as the Atlantic. Derek seized a pen and wrote the typically full-hearted headline ONE MAN AGAINST THE OCEANS OF THE WORLD.

Since my Chichester profile had already appeared, in the paper, my job for the *Magazine* was merely to write captions of technical information about the boat, its cold-moulded hull, self-steering gear, gimballed chair and pressurised beer-supply, so deepening the misconception that I knew all about sailing.

I'd already had the stupendous thrill of seeing my words turned into the *Magazine's* lovely chaste typeface ('Plantin', I discovered it was called) and published in the August 21st issue. The headline was simply 'Grandma Norman' – insultingly misrepresented by David King at the top of his voice throughout the production-process as My Grandad - with a 'by' byline, the very best kind. The illustration was a sepia photo she'd given me long ago of herself sitting in a deckchair in her back garden in Clapham Old Town, decades before she took over the Kiosk.

It fitted the *Magazine's* last two editorial pages without needing to be cut; indeed, there was room for Brenda Jones to insert two crossheads. The first was 'In bed she drank Guinness and gin', the detail people always seemed to like most. The second, a reference to a grisly Victorian self-abortion method – for our talks together had always ranged far and wide – should have been 'What you can accomplish with a crochet hook', but Godfrey had vetoed it as 'perhaps going a leetle too far.'

I never did meet Christopher Angeloglou, the picture editor who'd phoned me in Newcastle about the foreign assignment that was to have been part of my prize. He had left just before I arrived and been succeeded by his deputy, June Stanier, a red-headed woman with a faint look of Juliet Prowse (think, Elvis Presley's love interest in G.I. Blues) who, like most of my colleagues still showed no acknowledgement of my existence after almost three weeks. I presumed my being given a job had cancelled out the foreign assignment.

With my stubbornly Norman-blind colleagues, I decided to take the initiative, and introduced myself to one of the two assistant editors, Philip Oakes, while we both happened to be waiting for a lift. I told him how much I liked his work, which extended far outside the Sunday Times: he was a published novelist and poet, had worked on television programmes with the naturalist Desmond Morris and scripted Tony Hancock's film *The Punch and Judy Man*. Lantern-jawed, in a nice beige suit, he replied that he'd 'laughed like hell at Grandma Norman' and we were friends from then on.

No such easy transition took place with his fellow assistant editor and office mate George Perry, a man as tall as Michael Rand but bulkier, with a puggy face and a mass of unfashionably-greased hair. He had formerly been in advertising, when he was said to have invented the slogan 'Polo – the Mint with the Hole.' He never spoke to me, even if I was standing right beside him, and in this case I didn't have the option of saying I liked his work.

Nor did I even try with David Hillman, who'd looked like he wanted to murder me as I waited around on that first morning. He was yet another designer but on a rarified level that entitled him to work in Michael Rand's spacious room. Both of us were always in early and I watched him unpack his briefcase morning after morning without so much as a glance in my direction.

Among this crew of rampant egomaniacs, there was nothing resembling *esprit de corps* save in one respect: they all felt the same utter contempt for the newspaper one floor above. They called it 'the Steam Section', suggesting something as risibly outdated and laborious as George Stephenson's Locomotion Number One back in Darlington.

Some time in the past it had been laid down that all *Magazine* stories of a specialised nature be vetted by the relevant specialist on the Steam Section: its literary editor, J. W, Lambert, its political correspondent, James Margach, its industrial editor, Ian Coulter, or its foreign editor, Frank Giles. However, the specialists' comments were usually read aloud in funny voices – Giles's with especial gusto – before hitting the bottom of the bin.

Likewise, it was a given that writers on the paper were incapable of working for the *Magazine*. The two exceptions were Hunter Davies, whose name now signed the Atticus column, and his predecessor, Nicholas Tomalin, now the Vietnam correspondent who'd won huge praise that June with a dispatch about a Texan four-star general personally 'zapping' Vietcong guerrillas from a helicopter with an M19 carbine as if it was a turkey shoot.

I'd been wondering when I would bump into Tomalin so that I could thank him for his encouragement three years earlier, when I was on the *Hunts Post* and he the editor of *Town*, and to show I'd made it, as he predicted.

I finally met him coming out of Godfrey's office, now greying a little and wearing horn rimmed glasses that showed up a slight squint in those close-set eyes. He was perfectly nice, but clearly didn't remember me.

The ethos of the *Sunday Times Magazine* was nowhere better on show than at the 'ideas meetings' of its senior figures which took place about every fortnight.

I observed one of these initially just from the outside. At 12.30, a procession of young men and women in black – they were from Nick's Diner, London's most 'in' caterers – began carrying large foil-covered platters into Godfrey's office, a process that took some time.

Thanks to its opaque glass wall, nothing could be seen of the meeting but dark silhouettes, although the buzz of conversation, repeated pop of corks and frequent uproarious laughter carried clearly. Not until well past three did the participants emerge, rosy-faced and unsteady of step, most of the men smoking the large Havana cigars Godfrey had distributed. In a somewhat feudal touch, a half-demolished platter of rice salad and some oddments of fruit were then brought out and left on the top of the stationery cupboard for the serfs (which mostly meant the *Magazine's* young female secretaries) to fight over.

The next time a memo invitation to this event was circulated to Peter, Michael, Derek, Meriel, George, Susan, Brenda and June, I found Philip there, too.

The black worktop that ran the length of our editor's narrow sanctum, and was normally completely bare, now displayed a sumptuous cold buffet with an outsize game pie, every conceivable kind of avant-garde salad, French and English cheeses, long loaves, branches of pink grapes, peaches, nectarines and around two dozen bottles of red and white wine. Mineral water in those days wasn't yet considered a necessity.

'Come in, you young rips!' Godfrey greeted us, male and female alike. 'I hope everyone's good and hungry. Come in and dig in!'

That first ideas meeting taught me that 'ideas' were the last thing the *Magazine* sought, except from inside itself. In today's magazines, most stories are 'pegged' to some event, the premiere of a new film, the opening of a new play or publication of a new book. Under Godfrey the only pegs were the twice-yearly Paris collections covered by the fashion editor, Meriel McCooey, and the autumn Motor Show, marked by a bulky issue known as Automania, stuffed with car ads, put together by Derek Jewell. Otherwise, it decided for itself what it would do and when, heedless of the calendar and the blandishments of the PR industry.

Nor, like today's magazines, was it dependent on publicists for access to celebrities, doled out to all media at the same time in half-hour portions in a hotel-suite. For any film or theatre star (television being not much esteemed then) a request for an interview from the *Sunday Times Magazine* was the ultimate affirmation of their celebrity and almost never refused. It was understood that access would be unsupervised and unlimited; copy or picture approval were unknown and no guarantee of appearing on the cover ever given.

These days, famous faces routinely appear on several magazine covers simultaneously to plug their latest film or play. But to the *Magazine*, any similarity to its two arch-rivals was anathema: if ever it learned in advance that the *Observer Magazine* or the *Weekend Telegraph* had the same story - even if scheduled to appear *after* its own – the whole edition was pulped regardless of the cost.

Its characteristic feature expressed the Sixties' spirit of discovering the whole world anew. One Sunday just before my arrival, its cover story had been on Suffolk, a county which had been there for many hundreds of years (indeed, was the birthplace of my first editor, F.J. Johnson). Now page after page of sumptuous colour gave it a misty beauty and drama that had never been apparent before and somehow connected its ancient community and agricultural life to the swinging going on in London.

In everything it did, the *Magazine* pleased only itself and did not give a toss whether or not it pleased its audience. Every week, letters used to pour in from old-school *Sunday Times* readers, expressing outrage about something they'd been confronted with over their Sabbath breakfasts, such as a semi-clad fashion model or a Napalm-scorched Vietnamese child. All received the same formula reply from Godfrey, startlingly devoid of his usual bonhomie:

Dear --

Thank you for your letter. I am sorry you did not like our feature on --

Yours sincerely

Once everyone had helped themselves to food and wine, there was quite a scrimmage for the several but not quite sufficient armless black leather chairs, particularly those nearest Godfrey's desk. Michael Rand sat on the empty far end of the worktop, looming over the company like a hirsute offcut from Mount Rushmore. As the newcomer, I felt it behoved me to take one of the hard upright chairs brought in from the concourse and pushed up against the opaque glass wall at the back, where I was all but hidden from view.

Derek Jewell opened the proceedings with customary zest, offering up his latest enthusiasm for general discussion. 'For my money '(it was always for his money) the Beach Boys are the greatest poets of modern urban life since the Beatles.'

It surprised me how indifferent to pop music the others were, given the *Magazine's* place at the cutting edge. Brenda Jones in particular, who came from Liverpool, or near it, downplayed her newly-fashionable accent and was too cool to have been swept away with the rest of the world by her fellow Merseysiders' latest masterpiece. 'You'll be pleased to know I've finally heard *Eleanor Rigby*,' she told Derek, plainly relishing his incredulity.

There was no formal agenda, nor formality of any kind, although Godfrey's secretary, Sheila McNeile, perched on a stool, took notes of what was said, later to circulate a wonderfully deadpan resume.

First came a financial warning unlikely to be heard at any 21st century magazine conference: 'I have to tell you young rips we look like not spending our budget for Sixty-six,' Godfrey said. 'You know how twitchy the folks in accounts always get when that happens, so you'd all better think of some really big foreign trips to get in before the end of the year.

'And bear in mind that once you get to Bangkok, it's not really worth turning round and coming back. You may as well put a girdle around the Earth, as it were, and try to find something to interest our readers in Malaysia or Singapore or Indonesia.'

Next there were progress reports on the various single-theme issues in preparation; surveys of subjects on which, one might think, not a further word could be said but which the *Magazine* would give new freshness and fascination. The ones discussed that day were Middle Age, the Female Form and Scotland.

Here Peter Crookston took the lead, once more wearing his lovely pale green shirt with coordinated trousers. His particular charges were the *Magazine's* several distinguished American contributors, both writers and photographers - whom it paid on the same level as their own mighty Life or Look. It was quite a moment for me when he remarked in passing that he'd be phoning Norman Mailer that night.

I was still conscious of having failed to impress Peter, and believed it to be all my fault. At one point. he dropped a lump of game pie onto the red carpet and said 'Oh, Christ, I'm sorry' with such boyish Geordie charm, pushing his hair off his brow, that I resolved anew to earn his good opinion somehow.

The other theme-issue specialist was George Perry, who still hadn't spoken to me, even while we were spooning Coronation Chicken from the same dish. He was a man of encyclopedic knowledge, especially about the cinema and America, always calling films 'movies' and Los Angeles, 'LA'. He had just returned from an extended trip through Canada for an issue to be called 'Canada, A Question Of Survival' even though for the past couple of hundred years it had never had any discernible problem with surviving.

The material was already in production, yet there was a marked lack of enthusiasm for it among his colleagues, despite his fervent assurances that 'Calgary's a really cool place now' and 'You can take the most fantastic train ride through the Rocky Mountains.'

The actual 'ideas' part of the meeting proved the shortest. Godfrey took out a cardboard folder of suggestions from outsiders, freelance journalists or PRs, and read them aloud between popping pink grapes into his mouth. Every one was dismissed by a barely perceptible twitch of Michael Rand's beard or Meriel McCooey's nasal cry of 'Bor-*ring*!'

That bothersome ritual disposed of, Godfrey lit up an enormous Dunhill panatella and leaned contentedly back in his chair. 'Well now,' he beamed amid fragrant clouds of blue smoke, 'what's the gossip?'

Almost all of this concerned the internal politics of Thomson House and much of it revolved around Mark Boxer, the *Magazine's* founding editor who had handed it over to Godfrey a year ago and, it seemed, had been scheming and intriguing to win it back ever since. His office as the paper's Review front editor was also on the fourth floor, so his slim figure was constantly seen in the *Magazine's* vicinity, immaculately dressed and barbered but somehow melancholy, like a cheroot-smoking ghost drawn back to the scene of its greatest happiness.

The talk about Boxer reminded me of the great gap in my life. Godfrey had been at Oxford, President of the Union as one might expect; Boxer had been at Cambridge, like George Perry and Mrs Susan Raven, but had enjoyed one of the most glittering careers seen there in the 1950s, culminating in his being sent down for blasphemy.

Godfrey told the story with an indulgent smile, seemingly quite untroubled by Boxer's fell purpose. 'When he was editor of Granta, he published a poem that rhymed "God" with "sod". He was the first undergrad to be kicked out for blasphemy since Percy Bysshe Shelley.'

Several of the young rips had worked on the *Magazine* under Boxer and there was talk of his many eccentricities and prejudices and unashamed social climbing, for his wife was the daughter of the 18th Earl of Moray. Mrs Susan Raven, in particular, rhapsodised about 'Lady Arabella' - now a moderately well-known cookery writer - in terms that made me wonder if the Sixties were really so 'classless'.

I found I hadn't been alone in detecting that whiff of vicar's wife. 'She's probably hoping Lady Arabella will open her next jumble sale,' the waspish Brenda murmured.

As I also learned that day, no ideas meeting could pass without mention of C.D. Hamilton, the editor-in-chief of Thomson Newspapers, the creator of the *Magazine* as well as the paper's principal innovations like the Weekly Review, Insight and Business News, and the only person to whom Godfrey was accountable.

The *Magazine's* profitability was such that Lord Thomson kept it, metaphorically, hidden under his coat; a goose whose golden eggs never tarnished. Hence its complete separateness from the paper and its own autonomous editor. Thomson himself – that most atypical of press lords - never sought to influence or interfere with it and gave it complete freedom from managerial or budgetary restraint, so long as those golden eggs kept popping out.

The role of 'CDH' was defined simply as 'keeping an eye on it' for his proprietor - and to most of its excesses, that eye could be relied on to remain benignly blind. This was largely due, it seemed, to Godfrey's close personal relationship with CDH and understanding of his occasional odd little kinks. For example, there was currently awaiting publication an interview with a 'flasher' on Wandsworth Common, under an assumed name but with lots of grim detail, which David King had thought it hysterically amusing to give to the very beautiful but correct Gilvrie Misstear to lay out. Despite the explicitness of the subject matter, Godfrey anticipated no interference from the editor-in-chief.

'I thought CDH didn't like sex,' Brenda said.

'Ah, but this is *sad* sex … He doesn't mind *sad* sex.'

Later that week, I was called into Godfrey's office, its desk and worktop swept clean again, and found him standing and talking to a slight, rather dowdy man with an old-fashioned military moustache. "Denis,' he said, 'this is the winner of our writers contest, who's now joined us, I'm most happy to say.'

The reinventor of the *Sunday Times* was one of the shyest people I'd ever met, in journalism or out of it. Godfrey mentioned my connection with the North-East and in the brief, mutually awkward exchange that followed, I gathered that CDH had been born in South Shields and started in journalism on the *Middlesbrough Evening Gazette*. I never saw him again.

Lord Thomson himself was known to visit the building bearing his name only very seldom. But one day as I came through the front hall, there was a sudden stir among the commissionares, an urgent murmur of 'It's the Chairman', and a big elderly man wearing an old-fashioned black Homburg hat and thick pebble glasses, was ushered through to a concealed private lift somewhere on the left.

I never saw him again either, but felt his benevolence in many forms every day.

I hadn't used my prize money to buy a new suit, as the *Magazine's* readership had been led to expect; I'd bought two, along with a grey herringbone tweed jacket, an off-white corduroy safari jacket, two pairs of hipster trousers and four shirts. There was still quite a lot of change left from the £250.

Both suits were of a cut and colour I'd never dared before: one double-breasted Air Force blue, the other dark khaki with two rows of four buttons and Beau Brummel lapels, the perfect companion to a brown and yellow-striped shirt whose collar-points reached almost to my knees.

Hipster trousers that year were their lowest-slung ever, the 'rise' between abnormally thick belt and crotch no more than a couple of inches. If they were too long when you tried them on, the shop would send them around the corner to be shortened in about five minutes, one leg maybe a little shorter than the other, but who cared?

Most excitingly, I'd finally tracked down my first really tall Chelsea boots as opposed to the half-hearted ankle-huggers sold by the chain stores. David King wore such a pair, and I steeled myself to ask where he'd bought them. They were from Anello and Davide, a long-established maker of ballet shoes, and the first boot I tried slid on without any of the usual shoehorn heaving. Among the other customers, I recognised Crispian St Peters, currently topping the singles charts with *Pied Piper*.

On my next visit to Hungerford, I wore the off-white cord safari-jacket and the boots with a pink shirt and combed my hair forward like a Beatle's. At the sight of me, a look of mingled horror and disgust spread in slow motion over my father's face. I'd clearly reanimated his old suspicion that I was 'a nancy boy', as he put it – which had never been incompatible with suspecting me of eyeing up my stepmother, Joan.

It would later be said that by 1966, the best of Swinging London was already past, and cynicism and exploitation had set in. But despite the *Time* magazine article and the influx of young American tourists in their millions, there was still little commercialisation and virtually no inflation. Dinner for two in one of the countless new 'bistros', over a candle exploding with petrified wax, rarely cost more than £3. The 'in' drink, Mateus Rose, was 10 shillings (50p) a bottle – and *such* a bottle with its squat shape and label like a Renaissance painting. Black taxis with traditional flat-capped drivers, who called male passengers 'guv', went immense distances for under £1.

The city belonged to the young as it never had before, yet with a total absence of inter-generational friction. Older people just smiled to see the boys' frilly blouses and Zapata moustaches, the girls' wasp-striped microdresses, huge floppy hats and bare feet. Nor was it only clothes boutiques that pandered to this new mass elite: the very sandwich bars hung placards in their windows saying, 'JOIN THE SANDWICH SET.'

That summer was perhaps the greatest ever for pop music, with the Beatles' *Revolver* album, the Beach Boys' *Good Vibrations* and *God Only Knows* and a string of memorable one-hit wonders like Bobby Hebbs's *Sunny*, Los Bravos's *Black is Black*, Chris Farlow's *Out of Time* and the Easybeats' *Friday On My Mind*. All seemed to float in the air like electric pollen yet somehow upsetting no one.

Despite all the swinging-ness and an unprecedented tourist boom, Britain's economy was far from healthy, thanks to a lengthy dock strike and a huge balance of payments deficit resulting in strict controls on wages and credit. The fiscal downsides of life under Harold Wilson's Labour government even found their way into pop with the Beatles' *Taxman* and the Kinks' *Sunny Afternoon* ('Save me, save me, save me from this squeeze'). Nonetheless, London, had huge amounts of ready cash swirling around for those my age, above all, to scoop up.

Youth will always protest, but in this era Britain's cossetted and adulated youth could find nothing to protest about nearer than America's increasingly bloody and futile war-making in Vietnam (ignoring the fact that Wilson's government steadfastly refused to lend it military support). Even here - at least, to begin with - they met with indulgence, allowed to march and hold rallies scarcely checked by a still unmilitarised police force, and to agitate for revolution from the comfort of democracy and full employment.

In the bedsitter continents of Kensington and Earls Court, there was a party to go to every night, whether or not one knew the giver. Front doors were left open and one simply walked in and joined in. People made a steady living from rifling the pockets of the heaps of coats carelessly left on beds.

At one such gathering, I overheard a conversation between two young women that brought home what a brave and shame-free new world this was. 'Are you and Tony going on to the Cromwellian?' one asked.

'No,' her friend replied. 'We're going to bed. Honestly, I'm feeling *so* randy tonight ...' Different indeed from paramours in the North-East who'd thwarted my advances as often as not with a brisk 'Geroff, ya booger.'

My naivete at that time truly was pitiful. Several of my schoolfriends had been working in London all the time I was slogging around the provinces and one evening there was a reunion at the Bunch of Grapes pub in Old Brompton Road. Towards its end, I recognised Malcolm Davis, who'd been at the school only a short time and never been a particular friend of mine. But having both been boarders created a bond as between survivors of Colditz.

Malcolm was now a hairdresser, he told me, and when the party broke up he invited me back to his flat to continue our reminiscing. There was no need of a taxi; 'I've got an E-Type' he said carelessly.

The E-Type was custard-yellow and his flat halfway up a luxury block in Belgravia. A wonderful-looking girlfriend waited there and as we came in, he called to her that he was 'dying for a joint.'

I honestly thought he meant the kind Grandma Bassill cooked on Sundays in her little scullery, with Marmite added to the gravy.

Shortly after I joined the *Magazine*, it acquired a second recruit from Newcastle when Nicholas Mason moved down from the Thomson Organisation's *Evening Chronicle* to lighten Brenda Jones's load as its only sub-editor.

He was small in stature – though after meeting him, one never noticed it – with a domed forehead, very bright eyes and a wide, mischievous smile. According to Brenda, the other applicant for the job had been a former monk. presumably with some experience in cutting down illuminated manuscripts. 'But I took one look at Nick's merry little face and told Godfrey "*He's* the only one I want to work with."'

We'd never run into each other in Newcastle, for Nick had been largely shut away from daylight on the *Evening Chronicle* subs' table. Like me, he had merely been in transit through Geordie-land, having grown up in Surrey, won a scholarship to Charterhouse and read English at Mansfield College, Oxford, before joining Thomson's graduate training scheme.

He was six years older than myself, long married with three small children and another on the way. But our shared Tyneside experience drew us together as did our passion for P. G. Wodehouse (mine inherited from Grandad Bassill, whom I'd often seen chortling quietly in his wheelchair over the name 'Gussie Fink-Nottle').

He was a supremely gifted sub, with none of the grudge against writers harboured by so many of his calling and an erudition possessed by only very few. Behind that domed forehead was a vast store of knowledge, principally about cricket but seemingly excluding nothing: long before you could ask Wikipedia, you asked Nick Mason.

There still remained blind spots in my command of grammar, punctuation and spelling that Nick mostly put right. He it was who taught me always to remember how to spell 'surreptitious' from the Latin words 'sub' (secretly) and 'repti' (seized); that 'none' was followed by 'is', not 'are'; that i.e, was short for *id est*; and when quotation marks went to the left or right of a full stop.

He and his wife, Jane, lived in Morden, at the far northerly end of the Northern Line, the two of us usually travelled back to unswinging London together on those occasional evenings without a post-work champagne party. To save us the bother of changing trains en route, we'd be given a lift to Kennington by the *Magazine's* production manager, Stan Dawe, a voluble, moon-faced, man, as powerful in his way, as Michael Rand.

Stan remained apart from its junketings and often commented drily on their master of ceremonies: 'That Godfrey of yours is the last of the big spenders. Just wait until Christmas when you see him dance on top of a desk. You'd never think he had a weight problem.'

For the next four tube stops, before I got off at Clapham South, Nick and I would compare our observations as newcomers. He, too, had noticed the strange bareness of Godfrey's desk but picked up a detail I had missed concerning our editor's supposed masterly handling of C.D. Hamilton. 'Every time he goes upstairs to see Hamilton, he always puts his jacket on.'

Nick's first *Magazine* subbing job had been George Perry's 'Canada: A Question of Survival,' an experience he hadn't enjoyed. 'George,' he said, 'knows everything in the world that you don't want to know. He's like the top line of *The Beano*.' The comic we'd both read as children always used to print a one-line factual titbit above its title, such as 'When annoyed, the panda stands on its head' or 'Ants don't sleep.'

We agreed that a better coverline would be 'George Perry: A Question of Survival', never dreaming by what a distance he would out-survive us all

*   *   *

8

A bountiful, mirthful, pink-shirted Ghost of Christmas Present

For a long time after I joined the *Magazine*, I was half-afraid of being found out - of somebody noticing I didn't have a degree and had never edited *Granta* or *Varsity* and ordering my immediate expulsion. That dread was never greater than in the autumn and winter of 1966, as I discovered that beyond the flattery and applause initially lavished on me lay a wall of solid iron.

Following my Gipsy Moth IV captions, I'd got only two more pieces into lovely Plantin type. The first was about motor racing, a subject that interested me even less than boats. Derek Jewell sent me to Sheffield to interview Anita Taylor, one of the sport's few women drivers; my piece was headlined 'The Fast Lady' and the photographs showed her in a miniskirt, draped over the bonnet of an Aston Martin like a James Bond girl. Derek asked the art department to use the shot most emphasising her 'pristine thighs.'

My other appearance was a single-page essay entitled 'Yellow', the first of a series in which different writers celebrated their favourite colours. Godfrey's was supposed to have come next with 'Red'; however, after a first line 'Red is the king and bully of all colours,' he could think of nothing else to say and the series was terminated.

My next two assignments both failed ignominiously despite the seeming influence of their respective sponsors. First, Philip Oakes sent me to Elstree Studios to report on the making of a film called *Dutchman* by the black American playwright LeRoi Jones, about a white woman picking up an inoffensive black passenger on a New York subway train and publicly stabbing him to death. Then Derek Jewell sent me to the West End to interview the impresario Harold Fielding about his imminent new musical, *Houdini*.

That one never got beyond a first draft, for Fielding demanded copy approval and Derek told him down the phone to 'fuck off'. It would have been doomed in any case because, like the LeRoi Jones film, Michael Rand didn't like it.

I thought I was on to a sure thing when Godfrey himself requested a piece on domestic servants and how they were faring in the egalitarian Sixties. I interviewed a present-day butler, chauffeur and housekeeper and spent an evening undercover as a tailcoated footman at a cocktail party in a house on Bruton Street, offering champagne and canapes. The servility I'd learned in my father's employ came back at once, although these braying Mayfair types were infinitely worse than any daytrippers on Ryde Pier. At one point, a man in a black silk Nehru jacket flicked a burnt match onto my silver tray as I passed. Considerable self-restraint was needed not to smash it down on his head.

Everything looked good with 'Servants'. Godfrey praised it fulsomely at the next Ideas Meeting. Black and white portraits of my interviewees were taken by David Montgomery, a London-based American whose arrangement of his subjects in ironically formal poses suited the subject perfectly. But nothing was said about a publication-date.

Whenever I asked Godfrey about it, his reply was always the same: 'I'm afraid we're very short of space at the moment, dear boy.' As I'd learned from Nick Mason, the *Magazine* had more material in hand than it could ever hope to use: the 'overmatter' of articles commissioned and paid for - their authors often friends of Godfrey's or attractive young women he'd met at parties – represented expenditure of around £200,000 or £1 million by today's values.

The slim, evasive man I discerned inside that guffawing, all-embracing, Friar Tuck was always dodging someone or other who wanted to know when their piece was going in, a manhunt from which even the Gents afforded no refuge. Every male editor shared this same point of greatest vulnerability, the New Yorker's William Shawn going so far as to have a private corridor constructed between his office and the urinal to avoid being waylaid en route. But even if Godfrey made it there unwaylaid, he could still be caught in the act: usually there'd be quite a queue waiting for him to zip up.

Shortage of space never seemed a problem for Meriel McCooey, leaning on Michael Rand's shoulder, jokily calling him 'My Gran', while he did the next flat plan determining what would appear, in what order and at what length. Indeed, it seemed unlimited for her spreads on the latest Paris collections; the coolly unsmiling models in silver caps, fur necklets and white boots that to my uninformed eye, seemed little different from the previous Paris collections.

Nor was it any hindrance to Peter Crookston's coterie of contributors among whom, I noticed, was Francis Wyndham, the author of that style-changing interview with P.J. Proby when I was still in Darlington. Now he was writing about a suburban camera club and bringing out all its members' hilarious banality in the same way, just by letting them talk.

Peter hadn't yet asked me to do anything, I surmised because he thought me a too-hurried daily reporter - but it was he who usually broke it to me in his mild, regretful way that yet another of my pieces hadn't made it.

So, Sunday after Sunday, the *Magazine* came out in still greater glory for its 1.5 million readers without a word by me in it; my mother said, 'I couldn't find anything again' and my old schoolfriends jokily asked me whether I'd died.

I was not under supervision of any kind; no one demanded progress reports on what I was doing; I came and went without once being asked where I'd been or where I was going; if I didn't turn up at all, no one seemed to notice.

My unproductivity didn't stop the weekly £30 in blue fivers being shovelled out of that third-floor window and much more besides since each abortive assignment began with a pink slip for anything between £20 and £50 advance expenses. The subsequent accounting required no supporting receipts and nothing was ever queried.

I was therefore able to afford as many clothes as I liked and go everywhere by taxi, even the couple of hundred yards from Chancery Lane station to Thomson House. I drank champagne like Tizer at the after-hours office parties that happened at least once a week and, under Godfrey's tutelage, switched from Schimmelpeninck or King Edward cheroots to fat Havanas, Bolivars or Romeo y Julietas.

'Remember, dear boy,' he told me in the only piece of advice I can recall from him as my editor, 'the very best Havanas are hand-rolled by young Cuban girls on their bare thighs and some are said to have the additional aroma of a pubic hair accidentally rolled into them. Rather like finding a sixpenny-piece in your Christmas pudding.'

I told Grandad Bassill about Lord Thomson's largesse during one of our shove-halfpenny games, so discovering the first connection between our very different eras and branches of journalism. If anything, his expenses as a Pathe newsreel cameraman had been even more munificent that mine, some compensation, no doubt, for never having his name on the screen.

He told me that when he'd gone to India in 1912, to film massed maharajas pledging loyalty to newly-crowned King George V, he'd been given a money-belt containing 100 guineas in gold, enough in that era to buy a house. And after covering George VI's Coronation fleet-review at Spithead in 1937, he'd charged £5 as 'gratuity to admiral for bringing Fleet closer into shot.'

'Did Pathe stand for that?' I asked.

'Oh, sure,' he said with his ghost of a chuckle.

* * *

This chafing inactivity revived memories of Anthony Blond, the satyr-like publisher, who'd almost begged me to write a novel for his eponymous imprint. I'd always thought fiction meant making stories up, but when several people described 'Grandma Norman' as 'novelistic', I realised it could also be adding few light strokes to reality. And that my particular reality was stranger than any fiction. So, shutting my ears as far as possible to David King's 'fucks', I set about writing that novel, despite not having the first idea how to do it.

No one around me noticed what was going on nor would they have cared, for running a parallel freelance career from the *Magazine*, using its phones, secretaries and lavish stationery, was common practice. Philip Oakes wrote features for Nova magazine and poems for the *New Statesman*. George Perry – a rare exception to the Sixties' almost *de rigueur* leftiness - edited *Crossbow,* the journal of the high Tory Bow Group, from the room he shared with Oakes and was writing a history of comics (including *The Beano*) that his secretary, Jackie, typed chapter by chapter without being paid extra. Everyone in the Art Department regularly accepted commissions to design book jackets, record album covers or posters.

Godfrey himself had a separate existence as a novelist with one moderate success entitled the *Business of Loving* behind him. For obvious reasons, it had languished since he took over the *Magazine,* but he was said to be working on a new book, presumably at home because certainly not at his desk.

My rather predictable title was *The End Of The Pier*; its notional first chapter was about the time my father and some helpers, including me, had thrown a grand piano off the end of Ryde Pier to make space for the Pavilion's new Compton Melotone electronic organ and watched it float off towards the shipping lanes, doubtless to the astonishment of passengers on some passing liner. The names of the pier and its showman were changed; otherwise, nothing needed to be made up.

I sent it to Anthony Blond, whose office was in nearby Doughty Street; he wrote back immediately that he liked it, 'even though it's a bit breathless', and I could come in and 'talk turkey' whenever I liked. However, I was put off by the memory of his nascent tusks and instead sent it to *Argosy*, a long-established short story magazine in the format of a paperback book.

The editor, Andrew Byers, bought it for 40 guineas. I went and told Godfrey – who happened to be in the Gents at the time – ostensibly to check that I could appear in another publication, but really just to boast. He was obviously thankful not to be lobbied about 'Servants' yet again. 'Oh, no, no, no, that's perfectly fine, dear boy. Keep it up.'

At least I now had two friends in the *Magazine's* 'second eleven', as Godfrey jovially called everyone below assistant editor, even though Nick Mason and Brenda between them handled the whole of its production with never a hitch or a cross word.

The three of us usually went to lunch together, although not at the *Sunday Times's* pub, the Blue Lion, whose charms, like those of most newspaper pubs, were much exaggerated. The servings from its salad bar were miserly – especially compared to *Magazine* Ideas Lunches - and the landlord whipped your plate away in hopes that you'd vacate your seat before you'd quite stopped chewing.

Instead, we'd walk to the Lamb in Lambs Conduit Street, which still had its original Victorian wood and smoked-glass interior and sold real ale and home-made Scotch eggs. There we might be joined by Mrs Susan Raven, always something of an event for she had a packed social calendar and was celebrated for always leaving halfway through Godfrey's banquets and champagne parties, it was implied, to go on to something better.

Mrs Raven's hold on my erotic imagination had further dwindled with the colder weather, which had put her into a form-concealing coat and a headscarf and added on two full shopping bags that she took everywhere, including the more interesting parties for which she left Godfrey's halfway through.

Paradoxically, the greatest desire-dampener when she joined us at the Lamb was that the conversation – hers and Brenda's at any rate – tended to dwell heavily on sex. This was the dawn of the oral contraceptive and they speculated endlessly on which of the Magazine's secretaries were 'on the Pill.' Both of them were committed users, although it still couldn't be revealed to everyone. 'I always keep my Pill in a box marked "pills"' Mrs Raven told us in her crispest vicar's-wife tones, 'so as not to offend my Irish Catholic cleaning lady.'

Sometimes the talk took a turn that made poor Nick blench over his Scotch egg, as when Brenda mentioned how in 19th century New Orleans bordellos, the ladies would have all their teeth extracted to make oral sex totally risk-free for their clients.

Mrs Raven had evidently never heard of that particular sexual technique nor fully grasped the dental details. 'I really can't see why it should be such a big deal for a chap' she said, 'even if one did take one's teeth out first.'

The End of the Pier appeared in *Argosy's* October issue, billed as 'The first story by the winner of a recent nationwide competition for writers under 23'. The illustration depicted the end-of-pier showman as a beaming man in a striped blazer and straw hat. If they only knew, I thought.

Yet my dry spell on the *Magazine* seemed interminable. Nothing I put up at the Ideas Meeting stirred Michael Rand's beard with the faintest degree of interest, from 'Allotments' to 'A portrait of the BBC as the Ministry of Truth in George Orwell's 1984', and nothing for which I did get the go-ahead seemed to work out.

I interviewed Spike Milligan, whose gloriously lunatic and subversive Goon Show had lit up the po-faced mid-50s for everybody my age. Now he was to be found daily in Kensington Gardens, restoring the miniature animals and pixies carved into the trunk of an ancient oak. 'Come over at once,' he told me on the phone. 'You can't miss me - I'll be naked and wearing a reincarnation.'

I paid my first visit to Oxford to talk to a professor of literature named J. R. R. Tolkien, whose books about hobbits and wizards and talking trees were massively popular on American college campuses but still barely known in Britain. He was an unlikely creator of such fantasies, a tall man in a tweed suit and bow tie whose study was a garage next to his ordinary little house in Headington.

He told me that the apocalyptic battles in his *Lord of the Rings* trilogy (which I'd managed to read in a single day) were recreations of what he'd seen as a young lieutenant in the Great War. And that, like his hobbit hero Bilbo Baggins, he had a weakness for fireworks, which he would sometimes see from afar during college celebrations. 'I run to the window,' he said, 'every time I hear a "whoosh!"'

Under a table was a large cardboard carton filled to the top with a handwritten manuscript; it was the *Simarillion*, the prequel to the *Lord of the Rings* which would never be published in his lifetime. I got his wonderfully spidery autograph but later gave it to Philip Oakes's student son, Toby.

The Spike Milligan interview – exclusive, as it happened - never appeared, the Tolkien one not until more than a year later.

In November, I took part in a mass operation involving about 20 of the *Magazine's* writers and photographers, to chronicle A Day In The Life of Cambridge. We interviewed and photographed college heads, 'scouts', a selection of pictureseque undergraduates, the vicar of Great St Mary's and an editor of Varsity awaiting the call to Fleet Street, while Godfrey directed operations and held court in the restaurant of the Garden House hotel.

Reconnecting with the *Cambridge News* – and putting on maximum airs with my former news editor, Eddie Duller – I learned that a student had hanged himself the previous evening, a victim of the 'first-term blues' I'd always found incomprehensible. But Godfrey decided the story would spoil the feature's overall mood of indulgent amusement

When it came out, my byline was all but lost in the crowd. At the time, redundancies were being announced at several less affluent nationals and the *What The Papers Say programme* had great fun with this evidence of grotesque overstaffing, reading out the entire roll-call in a multi-voice babble.

Hope glimmered again when the *Magazine* was given exclusive access to the set of *Privilege*, a film starring Manfred Mann's ex-vocalist, Paul Jones. His character was a messianic preacher with rock-star charisma and I watched the filming of a massive stadium sequence that would have eclipsed the Second Coming with satirical phrases bubbling up inside me like a geyser. But then Michael Rand decreed a picture spread only, meaning captions only from me. When the proofs came back, Nick Mason softened the blow by writing in 'Commentary by Philip Norman.'

'He got a *credit,*' Brenda pretended to marvel.

I flew for the first time and then again, but still getting nothing into print.

A press trip to launch Dunhill's new range of men's toiletries took me to the Loire Valley for the day and at one point found me walking alone through an honour guard of French bagpipers with deer-antlers on their hats and up the steps of a beautiful chateau to be greeted by a white-bearded gentleman I took to be a vicomte named Alfre Du Nil but who was in fact the company's founder, Alfred Dunhill. Here no copy was expected; the *Magazine's* magic presence was enough.

Two weeks later, I was in Lerwick, capital of the Shetland Isles, watching men in horned helmets parade with fiery torches, in a somewhat less than sober state. It was the annual recreation of Up Helly Aa, the funeral rite of a Viking jarl, or lord, whose body would be carried in procession, lashed to his throne, then sent out to sea, Valhalla-bound, in a burning long ship. Only nowadays, burning boats were not allowed and the man playing the jarl had slipped a disc, so had to be borne through the streets lying prone on a shutter.

I was meant to have been writing for Derek Jewell's Scotland issue, but Michael Rand didn't like it.

Harry Evans, meanwhile, was making bigger and bigger waves. In three months, he had transformed the rather minor story of Francis Chichester's solo round-the-world voyage into an epic that gripped the whole nation and Chichester into a seafaring hero like none since the age of Drake and Raleigh. Especially to an older generation marginalised by rampant youth culture, wearied by a constant bombardment of pop music, miniskirts and the Pill, it had felt like a cleansing draught of salty air.

True, there remained Gipsy Moth IV's other commercial sponsors but in this era before onboard cameras, no one could see Chichester's Zeiss binoculars, his jumpers in 'pure, new wool' or his keg of temperature-controlled Whitbreads bitter. Battling the oceans of the world in his gallant little ketch, he was as much a symbol of the Sunday Times as of good old-fashioned British pluck and fortitude. Other media might snatch long-distance shots of him from ships or planes but the only inside account of his progress were the wireless reports, always on the paper's front page, which I'd once been offered the job of compiling and – stupidly, I now thought – refused.

There had been, as a result, another major surge in sales and Harry had been promoted from chief assistant to the editor to chief assistant editor, seemingly final confirmation of his being on course for the editor's chair. We hadn't crossed paths in a while, but I always felt his eye on me. It seemed that he knew about my problems on the *Magazine* and was trying to help when he asked me to take over Atticus for a week while Hunter Davies was on holiday.

I felt the mingled dread and joy, with joy uppermost, that he'd been the first to awaken in me, back in Darlington. 'Do you think I'm really up to it?' I asked.

'Oh, come off it,' he said with the impatience that was always so flattering. 'Haven't I always said it was your natural home? I'll speak to Godfrey about borrowing you for a week.'

Godfrey not only readily gave consent but announced my secondment at the next ideas meeting. 'Young Philip will be joining a distinguished company ... Sacheverell Sitwell ... Ian Fleming ... Robert Robinson ... Nick Tomalin. We should all be very proud of him.' The rest of my superiors continued helping themselves to food and wine without comment. 'Well, *I* am,' Godfrey added defiantly.

Dread taking over for a spell, I looked up some Hunter Davies Atticuses on that half-page well to the front of the news section. They usually consisted of two interviews with famous or weird people, written in an amused faux-naif style. A perfect example was one with a Japanese 'performance artist' named Yoko Ono about a film she'd made of nothing but bare human bottoms in a row.

Davies had an assistant named Tim Heald who got his own small credit each week – as in 'so-and-so told Tim Heald'. He was obviously good and I wondered why he hadn't been asked to stand in and whether he'd resent an interloper from the *Magazine*.

'I won't be around for half the week,' Harry told me, 'but you'll have Ron Hall to see you through to print.' I realised this must be the big, shambling man with the curly-stemmed pipe and issues with the letter 'r' who'd been waiting, rather impatiently, to talk to him that first dazzling day I'd spent inside Thomson House.

My week in the footsteps of Sacheverell Sitwell, Ian Fleming and Nicholas Tomalin turned out to be thoroughly enjoyable. Atticus had its own spacious, secluded office on the fifth floor and its own secretary. Tim Heald, a baby-faced recent graduate of Balliol College, Oxford, showed no sign of resenting me and we shared the work amicably.

In what I hoped was the right spirit of irony, I interviewed the comedian Arthur ('Hello, Playmates!') Askey and the pin-up photographer Harrison Marks; Tim did Leo Abse, a campaigning Labour MP with a taste for exotic waistcoats. We came up with, we thought, a good selection of one-paragraph jokes to break up the long pieces, viz *The High Court has just appointed a judge who's only four feet tall. Just one more of the little things that are sent to try us.*

Because Atticus was a self-contained department, its incumbent ranking as an editor, we subbed and headlined our own copy; the galleys came back on Friday afternoon and I was feeling pretty pleased with myself when I suddenly smelt pipe tobacco like prunes and custard and Ron Hall walked in.

Seated in a low chair and puffing steadily, he read through everything without a ghost of a smile, not even at the four-foot-high judge. His own judgement, delivered in a growly Northern accent, seemed to deflate the spirits of the very pot-plant on the window-ledge: 'A column like this needs a good, powerful newsy lead which, to be bwutally fwank, you haven't got.' I sensed that all his dealings with me in the future would have similar bwutal fwankness.

In the event, the column went to press as it was; Harry's eagerly awaited memo called it 'a stylish performance' but there was no mistaking a faint whiff of disappointment. I took no pleasure in its appearance on Sunday, certain I had blown any chance of being asked to do it again.

I returned to the *Magazine* to find preparations for Christmas well underway, initially from a purely work point of view.

A multi-part George Perry series, 'The Victorians' was to run in January and early February 1967, introduced by an issue devoted to the Victorian Christmas. Its main visual was a photographic reconstruction of a Christmas dinner in the 1890s featuring some of the *Magazine's* staff in period costume. Around the table with three children hired from a model agency, were Gilvrie and the researcher, Gilda Archer, in high-necked dresses and ringlets, Nick Mason in a stand-up collar and cravat, and Perry himself as a side-whiskered paterfamilias, carving an enormous turkey with an unfamiliar benevolent smile.

Nick told me that the rosy scene had taken hours to get right under punishing Strobe lamps and the succulent-looking turkey had been almost raw.

Then followed modern-day Christmas, Godfrey Smith-style, which literally was a *season* of goodwill.

It began in the first week of December when he took the male majority of his young rips to the Oxford v. Cambridge, or Varsity, rugby match at Twickenham. That it took place on a working day concerned no one. We went in a fleet of Sunday Times editorial cars and beforehand had a picnic of champagne chilled less than the air and four or five varieties of quiche in the car park.

Godfrey wore a Russian hat and a long fur coat whose vari-coloured vertical striations suggested that several protected species had been sacrificed for it. 'Get a load of God,' Derek Jewell murmured as we followed the jaunty, befurred figure to our row of premium seats in the grandstand, 'he looks just like some old queen out with his young men.' When the game started, a bottle of Bisquit brandy appeared from inside Godfrey's coat and we passed it back and forth. I shouted, 'Come on Cambridge!' as fervently as any BA (Cantab).

A few days later, the *Magazine's* secretaries were entertained to lunch in a private room at one of Godfrey's numerous favourite restaurants, the Gay Hussar in Greek Street, Soho. The intention was to thank the young women who'd slaved all year for the men they called their 'bosses' for little money and zero perks, not only answering their telephones and typing their letters and memos but making them tea and coffee through the day, fetching remedies for their hangovers, seeing to the payment of their household bills, being on call to their wives for all kinds of little services, sometimes even looking after their children.

In fact, it was a rather gruesome occasion, reeking of lordly male patronage and, for some of the guests, leading to the exercise or attempted exercise of *droit-de-seigneur*.

The climactic event was the Christmas party in the *Magazine* concourse on December 19. Invitations had gone out weeks before to notable names throughout Swinging London's interconnected worlds of fashion, art, photography and film. There was huge demand: reports continually came out of Godfrey's office of this or that celebrity who'd had to be turned down because the numbers were too great.

Last year's party had been a memorable one, so Ian Yeomans, the in-house photographer, told me. The actor Laurence Harvey had tried to pick a fight with Lord Snowdon; the painter Lucien Freud had 'started throwing glasses' and two of the *Magazine's* staff had had sex on the floor of Michael Rand's room. Ian told me who they were, then regretted it and swore me to secrecy.

The preparations took all day, what with the arrival of champagne and food in huge quantities, the assembly of a mobile discotheque and the pushing together of half a dozen desks to create an elevated dancefloor. Only David King, ever the rebel, continued working and calling to Lynn, the picture desk secretary – using her real name of Linda because he knew how she hated it - for 'a drink', meaning a cup of tea.

I saw little of the actual party since it took place in darkness but for the light show on the wall above the subs' desks. Terence Stamp, Mary Quant, David Hockney and Donyale Luna, the first black fashion model, were later said to have been there, but I caught no glimpse of any of them among the heaving, light-speckled crowd.

The climactic moment, came as the music started up with the Beach Boys' *Barbara Ann*, people began clambering onto the desk-top dancefloor and Godfrey appeared among them, bopping mountainously on his agile little feet and bellowing 'Ba-ba-ba Ba-ba-ber-Ann', a bountiful, mirthful, pink-shirted Ghost of Christmas Present.

'Like you said, he's the last of the big spenders,' I shouted above the noise to the production manager, Stan Dawe, who was standing beside me.

'I know,' he shouted back. 'And like I also said, you'd never think he had a weight problem.'

* * *

9

That young man seems very libel-prone

In January 1967, my six-month trial came to an end. Bruce Jeffcott told me I'd done well enough to join the *Sunday Times's* staff although, thankfully, there was no further talk of my being shuttlecocked around the paper. But they were still dark days of non-appearance in the *Magazine* and being asked by old schoolfriends whether I'd died.

There was a reshuffle of office space symbolising Peter Crookston's increasing importance and my lack of it. He moved from his outlying corridor into the concourse, where a cubicle next to Derek Jewell's had been specially built for him, while I lost my little foothold out there and was sent to the corridor to share an office with Mrs Susan Raven. I took comfort from the fact that my new desk was considerably bigger than the old one. And no longer being in earshot of David King.

Mrs Raven was not a restful office mate. Every time she left the room, she hurled the door shut behind her with a crash that reminded me of my first editor, F.J. Johnson. Her telephone conversations at the top of her voice seemed endless, many of them concerning her teenage son, Adam, a pupil at Bedales, the progressive school in Hampshire whose progressiveness he seemed to be testing to the limit.

Her duties included editing the copy of the *Magazine's* cookery writer, Margaret Costa, and there were many battles over its attempted humorous touches, usually puns about food. 'No, Margaret, I'm taking it out …*No*, Margaret, you've already made *two* steak-jokes…'

Yet the amorous flame in me hadn't completely died. One cold day, she was wearing a Foale and Tuffin mini dress with a shapeless woollen jumper over it. Too hot in our fiercely centrally-heated lair, she yanked off the sweater so roughly that the dress came off with it, leaving her in just underwear and tights. The sight wasn't at all a depressing one.

'Oh, Philip,' she said with her rather charming laugh. 'I'm *so* sorry.'

I used some of my too-ample spare time to write a second short story, this one set in Edwardian times, drawing on what Grandma Bassill had told me about her father, Alfred Skitterell, the stage manager at Gatti's music hall, and how she'd first met Grandad at Lambeth Liberal and Radical Club, cutting out a rival known as 'Chocolate Alice' who'd worked at a sweetshop in The Cut. The hero was called Frank and a cinema projectionist, as Grandad had been before joining Pathe, which made some amends for my glorification of Grandma Norman.

Argosy bought 'A Cinematograph King' for another 40 guineas. On my next visit to 63 Lynette Avenue Grandma said she'd read it aloud to him and her sister, Aunt Lou, during the latter's weekly visit. ''Ow much did you get paid for writing all that about us?' she asked. When I told her, she feigned a swipe at me and said, 'Artful little devil.'

Yet still that chronic shortage of space debarred 'Servants' and J.R.R. Tolkien from publication and every idea I suggested to Peter Crookston, from a profile of Burma's military dictator, General Ne Win, to a history of sweets, sounded irredeemably feeble when read out from my memo in his mild, unenamoured Geordie accent.

It was little comfort that other people did little or nothing in the office, yet lived a full and rewarding life outside it, derived simply from being 'on the *Sunday Times Magazine*'. A prime example was the researcher, Gilda Archer, whose sharp features and rueful expression were disconcertingly like those of my stepmother, Joan, although her accent was faintly Australian rather than faintly Birminghamian.

Gilda's research, mainly conducted behalf of George Perry's special issues, was known to be unreliable, sometimes dangerously so, and she spent most of her days in the same limbo I did. But by night, her magic credential made her an honoured guest at one or other of the press receptions held in Mayfair hotels or the film previews in West End cinemas.

Indeed, she frequently turned up at superior events at which George was present, treated by unknowing PRs as if they were of equal status. So irritated by this did he become that when they both received invitations to a reception for Alfred Hitchcock on the Savoy Hotel's riverside terrace, he forbade her to appear there.

In this, he was only partially successful. As he stood on the terrace, chatting to Alfred Hitchcock in undiluted Magazine glory, a riverboat chugged past with a noisy press launch for something or other going on in its open stern - and there was Gilda, drink and sausage-on-a-stick in hand.

January of '67 turned out to be the historic month when Lord Thomson bought *The Times* from the Astor family, so creating the connection to the *Sunday Times* which had been mistakenly surmised for decades past. *The Times's* editor, Sir William Haley – who'd latterly borne the burden of having the same name as the 'Rock Around the Clock' man – retired and his place was taken by the *Sunday Times's* deputy editor, William Rees-Mogg. At the same moment, Denis Hamilton, as had long been expected, turned over the editorship of the *Sunday Times* to Harry Evans.

A meeting was hurriedly convened in Godfrey's office – without food or drink for once –to hear what this might bode for the *Magazine*. But there was no need to worry, he reassured his young rips; CDH, now Chairman of the newly created Times Newspapers company, would remain the only person he answered to. The golden egg-laying goose was still safely hidden away inside Lord Thomson's coat.

The announcement that Harry's deputy editor was to be Frank Giles, the paper's former foreign editor, whom he had beaten to the 'chair', caused general astonishment. A decade older than Harry, bearing an uncanny resemblance to the Duke of Windsor, Giles was derided as a social snob even more extreme than Mark Boxer and likewise had a titled wife, Lady Kitty De La Warr. The story was oft repeated of their arrival at a French Embassy reception to be announced as 'Mr and Mrs Frank Giles.'

'Er, it's not *Mrs* Giles,' Frank demurred.

'That's all right, monsieur,' the major domo reassured him. 'We're very broad-minded here.'

'Why would someone like Harry want someone like Frank as a deputy?' Peter Crookston marvelled.

'Very astute move, dear boy,' Godfrey said. 'He knows he'll never be any threat.'

I wondered what Harry's elevation might bode for me, certain it would be something amazing. But with everything else he must have on his plate this clearly was no time to be bothering him. That's the kind of idiot I used to be.

In February, I left Grandma and Grandad Bassill's, long after I should have, to share a flat with Bryan Cooper, a schoolfriend and fellow Isle of Wighter now working for Procter & Gamble. The flat was a basement in Argyle Road, just off Kensington High Street. It had only one bedroom and a lingering smell of gas, but neither of us cared.

Austin Reed in Knightsbridge opened a new department for younger men named Cue, where I bought a purple satin shirt with a long, rounded collar and another in emerald green. And Godfrey gave me an outside chance of getting back into Plantin type.

It was a 'peg' story unusual for the *Magazine*: the approaching centenary of the birth of Stanley Baldwin, Britain's Conservative Prime Minister in the 1920s and 30s. My brief was merely to look into the subject with a view to writing something. 'I leave it entirely in your hands, dear boy.'

At that stage I knew only two things about Baldwin. Firstly, that he'd smoked a pipe, that symbol of wisdom and dependability being employed by our Labour Prime Minister, Harold Wilson - and belied for many years past by my own father. Secondly, that Grandma Norman still reviled him for his role in the Abdication Crisis of 1936, when King Edward VIII had given up the throne to marry the American divorcee Wallis Simpson. 'He was such a brute to the poor King,' I'd often heard her say. 'Oh, how I wanted to shake him.'

A return trip to the Morgue in the picturesque old quarter of Thomson House revealed how much more there was to say. Baldwin had been three times Prime Minister during a period of extraordinary turmoil not only including the Abdication but the 1926 General Strike, a social breakdown which in other countries had been the recognised prelude to revolution. After his retirement, he'd been branded an appeaser of Hitler and, in a petty gesture of reprisal, the railings in front of his house had been taken for scrap iron.

I interviewed the son who'd inherited his earldom, an unassuming, apolitical man who sucked Old Fashioned humbugs, and then visited his former family home in Bewdley, Worcestershire. Grandma Norman's 30 years of enmity proved undeserved when the present Earl Baldwin showed me a telegram from Edward VIII to his father, thanking him for his kindness and understanding during the Abdication. He also showed me a small grey pamphlet by Hitler which the Fuhrer had autographed to Baldwin, a barely legible black scrawl that prickled the hairs at the back of my neck.

Despite never having written on politics before, I decided Stanley Baldwin needed rehabilitation and I would be the one to do it.

When Godfrey called me back to his office, I assumed it was for a progress report. But not so. 'Dear boy,' he said. 'How would you feel about working behind a desk rather than being out and about as a reporter?' Then he told me Harry Evans wanted me to move to the paper as assistant to the literary editor, J.W. Lambert.

'I'm sure it would be very fascinating in many ways, and Jack Lambert is the nicest of men. But I'm very happy to keep you if you want to stay. And Harry can't insist. It's entirely up to you.'

Although I knew what my answer must be, I went through the motions of talking to Lambert's departing assistant, Michael Ratcliffe. He outlined the pressurised, sedentary life that could be mine; of sending out books for review, sub-editing the reviews and seeing the pages of reviews through production. The solitary perk would be a share in the sale of surplus review copies to a secondhand bookshop in Chancery Lane. And now and again I might possibly write a review myself. Altogether, I felt like someone expecting an Oscar who'd been offered a consolation prize for raffia work.

When I told Godfrey I wanted to stay, he shrugged, clearly not surprised. 'Very well, dear boy, I'll let Harry know,' he said, and I returned with a lightened step to Baldwin and the National Government of 1931.

The next day, I ran into Harry as he darted through the entrance hall to his private express lift, the first time I'd seen him since he became editor. 'Why'd you turn down that job I offered you?' he asked me abruptly. 'It would have been perfect for you. You'd have learned all about production ... gone on the stone on Fridays ... rubbed shoulders with literary titans like Connolly and Mortimer...'

I was engulfed by guilt at my ingratitude; he'd had my best interests in mind after all.

'I just ... like it on the *Magazine*,' I said feebly.

'Yes, you've got a great job,' he said with the same unfamiliar grimness. 'Only it may not last for ever.'

That Spring, as youth culture moved towards its apotheosis in a Summer of Love, I was buried in dusty, wing-collared names like Lloyd George, Bonar Law and Ramsay MacDonald, producing a 5,000-word manuscript which concluded beyond all doubt, all shades of black or white, that Stanley Baldwin had been unjustifiably maligned by posterity.

One night, I even dreamed I met Baldwin in the sepia of an old photograph yet so vividly that the next morning I felt it really had happened. It was on the tennis court I'd seen at his former home in Bewdley; he wore sepia-toned white flannels and thanked me for speaking up for him in the slightly bemused way that so eminent a figure might.

I was to have such a realistic dream encounter once more in the future: with John Lennon, 28 years after his assassination

In May, there was a crucial change in the *Magazine's* command structure only incidentally caused by Harry Evans's new regime on the paper.

It was at Harry's invitation that Philip Oakes went off to the fifth floor to become Atticus (much to my seething, hopeless envy.) But it was solely at Peter Crookston's behest that Francis Wyndham switched from star freelance contributor to Oakes's replacement as assistant editor (Arts). So, I finally got to meet my exemplar as a writer.

He was aged about 40, with a large, nearly hairless head and the ponderous features that in England denote high aristocracy, even borderline royalty. He did indeed belong to one of the country's noblest families, a sub-branch of which had detoured to literature and the bohemian life. His grandmother was Ada Leverson, the confidante of Oscar Wilde whom Wilde called 'The Sphinx,' and I guessed he must be related to John Wyndham, whose sci-fi stories like *The Day of the Triffids* I had devoured as a schoolboy.

At first glance, he seemed to be one of the relatively few gay men in those days who felt no need to hide the fact. However, with my growing awareness of the traps London could set, I wondered whether I might not merely be seeing an advanced form of patrician-ness or intellectualism. I therefore refused to jump to any conclusion and made an effort to picture him away from the office escorting strings of glamorous women friends.

Certainly, other things about him weren't what they seemed, for he was said to be wealthy as well as high born, which didn't always follow. Yet there were no signs of affluence, still less of Swinging London, in his shapeless grey trousers, blue short-sleeved Aertex shirts and sandals.

One thing I heard from all sides was how he encouraged and nurtured young writers, so at the first opportunity I told him how much his P. J. Proby interview had motivated and inspired me. 'Thanks awfully,' he said. But the conversation about semicolon use I'd been hoping for somehow didn't follow.

He was, of course, to write as well as assistant-edit and, despite its alleged dearth of space, the Magazine ran two pieces by him at express speed. One was an interview with the current Miss World, India's Reita Faria, the other an evisceration of BBC TV's famously inept talk show host, Eamonn Andrews. From Nick Mason I first heard the word 'camp' to describe this fascination with the tawdry, the mediocre and the banal.

At Ideas Meetings, the question as crucial as whether Michael Rand liked it was now 'What does Francis think?' Often, his only reply would be a loud belch, followed by an unrepentant 'Excuse *me*', which I took to be a further prerogative of aristocracy and intellect.

There was an extra dimension to Francis, illustrative of how totally the old social order had been upended by Swinging London. For this unequivocal blueblood knew the East End's most powerful and violent gangsters, the Kray Twins, Ronnie and Reggie. On the strength of his *Magazine* work, the Krays – who were as image-conscious as any film-stars – had asked him to write their biography, but he'd declined and the job went to another *Sunday Times* writer, John Pearson, whose masterly study, *The Profession of Violence*, would appear in 1972.

However, Francis had stayed on good terms with the twins and even profiled their mother, Violet, in the *Magazine*, so forming a direct link between them and his friend, the Queen's brother-in-law Lord Snowdon. How's that for 'classless'?

Reggie Kray, marginally the less psychopathic twin, even came to a *Magazine* Christmas party also attended by Snowdon. With him he brought a man and woman, not dressed up and noticeably ill-at-ease among the champagne drinking and desktop-dancing. According to David King later, they were a husband and wife who ran one of the pubs from which the Krays extorted protection money.

'That evening, when Reggie dropped in to collect, they hadn't got the money to pay him, so he said, "I'll have to think what I'm going to do with you two, but first you're coming to a party with me." That's why they looked as if they were shitting themselves.'

It provoked the loud, hacking laughter devoid of all humour in which every pustule on King's face seemed to join – but I felt slightly sick.

I was now in more buoyant spirits, for Godfrey had praised my 5,000-word defence of Stanley Baldwin and Michael Rand had liked the visuals – in particular, a 1920s advert for Swan Vestas matches showing Baldwin lighting his pipe with the caption 'The Prime Minister uses them' – so a major transfusion of lovely Plantin lay somewhere ahead.

My follow up, I decided, must make Francis Wyndham think me a young writer worth encouraging and nurturing; a piece in his narrative style, reliant on dialogue more than description, about someone meeting his highest, or lowest, ideal of camp.

I immediately thought of Diana Dors, the platinum blonde film actress known in the Fifties as Britain's Marilyn Monroe and the bestower of wet dreams on every schoolboy of my generation. Now she seemed to have been eclipsed by Sixties screen-goddesses like Julie Christie, with their non-blonde hair and hollow cheeks, and was in the papers only for owing £30,000 in income tax. Altogether, the camp potential looked unlimited.

'Fine by me, dear boy,' Godfrey said. 'But you'll have to see what Francis says.'

'Great,' Francis said. If people in those days had punched the air and gone 'Yesss!', I would have done it.

Diana Dors was naturally more than happy to be interviewed by the *Sunday Times Magazine*, despite the obscurity of the interviewer, and her publicist arranged for me to see her at her home in Sunningdale, accompanied by a photographer. His name was Malcolm Hart and he was a perfect couture hippy, chiffon-scarved, amulet-hung and alligator-booted. With him he brought a curly-haired assistant called Ray, a Bob Dylan lookalike who until very recently had been a New York policeman.

They'd worked with Francis on the Miss World story, and Malcolm had been profoundly impressed. 'There's a guy without one bit of aggression in him. He just listens to people, never saying anything but "How *interesting*."' I stored that one away for future use.

On the journey to Sunningdale, squeezed into Malcolm's Lotus Elan, Ray told me how he'd persuaded Miss World to consult the I Ching, an ancient Chinese book of supposedly oracular power. 'The part the I Ching guided her to was about the unimportance of physical beauty. Blew her mind, man.'

We arrived outside Diana Dors's Hollywood-style bungalow much too early so went to a nearby Trust House hotel to have coffee. But Malcolm's chiffon scarf created such alarm that we were refused service.

It was an overwhelming experience to meet the real-life version of the black-and-white pin-up I'd ogled so often in *Reveille* or *Tit-Bits* magazine, usually sitting on the toilet at Grandma Norman's dreadful Castle Street flat with its uninterrupted view of rock cartons piled high.

The last thing I expected her to be was a friendly, jolly, highly articulate woman who answered all my questions, often hilariously, and regarded her glamour-icon status as a rather tiresome joke. Camp couldn't find a foothold anywhere.

We spent the afternoon beside her swimming pool with her much younger boyfriend, a would-be pop singer named Troy Dante, while Malcolm busied himself with what he unpretentiously called his 'snaps'. Inside the house, the Beatles' just-released new album was playing; I can still picture the most famously erotic lips before Mick Jagger's, singing 'Sergeant Pepper's Lonely … Sergeant Pepper's Lonely …'

My piece went in almost at once, albeit under a condescending headline, 'The Last of the Big Blondes'. Even so, she sent me a nice letter about it, ending 'keep up the good work of writing. Diana D.'

It had, of course, been aimed at one person only and his verdict was the only one that mattered.

'Great,' said Francis – which in that moment I realised wasn't much of an improvement on 'fine'.

At least, I finally seemed to be making some headway with Peter Crookston, whose special issue on Middle Age was now in preparation, exploring all its laughable and pitiable implications in this time of omnipotent youth. To lighten the anthropological and statistical content, he wanted something about middle-aged people stubbornly continuing to have sex, in particular illicit sex outside marriage. And at the last Ideas Lunch, Godfrey had suggested how amusing it would be if someone of my age were to write on 'The Middle-Aged Affair'.

Acquaintances of Godfrey's, Derek Jewell's and Mrs Susan Raven's proved to be positively lining up to tell the *Sunday Times Magazine* about their middle-aged affairs, albeit under assumed names. I chose an American woman Derek knew vaguely, who'd been cheating on her dentist husband with a welder from St Albans below her both in age and class, and to whom I gave the alias of 'Janine'.

When I returned from interviewing her in a pub in Fulham, Bruce Jeffcott came out of his office to intercept me. 'Has anyone spoken to you,' he said, 'about flying to Nice?'

My first foreign assignment, like the Francis Chichester profile, arose from the misconception of me as a man of the sea, but this time the subject would not be on it but under it.

Following that huge success with Chichester, the *Sunday Times* was sponsoring an American long-distance swimmer named Mary Margaret Revell in her bid to become the first person able to exist on the seabed for extended periods like an astronaut in space, so consequently an 'aquanaut'.

What the paper had dubbed Operation Mermaid was to take place beneath the Mediterranean at Villefranche, between Nice and Monaco. I was not only to cover it for the Magazine with my supposed expertise in all things maritime, but also hand over the £1,800 balance of the sponsorship money on its successful completion.

As the BEA flight curved in over Nice bay and the window filled with almost blindingly beautiful blue, the young Frenchwoman next to me began bouncing up and down in ecstasy in what was obviously a homecoming after long absence. She was like a ventriloquist's dummy, channeling my own joy and dread with joy, as always, uppermost under my emerald-green, round-collared shirt.

The 'Mermaid' had streaky blonde hair and the powerful build to be expected in the first woman to have swum the Straits of Messina, combined with a hippy artiness; one of her planned underwater activities being to paint a picture. Apart from on the seabed, she was accompanied everywhere by her husband/manager, Irwin Goodwin, a short, bald man, on leave from his job as a correspondent for *Newsweek* magazine, who would increasingly look as if he wished he were back there.

The operation was to take place on a secluded stretch of Villefanche's famously deep-water harbour, off a jetty belonging to the Observatoire Oceanographique, a centre devoted to the study of small marine life, especially sea urchins and jellyfish, that had been set up at the impetus of Charles Darwin.

I arrived to find the jetty already crowded almost to its limit. The operation was overseen by La Spirotechnique, the company owned by the great French underwater explorer, Jacques Cousteau, who, although not present himself, had sent a six-man team equipped with stopwatches and talkative walkie-talkies, and a truck towing a gigantic decompression chamber.

There were two Italian divers who had watched over Mary Margaret in the Straits of Messina - and who, it was said, would lay down their lives for her – supplementing a contingent of local French ones to keep her under round-the-clock observation. Least welcome to me was a film-crew from BBC TV's *24 Hours* programme, which was also funding the project.

Accommodation had been booked for me at the Observatoire but I found this to be an open dormitory with the French and Italian divers, so booked into a small hotel up the hill behind it.

That evening, there was a briefing for the BBC crew and me by Irwin Goodwin. The plan, he said, was for his wife to spend up to three days as 'a free-ranging aquanaut', studying undersea life, painting her picture, taking minimal rest periods in a plastic shelter known as 'the bubble'. Anticipating the obvious question, he said she had been on a course of doctor-prescribed enemas, so would never need to 'evacuate'.

The next morning, a substantial crowd on the shingle beach as well as the jetty watched Mary Margaret wade into the Mediterranean in flippers, a parti-coloured wetsuit and large white goggles with Michelmas daisies threaded through them. But after barely an hour, her submersion was cut short by unfavourable sea and weather conditions.

So it was the next day, too. On the day after that, the sea and the weather were perfect and she ducked under, seemingly to stay. As the *BBC* crew and I hung around the jetty, wondering what to do with the indefinite number of hours to come, the sound recordist switched on a transistor radio and we heard that Israel had launched a devastatingly successful pre-emptive strike against its three hostile Arab neighbours

But after another brief spell, the Mermaid re-emerged from the waves for reasons not immediately clear in the blare of French walkie-talkies. The only English-speaking French diver told us she'd spent little of that time free-ranging and rather a lot of it inside the 'bubble' supposedly intended for brief rest periods.

I'd arranged with the *Magazine's* picture editor, June Stanier, that I should suss out the visual possibilities before she sent a photographer out to join me. I was starting to have misgivings about Mary Margaret but, as a non-swimmer, had no way of studying her in action or inaction. I phoned June from the hotel and requested a photographer who could dive, thinking it a tall order. But twenty minutes later, she called back and told me to expect Terry Le Goubin.

This proved not to be a Frenchman but a heavy-set, slow-moving Londoner who seemed to have little of the merman about him. However, after I explained the situation, he borrowed a wetsuit from the Observatoire and the next time Mary Margaret went under, followed after her with a confident upkick of flippers. When he reappeared, it was to say, 'She's in the bubble.'

Among the crowd on the jetty, a certain ennui began to take hold. The French divers no longer spoke of 'Operation Mermaid' but 'Operation Merdeuse', which I don't suppose I need translate. The near-skeletal one nicknamed Sacdos (Bag of Bones) started taking bets on how long Mary Margaret *wouldn't* spend free-ranging about the seabed, on the principle that 'time in the bubble counts double.' Even the two Italian divers said to be willing to lay down their lives for her were looking distinctly pissed off.

During her absences, the BBC sound man beguiled the time by writing lampoons of the operation in supposedly *Sunday Times Magazine* style – 'Yesterday, intrepid, insipid blonde mermaid Mary Margaret Revile began another intrepid day on the seabed but was forced to admit de-feet after stubbing one intrepid toe on a starfish' and the like. I returned to a pastime I'd all but given up, drawing caricatures of her and Irwin as grotesque fish.

Her final submersion ended late at night, far short of the planned three days. As she came out of the water into a glare of television lights, the *24 Hours* reporter, David Lomax, as good as accused her of malingering.

Before she was even quite dry, she asked me for the £1,800 balance of her *Sunday Times* sponsorship money. I refused to hand over the cheque on the grounds that she hadn't adequately fulfilled her side of the bargain.

After an acrimonious scene, half-expecting trouble from her Italian divers, I fetched the bag I'd already packed, sprinted up the hill into Villefranche and took a taxi to the airport.

* * *

That summer, the *Magazine's* shortage of space where I was concerned suddenly ended, to an extent which taught me an important lesson about writing for it. If there was one thing worse than not getting one's pieces in, it was getting them in.

To begin with, I naturally felt triumphant. Peter Crookston's issue on Middle Age included 'The Woman Who Ran Away', my interview with 'Janine' about her extra-marital affair with her welder from St Albans, (disguised as a plasterer from Colchester).

Three weeks later, in an admittedly small issue, there was only one thing not by me – and that just a picture story on the wooden hut used by Scott of the Antarctic on his doomed journey to the South Pole, where the cold had kept everything in the same pristine state as in 1911.

The centre of the *Magazine* was filled by my 5,000-word defence of Stanley Baldwin, lavishly illustrated by sepia photographs of the General Strike and headlines from the Abdication crisis of 1936. The opening piece was my satirical report on Mary Margaret Revell as an aquanaut, headlined 'The Blonde in the Bubble'. The top half of the cover showed her white-goggled face, the bottom half, that of a present-day Antarctic scientist in a fur-lined hood. 'Under the world: the men who stayed' read the caption to that one; 'Under the sea: the mermaid who 'didn't', read the other.

The Baldwin piece brought a letter from the Liberal politician Lady Violet Bonham Carter, saying she had read it 'with pleasure and agreement.' 'The Blonde in the Bubble' brought a writ for libel from Mary Margaret's lawyers.

I had never faced this terror before, and quickly discovered how utterly alone it made one feel. Apart from Bruce Jeffcott, who broke the news of the writ's arrival and made me an appointment with the *Sunday Times's* lawyers, no one on the *Magazine* ever mentioned it. Even Godfrey, who had been vastly amused by my refusal to pay Mary Margaret her £1,800, uttered no word of reassurance or censure. The general determined myopia strangely recalled that time when the Hunts Post had printed 'whanked' instead of 'thanked'.

By a coincidence in which I could take no pleasure, the *Sunday Times's* lawyers were the firm of Theodore Goddard whose founder had advised both Stanley Baldwin and Wallis Simpson during the Abdication. There I was seen by a man named Mr Calderan who possessed the unnerving ability to raise each eyebrow independently of the other. They both kept going up and down like railway signals as he questioned me about the events in Villefranche.

'I don't think you're going to have a defence of fair comment,' he said, 'because the other side are claiming malice aforethought on your part and say they're in a position to prove it.'

Three days later, a long brown envelope was pushed under the front door of my shared basement in Argyll Road. In it was a writ for libel from the dentist husband of 'Janine', to whom I'd given the name of 'Douglas' in my piece about her middle-aged affair. It claimed that nonetheless he'd been recognisable to all his friends, professional colleagues and patients and that everything said about him was untrue and held him up to 'ridicule and contempt'.

So I *had* been found out, but in a way beyond my worst nightmares. I assumed this meant the end of me at the *Sunday Times* and probably my journalistic career. I could imagine what fun *Private Eye* would have with it in their Street of Shame column: 'Red faces at the *Sunday Times* Colour Mag where their much-vaunted Young Writer of the Year has landed them with not one but two libel-actions …' Brenda Jones, who dealt regularly with Mr Calderan, passed on his damning judgement: 'That young man seems very libel-prone.'

As it turned out, 'Douglas's' writ went away (without Peter Crookston ever having mentioned it.) But the Mary Margaret case not only continued but grew in complexity, for the *Sunday Times* was now counter-suing her for the return of the sponsorship money it had already paid her. Depositions were taken from material witnesses, like the photographer Terry Le Goubin and the BBC film crew, then rolled up like parchments, secured with green sealing-wax and tied with pink string, all at unimaginable cost.

Then one day, Mr Calderan showed me a bundle of photostats with the evidence of my supposed malice aforethought. They were the lampoons of Operation Mermaid which the BBC sound-recordist had written in mock *Magazine*-ese. Her husband must have found them lying around the jetty and assumed I was their author.

When I told Mr Calderan, the eyebrows for once didn't come into play. 'In that case, this is what our answer to them will be,' he said, and made a sweeping V-sign.

In the 21st century, all this sounds very like the oppressing of a courageous woman – the first, after all, to have swum the Straits of Messina – by a lot of bullying, patronising men. I don't exclude myself. It wasn't my £1,800 and she'd obviously been short of money; I could easily have handed it over, so helping Operation Mermaid on its way, perhaps into the *Guinness Book of Records*.

At the time, such thoughts never crossed my selfish, self-obsessed 24-year-old mind. I just thanked God no one had found the scurrilous - a judge might even have said malicious – caricatures of her I had drawn to illustrate the BBC man's words.

*   *   *

10

How would you like to go to America?

One of the best things about the *Magazine* was the space it devoted to great art and artists, not just as tasters for some forthcoming exhibition but, in its usual random, extravagant manner, giving Caravaggio or Breughel or Lawrence Alma Tadema or Jackson Pollock the same lush colour spreads as fashion and the Vietnam War – and often the cover as well.

To choose the artists and the illustrations, anywhere else would have had a mere fine art consultant. But the *Sunday Times Magazine* had David Sylvester.

I'd of course never heard of Sylvester, but my omniscient friend Nick Mason on the subs desk soon set me straight. He was considered by a long way the greatest living critic of modern art and had curated major exhibitions of giants like Matisse and Henry Moore in most of Europe's major galleries. 'He doesn't just know all about them, he knows a lot of them personally, like Picasso and Magritte,' Nick said. 'And he pretty much invented Francis Bacon.'

He was about Godfrey's age and practically Godfrey's girth, although his lurked under an enormous unstructured dark brown suit. He wore a piratical black beard from which a few stray tentacles arched over his skull and his brown eyes were of a curious intensity as though constantly sifting the genuine masterpiece from the fake.

In contrast with his general air of dishevelment and chaos, his prose was elegant and precise, and imbued with a passion that could make one rush to a painting he had described as if to a lover's tryst. However, even the shortest piece caused prolonged agony which regularly made him miss deadlines by as much as a year.

He was paid the *Magazine's* top rate of ten shillings per word and, it was said, always used the shortest words possible to make the bargain feel even better. By a unique arrangement, his earnings were sent directly to his wine merchant.

His expense claims were among the very few ever to be challenged. 'He's a genius,' Godfrey would shrug, handing them back, countersigned, to a stupefied Bruce Jeffcott. 'They say that the price of liberty is eternal vigilance. Here our watchword should be "the price of Sylvester is eternal vigilance."'

I expected such a personage to have little time for someone to whom 'Francis Bacon' still meant the 16th century essayist many people believed to have written the works of Shakespeare. But one afternoon, as we passed in the passage to the Gents, he addressed me in tones as solemn and sonorous as an archbishop's. 'I liked your piece about your grandmother, but I was fascinated by the one on Diana Dors. I must have beaten my meat while looking at pictures of her enough to go blind about ten times over.'

After that, we always talked when he came into the office or, rather, he talked and I listened. Each time, another gap in my aesthetic education was closed; I learned to tell Monet from Manet, that there was a Picabia as well as a Picasso, that the Bauhaus hadn't been a German beer hall, Le Corbusier was an architect not a brand of Cognac and Man Ray a photographer not a flatfish.

The catholicity of his interests was almost the equal of Nick Mason's and he would discuss the latest James Bond film or Tottenham Hotspurs' chances for the Cup with equal seriousness and knowledgeability, chainsmoking a brand of aromatic yellow cigarette named Doctor Bustani, which he said, could be bought only in Egypt.

Despite his size, he fancied himself mightily as a sportsman – as a cricketer above all, though there were suggestions that his brilliance in other fields might not extend to this one. The illustrator Roger Coleman later told me how the two of them had been walking through the East End one day and seen a group of small boys playing on some waste ground with a home-made bat and stumps.

'David went up to them in his grandest manner, grabbed the bat and said, "A pound for the first boy to get me out." I walked on, but a few minutes later he came after me and said "Roger, can you lend me five pounds?"'

That autumn of 1967, there were major projects afoot at the *Magazine* in which I expected to play no part whatsoever.

Among the relatively few international celebrities in those days, none had more glamour and fascination than the British-born film actress Elizabeth Taylor. Her unique violet-coloured eyes with double sets of lashes, her constantly changing husbands, her legendary extravagance and periodic life-threatening illnesses had kept her in the headlines for twenty years and still did, despite all the latter competition from 'swinging' screen-sirens half her age.

In 1961, she'd been paid an unprecedented $1 million to play the title-role in Cleopatra, a shambolic epic that all but bankrupted the 20th Century-Fox studios. It had gained equal notoriety from her public affair with her co-star, Richard Burton, although both had spouses at the time, which titillated the whole world and brought an official condemnation from the Vatican.

Burton had since become her fifth husband and the couple had begun making films together, each in some way a reflection of their so-called 'Marriage of the Century', to which the public flocked.

Now the *Magazine* had decided to do a profile of Taylor: as usual, not to coincide with any film release, just because it felt like it. Even to a star of such dimensions, its lure was irresistible. She had immediately agreed to be interviewed without setting any time limit or seeking copy approval, although her filming commitments, would delay it a few months. Meantime, her office had provided a list of the people closest to her who could be talked to for background research.

Godfrey's young rips were to do these supporting interviews in Britain, France, Switzerland and America, then he himself would have the conversation with Taylor and write the profile, at around 5,000 words.

The second major project in preparation was one I expected to observe from even further afar. Early next year, true to its policy of discovering the whole world anew, the *Magazine* was to do a three-part series on America. It was a land still inaccessible to most British people and as yet had spread its culture to few places outside London. This would be the definitive portrait of such national institutions as football played in helmets and hot dogs, gorgeously illustrated but with a characteristic satirical edge.

Peter Crookston and Derek Jewell were the co-editors and both would be travelling there, along with a team of the *Magazine's* top photographers. Among them would be the one still known as Donald rather than Don McCullin, taking a break from covering the Vietnam

War. I caught my first glimpse of him in the Art Department, a dead ringer for Steve McQueen in an olive-coloured suit and purple shirt, over whom Michael Rand and even David King positively slavered.

At the time, David Sylvester was much in evidence around the office, organising a special issue he'd talked Godfrey into that had nothing to do with art. Its premise was that every important figure in the 20th century had had a surname ending in 'stein', from Albert Einstein, who'd developed the theory of relativity to Brian Epstein, who'd developed the Beatles. I'd hoped he'd ask me to write about Epstein, but so far the call hadn't come.

I thought it had late one afternoon when Sheila McNeile summoned me to Godfrey's office just as I was about to go home. Instead, he beamed at me from behind his unencumbered desk and said 'How would you like to go to America?'

I was to be absorbed into the American series after all, with an assignment that, all these years later, still makes me shake my head in disbelief. 'We want you and a photographer to drive along Route 66 – you know, the famous highway from Chicago to Los Angeles – and write about all the places along the way and the people you meet.'

How my elevation to that elite transatlantic taskforce had come about was explained the next time I saw Sylvester. 'You can thank me,' he said. 'I went to Godfrey and told him, "You *have* to send that boy to America."'

I also had him to thank for a second assignment, almost as thrilling, to which he'd already secured Godfrey's agreement. While in New York, I was to do a story on the Apollo Theatre in Harlem, which had given almost every major black American music legend from Ella Fitzgerald to Sam Cooke their first big chance.

I was amazed by this fresh evidence of his cultural versatility. 'I can't believe you know about people like Ella …and Sam Cooke… and Bo Jingles Robinson …'

'Bo *Jangles* Robinson,' he corrected me.

A third assignment materialised from Godfrey that was more in the realm of normality: interviewing some of the American sources for his Elizabeth Taylor profile, including her parents in Los Angeles. (Except what could be normal about being in Los Angeles?)

Six days later, I flew to New York first-class on Air France – some kind of PR promotion I never quite understood – with my smallpox inoculation still suppurating on my arm and a book of American

Express travellers cheques totalling $2,000 in my pocket. If Grandad Bassill could see me now, I thought.

In America then, Anglophilia was at its all-time high. Visitors from Britain were invariably asked whether they knew Winston Churchill (although he'd been deceased for two years) or the Beatles. But my first encounter with it was peculiarly charming.

The Magazine had booked me into the Hotel Algonquin on West 44th Street, which I'd read about in James Thurber's book about Harold Ross, his editor at the *New Yorker*, the one with the private corridor from his office to the gents'.

On the evening of my arrival, I was sitting in the lobby Thurber and Dorothy Parker had once frequented, sipping a Pimms Number 1, over here called 'Pimms Cup' and served in a little copper tankard. At a nearby table were an important-looking white-haired man and two women.

The younger one was rather pretty and I couldn't help repeatedly glancing her way. When the older one rose and came over, I half-expected her to ask what the hell I thought I was staring at. 'Pardon this intrusion,' she said, 'but we're such fans of your movies, we wondered if you'd do us the honour of having dinner with us.'

I may have borne some faint resemblance to the new young British screen idol David Hemmings, but I think it was my Take 6 suit, floral shirt and cerise silk kipper tie that did it. At all events, I was hungry and the hours ahead were completely empty.

'Thank you very much,' I said. 'I'd be delighted.'

They were Judge Howard Burns, his wife, Peg, and daughter, Sandy, from Cincinnati, Ohio. Thinking this a rare departure from the celebrity's usual craving for privacy, they steadfastly respected mine, never once referring to my 'movies' nor giving any clue to as to who they thought I was, so I was under no pressure to play a part or to lie.

On that basis, it was a thoroughly agreeable evening for all of us. They took me to an Italian restaurant a couple of streets away where, for the first time, I heard spaghetti referred to as 'pasta' and discovered it could be green, pink or white as well as yellow. Judge Burns was a bit pensive at first, making me suspect the invitation hadn't been his idea, but he brightened when we discovered a mutual love of Gilbert and Sullivan, and together mimed polishing up the handle on the big front door from HMS Pinafore.

Most people remember their first visit to New York as almost unbearably exciting, but for me it was the opposite. Everything was vastly bigger and louder than back home, but somehow not strange, even reassuring; at times, the very skyscrapers seemed to lean down to form a protective bower over my head. I suppose it was the legacy of my upbringing in a wild seascape, with no roots but iron pier legs, that the greater the metropolis, the safer I felt.

To someone who'd known Clive Norman's grim portion control, the liberality of New York catering was staggering. In bars, whisky, gin or vodka, known in Britain, appropriately, as 'shorts', came in full tumblers, garnished with whole salads or fruit-salads. At chain-restaurants like Schrafft's, a main course entitled you to both a salad starter and a dessert; in sandwiches at Wolf's or the Carnegie Deli, bread was a mere afterthought to the great mound of salt beef or pastrami.

My first priority was to connect with John Bulmer, the *Magazine's* very senior photographer with whom I was to drive along Route 66. After a couple of days, he dropped by to see me in my room at the Algonquin, which gave onto a ventilation shaft and so looked out at darkness around the clock.

He was several years my senior, with a pointy face, very curly hair and an unmistakable whiff of either Oxford or Cambridge. But he'd had many previous assignments in America and driven over large areas of it, which I was relieved to hear since that aspect of our journey scared me stiff. A few years earlier, there had been an American TV series called *Route 66* about two young men freebooting along it in an open sports car and Bulmer suggested we emulate them by renting a two-door Ford Mustang. I wasn't to see him again until we took to the road in Chicago.

Working in New York proved no different from anywhere else, apart from the yellow cabs, the incessant traffic-wail, the pervading smell of burnt toast, the flashing signs at pedestrian crossings, brusquely ordering WALK or DON'T WALK, the police in their cross-buttoned dark blue tunics with deep side-vents that could have come straight from Carnaby Street.

I interviewed Elizabeth Taylor's lawyer, Aaron Frosch; her child co-star in *Lassie Come Home*, Roddy McDowall, who had me to breakfast at his apartment overlooking Central Park; and Mike Nichols, who'd directed Burton and Taylor together in *Who's Afraid of Virginia Woolf*, America's top-grossing film of 1966. The name of the *Sunday Times*

Magazine, usually rendered as 'the London Times', didn't open so much as kick down every door.

Harlem in those days was not somewhere it was advisable for white people to go, but once I'd persuaded a yellow cab to take me to the Apollo Theatre on 125th Street, Englishness and naivete and 'the London Times' were better protection than a phalanx of bodyguards.

I spent two days around the theatre, talking to its (white) owner, Frank Schiffman and Honi Coles, the amiable compere of its famously uproarious weekly Amateur Hour, where Ella Fitzgerald and so many other legends had been discovered. In Mr Schiffman's office I was introduced to Willie-Mae ('Big Mama') Thornton, whose version of *Hound Dog* as a wife berating an idle husband had preceded Elvis Presley's and was preferred by many.

I also witnessed a performance by James Brown, 'the Hardest-Working Man in Showbusiness', as he proved by erupting onto the stage without any warm-up act and doing two screaming, sweating, begging, pleading hours on the moving staircase of his own feet until something like a seizure brought him to his knees and two of his band wrapped him in a cloak and half-helped, half-coerced him towards the wings.

It was pure showmanship: at the last moment, he threw the cloak aside, strutted back into the spotlight and carried on.

* * *

On my journey with John Bulmer down 2,000 miles of Route 66, through Missouri, Kansas, Oklahoma, Texas, New Mexico, Arizona and California, one scene constantly repeated itself. We'd stop at a diner for a cold drink and be served with glasses of iced water directly we sat down. In British restaurants then, one almost had to beg for water, which never came iced, so this was an event in itself. Then, having quenched our thirst for free, we'd guiltily leave without ordering anything.

'Get your kicks on Route 66,' says the Bobby Troup song, later covered by the Rolling Stones. In our case, rather miraculously, the kicks weren't that hard and none caused lasting damage.

It took just over two weeks to 'motor west', with Bulmer doing most of the the driving, and for the first thousand or so miles each day felt much the same, whatever the state. Yet another eight hours or so of dead-straight white highway beyond the Mustang's slightly elevated front, stretching to infinity and boiling like milk in the heat. Then with the sudden chill of evening, yet another Holiday Inn or TraveLodge, both still unknown in Britain. Another pair of rooms exactly like the last with their two king-size beds for one person, and airborne colour TV and paper strip across the toilet bowl saying 'Sanitized For Your Protection'; in the floodlit dark outside, another frantic fizz of cicadas.

I grew accustomed to the huge skies shared out among every state but with a bonus for Texas; the amazing choice of music on the radio compared with the stingy BBC back home; the sublime sunsets and dead skunks in the middle of the road; the passing signs for 'Genuine Indian Curios', Rattlesnake Farm' and the peculiarly persistent Denny's restaurant chain: '5 miles to Denny's for shakes and fries …3 miles to Denny's for shakes and fries … 1 mile to Denny's … Heck, ain't you *hungry* yet?'

Each state line meant a different Ruritanan uniform for the police and the Highway Patrol, sometimes a mixture of chocolate and café-au-lait, sometimes dark blue with a pale blue bow tie, often surmounted by the kind of broad-brimmed hat with pinched-in crown worn by British Boy Scouts. We were pulled over for speeding near Joplin, Missouri, then again near Tulsa, Oklahoma, but England and the London Times did their usual magic and we were let off without a 'citation' and told to have a nice day.

Despite the Mustang, we hardly cut the romantic figures of those two young adventurers in TV's 'Route 66.' John Bulmer's curly hair led to a frequent assumption that we were 'faggots', a word that in Britain still meant meatballs. Narrowed eyes were turned on us in most wayside eateries and in one midnight-black bar, as Country and Western music played on the jukebox, an enormous truck driver came over and asked Bulmer if he'd care to dance.

At Bulmer's suggestion, I left him and the Mustang in Amarillo, Texas and hitchhiked 300 miles to rejoin them in Alburquerque. New Mexico – even for those days, a piece of utter lunacy that still causes me the occasional night-sweat. But the gods of Route 66 continued to smile on naivete, Englishness and the London Times.

My first ride was in another Mustang, with an oil worker from Louisiana named Bud Epperson, a dead ringer for Jack Nicholson, who drank cans of beer non-stop from a case between his feet. He took me almost 200 miles and the remaining 100 I did in a puttering

Volkswagen Beetle beside an elderly man with a racking cough, whose name sounded like 'Fritz Wheelhouse' and whose holstered .38 handgun, dangling from a peg behind his left ear, I initially mistook for a transistor radio.

Once I'd rejoined Bulmer and we'd put Texas behind us, the continent suddenly seemed to open up. I saw the Grand Canyon, the Painted Desert and the Hoover Dam, from which we made a 30-mile detour to Las Vegas, where fruit machines grew by the million and, unlike my father's half-dozen, had no limit to their jackpots. As I stood on the never-unlit main street, watching Bulmer tirelessly at work, a passing punter with a woman clinging to each arm snarled, 'Looka those two fuckin' queers.'

In New Mexico, I met an old rodeo performer named Rusty Ryan who - unsuccessfully – tried to teach me to crack a bullwhip, and a Hopi Native American boy with a cardboard sign saying 'MY NAME IS BERNARD J. JOHNSON. TAKE MY PICTURE FOR A DOLLAR' and a stripper named Zola Goyer, filling in between engagements by driving a huge truck, tiger-striped in silver and black and carrying 3,000 frozen TV dinners.

I can't say I ever felt close to John Bulmer (and, in fact, never partnered him again) but the way he worked as a photographer taught me invaluable lessons no fellow writer ever had. Never regard a story as over … keep your ears open at all times … always make the phone-call, even if it seems hopeless… don't take 'no' for an answer.

I was thinking the story pretty much over, in the sense that nothing else could possibly top it, when Bulmer proved his point that there could always be something more.

In Albuquerque, we learned from its daily Journal that a rancher named George Farr was about to drive 500 longhorn steers across the desert to the city's stockyards as his family had done for generations at this time of year, although latterly with herds much reduced in size. This age-old trail lay across what was now the U.S. military's White Sands missile range where, in deference to one of the Old West's most hallowed rituals, firing would be suspended for a week.

We drove to the Farr ranch in Datil to find a scene John Ford might have choreographed. There were cowboys on horseback, in perfect Hollywood detail except for the gleam of watches on their wrists; there was even a traditional chuck-wagon hitched to a Chevrolet pick-up.

I talked to Mr Farr's son Roy as he sat on his palomino, ready to move 'em out. 'You've asked me a lot of questions,' he said, 'now I'll ask you one. Why ain't your hair same as mine?' He doffed his Stetson to reveal a scalp cropped almost to the bone.

We'd arranged to meet up with the drive at its first night's camp, but John missed the way; we drove off the road and actually into the desert, at one point along a seemingly endless dry riverbed. I was imagining how it might feel to be eaten by the coyotes we could hear when, to my ineffable relief, a campfire glowed ahead.

The cowboys treated the appearance of a Ford Mustang from the darkness as nothing untoward and a classic 'old-timer' with a walrus moustache took us to the rear of the chuck-wagon to wash off the dust. The soap came in a curious whitish receptacle. 'Hollowed-out skull of a yearling heifer,' he explained.

They sat us by the campfire and gave us a supper of huge T-bone steaks and black coffee, neither of which I much cared for as a rule. But in the desert air, under the stars, nothing had ever tasted so wonderful.

We reached Los Angeles on Hallowe'en - which at that time meant nothing in Britain. All the way into the city there were giant billboards for Elizabeth Taylor's new film, *Reflections In A Golden Eye*. When we checked into the Hollywood House Motel on Sunset Boulevard, the background talk about 'trick or treating' was a mystery to me.

Peter Crookston arrived the next day from New York, where he'd persuaded a photographer named Diane Arbus to work for the *Magazine*. His shirts were more brilliant and his manner more amiable than ever and I hoped that, away from the office and with such a journey behind me, I'd finally succeed in impressing him.

This I certainly did when the three of us went for dinner at the International House of Pancakes opposite our motel and Bobbie Gentry's *Ode to Billie-Joe* began playing in the background. Peter had never understood what had made Billie-Joe McAllister jump off the Tallahatchie Bridge; I suggested it was remorse for having murdered the illegitimate baby born to the singer and himself, and their disposal of its body into the same 'muddy waters'. He listened in fascination and I hoped my copy might one day have a similar effect.

He and John Bulmer were old friends and it was no surprise when they went off together to watch the former Hollywood child star Shirley Temple campaign for a seat in Congress – almost as bizarre an idea as a former Hollywood semi-star, Ronald Reagan, having recently become Governor of California.

Left to myself, I rounded off Route 66 by persuading radio station WABC to let me accompany its traffic reporter Dawn O'Day (not her real name) on her early-morning helicopter patrol above the loops and figure-eights of teeming highway glistening in the smoggy sunshine. En route she took time to inform her sweating, gridlocked audience 200 feet below, 'My passenger today is Philip Norman of the London Times ... great to have you with us, Philip.'

Finally, and least interestingly I expected, there were two further pre-arranged background interviews for Godfrey's Elizabeth Taylor profile – the first with a man I'd never heard of named Bennie Thau, the second with her parents, Francis and Sara.

The tiny, wizened Thau had formerly been head of MGM studios, Taylor's first screen home, and one of Hollywood's principal power brokers for thirty years, reputedly the only producer Greta Garbo ever trusted. He seemed not much interested in talking about Taylor in *Lassie Come Home* but then, unexpectedly, took me to lunch at a country club whose intense low-keyness – Englishness in fact - proclaimed the vast wealth and influence of its membership.

While we were having dessert, a merry-looking man with a moustache stopped by to chat. He was the director Pando S. Berman, whose *Prisoner of Zenda* I'd sat through, enthralled, five times at Ryde's Scala cinema.

I was to see the Taylor parents at their home in Bel Air – extraordinarily, it seems now, without any PR person there to censor my questions or limit the time. My taxi arrived outside their vast white bungalow far too early and I decided to go for a walk around. Within minutes, a police car drew up beside me and I was brusquely asked for some identification. In this wealthiest and most exclusive of star enclaves, anyone on foot was *prima facie* up to no good.

Francis and Sara Taylor had settled in Los Angeles so long ago – he as an antique-dealer, she to get her only daughter into the movies – it was hard to believe they'd started out from Hampstead, north London. Francis was tall and what used to be called ''distinguished-looking'; Sarah was small and voluble, like an early sketch for the masterpiece they'd produced between them. He was still recovering from a stroke that had left him slow of speech and prone to loud, unapologetic belches. 'Well, better out than in!' she kept saying in a way that reminded me of my Grandma Bassill.

Without any PR to censor or call time, we had a pleasant hour-long chat. Francis Taylor told me what a healthy appetite Hollywood's sloe-eyed Cleopatra had; how she thought nothing of eating five hot dogs 'with everything' at a sitting. Sara said how much she and 'Daddy' both loved their new son-in-law, Richard Burton, not least for his effect on their daughter's chronic untidiness that I knew (from cuttings) had helped see off at least two of her four previous husbands.

'I've actually seen her emptying ashtrays,' her mother said. 'That's something she never would have done before she met Richard.' On a side table stood a jointly-signed photograph of the couple, she in an armchair, wearing mink and net stockings, he perched on one arm; a typical before-Sunday-lunch kind of pose with bookcases in the background. 'Wait until you see the library we're going to have in Switzerland,' his inscription said. 'From Elizabeth,' hers said, 'with more love than all the books in the world.'

'That's so nice,' I said to Sara. 'Do you mind if I copy it out?'

'Of course not, dear,' she said.

*　　*　　*

Part Three

* * *

11

Take it from me, kid, Godfrey runs the warmest stall in town

I arrived back in London to find the Foundations' *Baby Now That I've Found You* at the top of the singles charts and a new arrival at the *Magazine*, occupying the formerly empty third desk in the office I shared with Mrs Susan Raven. His name was Dick Adler; he looked almost a caricature of a fat, bald, cigar-chomping American, the archetypal crude, philistine Hollywood producer or agent. And what you saw was what you got, except for the crudity and philistinism.

I knew of him already from the masthead of *Town* magazine, that dream workplace of my *Hunts Post* days. Since then, Town had dwindled to a mere shadow of its once super-cool self, largely thanks to unbeatable competition from Lord Thomson's golden egg-laying goose. Dick had been its last editor, brought over from New York in what proved a vain attempt to halt the slide.

Soon after *Town* folded, he happened to meet Godfrey at a party and mention he was currently without a job and planning to return to the States. 'No, don't do that, dear boy,' Godfrey had replied with typical expansiveness. 'Why don't you join us at 200 Gray's Inn Road?' In his gratitude and relief, Dick had come to the *Magazine* without a title or any clear-cut role, but his understanding had been that he would write.

I warmed to him immediately, for he talked like a mixture of Raymond Chandler and Groucho Marx and shared my addiction to puns, the groan-worthier the better. In our very first conversation, he told me he'd once worked for an American girlie magazine where he had to invent names for the models to spare their families' blushes back in Topeka or Wichita Falls. One of them he'd called Myra Gards, so as to be able to write the headline 'Give Myra Gards to Broadway'.

He seemed completely at ease with both his size and hairlessness; indeed, was full of *joie-de-vivre* that frequently made him burst into song in a pleasant tenor. At that time, his favourite was Simon and Garfunkel's *Mrs Robinson* from the soundtrack of *The Graduate*, adding a special yearning tremolo to 'Where have you gone, Joe DiMaggio...?'

His charm, evident to me in so many ways, was completely lost on Mrs Raven, with whom he had already been *tête-à-tête* for about three weeks. The occasional verbal sally he directed at her had much the same effect as a pin glancing off a Centurion tank, eliciting only a puzzled frown and a peremptory '*What?*'

'I'm just not getting through to that lady,' he said the next time the door crashed shut after her. 'She's got a kind of deafness about her ... I don't seem to register at all.'

He was six or seven years my senior, which still put him only just over thirty, although, constituted as he was, he could have been in his fifties. As a result of editing *Town*, and several senior magazine jobs in New York before that, he had a vast acquaintanceship in film and literary circles on both sides of the Atlantic, including major writers like Richard Condon and Mordecai Richler whom he refused to treat with the fawning reverence they were accustomed to. Richler phoned him at the *Magazine* one day and said 'Hi, Dick, it's Mordecai,'

'Mordecai who?' Dick barked back.

Despite such competition, I found I'd acquired a second outsized mentor and friend who could teach me just as much as David Sylvester, in a less elevated sphere, 'You're kind of like my younger brother,' he once told me. (beat) 'Kid was a fairy ... we had to shoot him.'

His unabashed devotion to food and pleasure was an education in itself to one conditioned to feel guilty about both. Lunch with Dick in Soho only started off at his favourite Chinese restaurant, the Dumpling Inn. After vast amounts of dumplings resembling steamed or grilled dental-plates, we'd go to Patisserie Valerie for dessert, then to Bar Italia for espressos. Last stop would be the Coleman Cohen cigar store in Old Compton Street, where we bought Romeo y Julietas or Bolivars, lighting them at the naked flame that spurted all day from an airborne brass nozzle.

He lived in Primrose Hill with the British journalist Jane Wilson, who'd worked for him at Town and was now a well thought of profile writer for the *Magazine* on the likes of Paul Newman and Julie Andrews. An Oxford graduate, very pretty and very English, she had a simple rationale for so unlikely seeming a lover. 'I'd always adored Guy the

Gorilla,' she would explain, referring to the enormous silverback whose gentleness and dignity had made him the star attraction at Regent's Park Zoo.

Dick Adler was to do many things for me but one of the biggest came at the very beginning, when he passed me over a small book with his finger holding a page open and said, 'Don't you think this is the best writing there could ever be?'

It was the final page of F. Scott Fitzgerald's *The Great Gatsby*:

'… He had come a long way to this blue lawn and his dream must have seemed so close that he could hardly fail to grasp it. He did not know that it was already behind him, somewhere back in that vast obscurity beyond the city, where the dark fields of the republic rolled on under the night.'

After that I flew to Fitzgerald, never to leave him.

Dick also made me realise the snare of our over-heated room, where there was no pressure to do anything but wait for the next trip to Cashiers for another transfusion of blue fivers and take another taxi to lunch.

'An old City editor I knew on the *New York Herald* used to say that working for newspapers was like the story of Black Beauty. Sometimes, Beauty has a cruel owner who beats and starves him and keeps him chained up in the rain; sometimes a kind owner who gives him a nice warm stall and plenty of bran mash to eat. Take it from me, kid … Godfrey runs the warmest stall in town.'

Godfrey's Christmas festivities began, as last year, in the first week of December with his young rips' champagne, quiche and Cognac-fuelled outing to the Varsity rugger match at Twickenham, followed a few days later by the Secretaries' Lunch in all its droit-de-seigneurial condescension at the Gay Hussar.

This year there was the added spice of 'Thank U Very Much', a hit single by the Scaffold (two Liverpool poets and Paul McCartney's younger brother) which named '*The Soonday Toimes*' among its reasons to be thankful. Ironic or not, getting onto a pop record was an unprecedented accolade to which the *Magazine* and the paper each laid sole claim.

However, the usually climactic Christmas Party was somewhat

marred when a group of drivers from the editorial car pool gatecrashed it several hours too early, helped themselves to champagne, then sat down in the concourse, with Art Department business still going on around them, and called impatiently for some 'action'.

The Sixties might be classless but Thomson House definitely was not, so there could be no question simply of asking them to come back later. Since the building had nothing resembling security, the task of getting rid of them fell to Godfrey and Dick Adler, with myself hovering in the background. I thought it might help my career were I to stop a punch intended for my editor.

The intruders finally left after a ticklish scene out by the lifts when Dick's Chandleresque tough-guy act and Godfrey's 'Look here, you chaps, don't be silly' met with equal scorn. The hardest-looking of them gave the combined body mass of his two would-be chuckers-out a disparaging glance. 'You don't want to start a bundle with me,' he advised them.''Cos you don't look too fit.'

In January, a heavy rainstorm flooded the basement flat off Kensington High Street that I'd been sharing with my schoolfriend, Bryan Cooper. Its one bedroom had severely limited our love lives, making frequent coitus-interrupters of us both, and we decided to go our separate ways, dividing our few possessions in common without rancour. He took the little wooden manikin with articulated limbs, I the back copies of *Playboy*.

Rather than go on sharing, I'd decided to return to bedsitter-land, and struck lucky first time in Scarsdale Villas, just the other side of High Street Ken. It was a ground-floor front room that had evidently once been a small cocktail bar, although the house showed no other sign of an earlier life as a hotel. It was red-carpeted and panelled in wood, with inset gilt Tudor roses, and one panel opened to reveal a small washbasin and mirror.

Its large bay-window was only a couple of feet from the house's front steps and the nearest pane, for some reason, opened like a French door. This I kept unlocked and used as my own private entrance. In the fourteen months I was there, I never had a thing stolen.

The *Magazine's* discovery of America ran in three parts during January and proved yet another major circulation-builder. John Bulmer's Route 66 photographs were sumptuous – particularly one of cowboy silhouettes looming through the faintly golden dust of their longhorn herd – but the one cover of the series went to Don McCullin's portrait of huge-shouldered black football-players, from Derek Jewell's story on the all-conquering Green Bay Packers. The art department's double-page spread of a hot dog smothered in mustard had even winkled Godfrey out of his office to congratulate them.

As I now knew, January was the time to be planning major series for the summer and autumn, as always free of any interference from higher management, pressure from the advertising department or any considerationof what the readers might want, and as always regardless of expense.

The ever-energetic Derek had come up with the Second World War's North African campaign, in which the British Eighth Army's victory against the Italians and Rommel's Afrika Corps in Libya and Egypt had first presaged the turn of the tide against Hitler. With his usual zest, he was already bursting with fascinating facts about Tobruk and the Desert Rats and the Italian general whose wild moustachios led British troops to nickname him 'Electric Whiskers Berganzoli.'

The main participant in the series was to be no less than the desert war's great victor, Field-Marshal Viscount Montgomery of Alamein. C.D. Hamilton, the *Magazine's* self-effacing *eminence grise*, had served under 'Monty' as a junior officer, kept him touch with him after the war and bought his memoirs for a huge sum to launch the *Sunday Times's* Review section, since when he'd been regarded as more or less the paper's property. Derek's 'Alamein and the Desert War' was therefore to kick off by taking him back to the scene of the decisive battle near a lonely Egyptian railway stop from which he had taken his title.

I'd mentioned that my mother's brother, my Uncle Frank, had served with the Eighth Army (although pulled out of the line on the eve of El Alamein to keep a dental appointment) and Derek had me standing by to write one of the supporting historical pieces, yet to be decided. So it came about that, 18 months after officially becoming a colleague of Lord Snowdon, I finally saw him in close-up.

This seeming epitome of Sixties classness had always insisted his work as a *Sunday Times* photojournalist was quite separate from his quasi-royal role as the Queen's brother-in-law. The reality was that when Snowdon went on assignments, red carpets tended to be unrolled and railway station masters to put on ceremonial top hats. But one barrier between his two lives seemed impermeable: in seven years of marriage to Princess Margaret, he'd never been known to utter an indiscreet word about her, her family or any other matter of public interest.

Snowdon had been given a vast office on Thomson House's

executive sixth floor but seldom used it, and his visits were as rare and unpredictable as those of Lord Thomson himself. It was therefore a complete surprise when he walked into one of Godfrey's Ideas Lunches when 'Alamein and the Desert War' was under discussion and began helping himself from the cold banquet on the worktop.

As a televised royal personage, always the immemorially prescribed one step behind his wife, he'd seemed handsome in an old-fashioned keen-jawed way, but in person he was small and colourless and wearing curiously high-waisted grey trousers.

Godfrey and Francis Wyndham greeted him as 'Tony' but otherwise there was no acknowledgement of his presence, eating salmon mayonnaise, not exactly with royal good manners. Derek Jewell went on talking about his impending trip to Egypt with Britain's most famous and famously cantankerous old soldier.

'So… around the beginning of May, before the heat gets too bad, we take Monty back to the desert…'

'And leave him there?' suggested Lord Snowdon.

* * *

Godfrey's profile of Elizabeth Taylor seemed to be going swimmingly. 'He's been spending time with her and Richard Burton in Cap Ferrat,' I heard Michael Rand say to Meriel McCooey, who'd done background interviews with various couture celebrities about Taylor's clothes. 'The other day, he was driving around with them in their Rolls, drinking champagne out of crystal goblets.'

A couple of days later, I was sitting idly at my desk, Derek still having not decided on my contribution to 'Alamein and the Desert War', when Sheila McNeile phoned and said, 'Please could you come and see Godfrey?'

I found my editor devoid of his usual boundless bonhomie; instead, the jumbo-cherub face wore an almost shifty look. 'Dear boy,' he said, 'for reasons I need not go into, I'm unable to write our profile of the very charming Liz Taylor.'

The reasons really did not need going into. Weaving his first-hand encounter with the Burtons and the research files provided by his young rips into a seamless narrative of 5,000 words would be a lengthy and arduous job. And while his aptitude for riding around Cap Ferrat in a Rolls-Royce and drinking champagne from crystal goblets was beyond question, Godfrey did not do lengthy or arduous.

Someone else would therefore have to pull the profile together from the voluminous 'background', which was why I thought he'd called me in, just an anonymous rewrite job.

But not so. Such was Elizabeth Taylor's desire to accommodate the *Magazine* that she was offering a further interview, which obviously couldn't be passed up. In view of Godfrey's defection, it had been thought only polite to let her choose his stand-in from among the background researchers. And she'd chosen …

'You seem to be the natural candidate, dear boy. Apparently, you made a good impression on her mum when you were in LA. So, from here on, it's your piece.'

I sat there in a kind of fog, barely taking in the details that followed. I wouldn't be seeing her in Cap Ferrat but in Austria, where she'd be with Richard Burton while he made a film that, for once, didn't co-star them, set during the Second World War. I was expected at its Alpine location three days from now.

Sheila had already made the arrangements with her usual calm – and calming – efficiency. 'You'll fly to Munich, then go by taxi across the Austrian border to Salzburg. I've booked you in at the Osterriechischer Hof, where the Burtons will be staying. And here's Godfrey's research-file.' She handed me a red cardboard folder bulging with contributions by people in every case senior to myself, from which I was to choose what I considered the most apposite quotes.

Dick Adler knew all about the Richard Burton film, having just read a piece about it in Variety. 'Oh, sure … *Where Eagles Dare*, from the Alistair MacLean novel. Shooting at some schloss in the Alps. Better pack your snowshoes, kid.'

He might have been expected to be given the assignment, especially since he already knew the film's American co-producer, Elliott Kastner. But he showed no resentment over my surprise casting and did everything he could to prime me in the short time available, lending me two paperback biographies of Taylor and feeding me all kinds of juicy snippets about the calamitous *Cleopatra* epic in which, he said, 'she had a lovely asp.'

The red folder showed my superiors' interviewees to have taken broadly the same line as mine: that her high consumption-rate of husbands indicated a deeply moral outlook ('She has to marry them before she'll sleep with them,' as Roddy MacDowall had told me), that her extravagance and appetite for jewellery were colossal and her beauty, particularly those double-lashed violet eyes, tended to blind people to what a fine actress she was.

There, too, I found Godfrey's own notes, dictated to Sheila, not only of driving around Cap Ferrat with the Burtons and the crystal goblets but also a dinner with them at the Eden Roc Hotel when Burton had toasted him as 'the editor of the best magazine in Europe.' 'It was quite an evening,' Godfrey's account ended with typically graceful understatement. How could my postscript of an interview come up with anything remotely as good as that?

I flew to Munich first class on BEA, luxuriating in a vast padded seat and enjoying service that only just stopped short of being bathed in asses' milk. You had to order that in advance.

Just after takeoff, a dark-haired, rather Spanish-looking woman came from the rear of the plane and introduced herself as a friend of Godfrey's in a way suggesting she meant girlfriend. She turned out to be in the film business and also travelling to a location, although not that of *Where Eagles Dare*.

'When darling God found out we were on the same flight, he asked me to wish you all the luck in the world with Liz Taylor – and to give you this.' She handed me a box of 25 Romeo y Julietas.

During the flight, when I could spare the time from Krug champagne, vintage claret, Beluga caviar and Tournedos Rossini, I re-read the synopsis of Where Eagles Dare. 'It is 1942, the Nazis have captured a high-ranking American general and taken him to a remote Austrian castle for interrogation … Burton, as Captain John Smith of the Grenadier Guards parachutes in with a crack commando team to rescue the prisoner disguised as German soldiers …'

At Munich Airport, there was deep snow and the cold sliced through me as I came out of the terminal in my skimpy Beau Brummel jacket and thin-soled boots. I hadn't brought an overcoat for the simple reason that I didn't own one.

From there I travelled by pre-booked Mercedes taxi across the Austrian border to Salzburg. The journey lasted almost two hours and I took my usual precautions against the car sickness that had plagued me since childhood: keep a window open, suck Polo mints, never look anywhere but straight ahead.

There was no doubt about whose birthplace Salzburg had been. Almost every shop window displayed Mozart's white-wigged face many times over on boxes of the Kugeln chocolates I remembered wealthy foreign boys having at my boarding school - yet another of the recurring reminders how infinitely times had changed for the better.

The Osterriechischer Hof was an intimidatingly grand hotel, doing its best to maintain dignity in the noisy, hyperactive invasion of film-making folk. Beyond the lobby was an enormous atrium with galleries of bedrooms seemingly rising to infinity.

As I waited to check in, I realised I was standing next to Anton Diffring, who'd portrayed the definitively cold-eyed, sadistic Nazi officer in Albert RN and many other World War Two prison camp dramas I'd seen at Ryde's Scala cinema. Only now he wasn't clicking his heels and sneering 'You must understand, escape from Colditz is impossible', just asking politely about some missing dry-cleaning.

That night was the first I ever spent under a continental down quilt instead of bedclothes that tucked in. I was feeling my usual pre-assignment mixture of joy and fear but this time with joy *not* uppermost.

*   *   *

12

Richard and Elizabeth send their love

At 9.30 the next morning, my bedside telephone rang. Eventually finding my way out of the continental quilt, I picked up the receiver. 'Mr Norman?' a quiet voice said. 'My name is Bob Wilson. I understand you need a ride out to the location?'

Mr Wilson was waiting for me in the lobby; as I had surmised, an African American of some seniority. With the same grave politeness, he told me he was 'Mr Burton's dresser'.

He led the way to a chauffeur-driven station-wagon and within a few minutes we had left Salzburg and its Mozart chocolatiers and were in the snowy Alps, continuously climbing almost vertical hills and hairpin bends without safety barriers despite the drops of hundreds of feet below. On the bright side, travelling uphill never made me car sick.

After about an hour, we reached a grim medieval fortress that seemed carved out of the crags that surrounded it. 'Welcome to Hohenwerfer Castle,' Mr Wilson said. 'Schloss Adler in the movie.'

To my surprise, he took me to a small and very basic café outside its walls where about two thirds of the wooden booths had been commandeered by the film-unit. In the largest of them sat Richard Burton, dressed in a Nazi officer's field-grey uniform, half-unbuttoned to reveal a bright red undervest. The familiar craggy, rather pockmarked face, under its thick makeup, looked heavily hung-over. On the bench beside him were a high-crowned cap and a pair of grey woollen gloves; on one jodhpured knee was a copy of *The Times*, open at the crossword.

'I thought Miss Taylor would be here,' I whispered to Bob Wilson,

'She'll be by,' he said. 'Just have a seat.'

He put me firmly in an empty booth, three away from Burton's. Since, clearly, no formal introduction was to be made, I was going to have to engineer one.

After a few minutes, he threw the paper aside. In the majestically posh-Welsh voice that seemed made to narrate Dylan Thomas's *Under Milk Wood*, he said, 'I thought I'd got inside this guy's head, but twenty-three across is an absolute bugger. "Newt-loving visitor to mansions where nightingale sang."'

I did a quick letter-count on my fingers, then looked over the edge of my booth and quavered, 'Gussie Fink-Nottle.'

'I beg your pardon?' Burton said as the people around him visibly shuddered at the intrusion.

'It's P.G. Wodehouse. Bertie Wooster's flat is in Berkeley Mansions. The nightingale sang in Berkeley Square. And Gussie Fink-Nottle was Bertie's friend who liked newts.'

His face cleared or, at least, looked fleetingly less hung-over. 'Fink-*Nottle*! Of course!' He filled in the blank squares, then gave me something between a scowl and a grin. 'Young man … come here and sit by me.'

We had just worked out the final clue ('Could be used for arranging the rice in Bengal,' nine letters, answer: currycomb) when there was a commotion outside and two or three film people jumped up to open the café's folding doors. In with the gust of icy air came a small, hook-nosed man wearing a black Basque beret and carrying a white Pekinese, followed by Elizabeth Taylor.

There was little outward sign of the serial seductress who'd bewitched George Sanders as Sir Brian Dubois Gilbert in *Ivanhoe* (seen three times by me at Ryde's Scala cinema) taunted Paul Newman as 'Maggie the Cat' in *Cat On A Hot Tin Roof* and been unrolled semi-nude from a carpet for Rex Harrison's Julius Caesar in *Cleopatra*. She wore a mink coat, a purple mohair sweater with a roll-collar, pale blue Lycra ski-pants and white moon boots. Her face was obscured by outsize sunglasses, her black pompadour dragged shapeless by the pink chiffon scarf knotted under her chin.

With a schoolgirlish squeal, she rushed over to Burton, who had chivalrously risen, and threw both arms around his neck, kicking up one moon boot behind her. 'Hi, Boofy!' she cried.

He tactfully disengaged himself and scooped up the Pekinese. 'E'en So!' he said to it adoringly, then to her: 'Did you have a good sleep?'

'Uh-huh. But I got so thirsty, I've just eaten three tangerines.' Her fluting American accent still had a whisper of her north London origins.

Burton indicated me. 'This is the new man from the *Sunday Times* colour thingy. Got a bit better figure than his predecessor, hasn't he?'

She took off her sunglasses and I met the gaze of violet eyes in double rows of lashes like starfish with amethyst centres, True beauty, rather than mere prettiness or attractiveness, affects the vision of the beholder, so her face momentarily seemed to swim in a mist.

'… Only, the dolt thinks he can come to the Alps in January without a proper coat. I've already told him he must be off his head.'

A plump little hand, frosted with diamonds, felt the pathetic thinness of my Beau Brummel lapels. 'Honey, you'll freeze,' she told me rather like a reproving mum, 'especially when we're up at the castle. Let me see if I can get you something from Wardrobe.'

Ten minutes later, Bob Wilson, now temporarily *my* dresser, helped me into the dove-grey, gold-buttoned, velvet-collared greatcoat of a Wehrmacht field marshal. It certainly was lovely and warm.

Nowadays, stars of such magnitude – if there still *were* stars of such magnitude – would be fenced about with publicists and PR people, censoring, curtailing and dripping their deadly treacle over everything. But I was to spend something like eight hours continuously around the Burtons without a PR or minder in sight.

This turned out to be the last day of filming at Hohenwerfer Castle, though the interiors remained to be done at MGM's British studios. The afternoon was taken up by an action sequence with Burton in his Nazi officer disguise being driven round and round the castle's interior courtyard in a motorcycle sidecar. 'Bessie', as he called her, watched from the window of a dungeon-bare turret room, without any role in the production but nonetheless playing its undisputed lead.

In one corner, she'd set up a table with loaves, cold meats, cheeses and packets of biscuits and a portable griddle on which she made relays of toasted sandwiches and hot dogs for the cast members and crew. I can still picture those diamond-frosted fingers, by now rather greasy, folding bread around a wedge of cheese and handing it to me, followed a few minutes later by a chocolate wafer biscuit. Every few minutes, she'd run to the window, lean out and go 'Hi, Boofy!' in her joke schoolgirl squeal while Burton smiled up tolerantly from his sidecar and the director pretended not to mind the ruination of the shot.

The idea had been that my interview with her would be at the castle and at one point the two of us – only the two of us – went into an even smaller dungeon for that purpose. It was a miserable failure; I found that facing the violet eyes at close quarters drove every question completely out of my head and I felt rather relieved when she was called away to speak to one of her many children on the telephone.

However, she came back full of apologies for not giving me what she called 'a fair shake' and suggested that at the end of the day's filming, I should finish the interview in the back of her limousine on the return journey to Salzburg. We'd be completely private, she said, but for her Basque chauffeur, Gaston Sanz, and her Pekinese, E'en So.

The limo was parked at the bottom of a long flight of icy steps. As I picked my way down beside her in my Field Marshal's greatcoat, with E'en So in my arms, I couldn't help laughing.

'What?' she said.

'I was just thinking … this time tomorrow, I'll be back in my bedsit in Kensington.'

I soon felt very little like laughing, let alone interviewing the world's most beautiful woman, for Gaston drove at high speed, rounding the downward hairpin bends with barely a touch of the brakes. The heater was on full blast, every window was closed and the heady scent of her perfume was yielding to that of flatulent Pekinese. As carsickness sent its early warnings - first a dry mouth, then repeated yawning - my only hope was to focus on what I could see of the road ahead, going with each twist and turn like a bobsleigh rider.

I realised the incongruity of interviewing Elizabeth Taylor with averted eyes, and thought I had better confess what ailed me. 'Please don't think me rude for staring at the road like this,' I said, 'but I'm afraid that if I look at you, I'll be sick.'

She guffawed so explosively that E'en So started barking and Gaston glanced backward to check that nothing was wrong, almost taking us over the next precipice. My stammering mortification, in fact, cancelled out the nausea and, groping in my back pocket, I found the stump of a tube of Polo mints so old that they resembled grimy mothballs.

I offered her the top one out of politeness; she said, 'Mmm, Heaven!' and picked at it determinedly with a silver fingernail when at first it refused to be dislodged.

In the Hotel Osterriechischer Hof's rococo restaurant, a long table had been prepared for the 'wrap' dinner the Burtons were giving for the principal cast members, to which I'd also been invited. Burton sat down still in costume, as did all the men; I thus found myself eating Weiner schnitzel and drinking hock with every Nazi villain I'd ever booed from the stalls of Ryde's Scala cinema.

Anton Diffring was seated near me, together with Victor Beaumont, who had black-ringed eyes like Rudolf Hess, and the more smoothly sinister Ferdy Mayne. It was bizarre to hear them, with their SS thunderflash insignia and Iron Crosses, gossiping like typical luvvies about producers and agents and working for the theatrical impresario 'Binkie' Beaumont.

On my right sat the young American actor cast as Burton's deputy in the commando raid, whom I remembered from the TV Western Rawhide. I thought him rather boring, with his feeble W.C. Fields impersonations, so made little effort to talk to Clint Eastwood.

The Burtons presided jointly at the top of the table, he in his Wehrmacht field-grey, she in the purple rollneck that her eyes eclipsed, alternately canoodling and verbally sparring.

It turned out she'd been the one to turn him on to P.G. Wodehouse, that lucky cue for me in the castle café. He gave a little recital of Wodehouse quotations, almost crying with laughter over 'if not actually disgruntled [Jeeves] was far from being gruntled' and 'He spun round like an adagio dancer who'd been caught watering the cat's milk.'

Another revelation was that when she'd married him, she'd learned to speak Welsh (just as when she'd married his predecessor, the singer Eddie Fisher, she'd converted to Judaism) and since then had called him 'Dicon', the Welsh diminutive of Richard. 'I love talking Welsh,' she said. 'It's such a great language to swear in.'

Only once was there any mention of my being a journalist and a great deal of what was said being implicitly off the record. Burton recalled how, on a journey to their home in Gstaad, his brother Ivor, had been carrying two million dollars' worth of Taylor diamonds in a paper bag, had put it down on the pavement at the airport while loading the car, then forgotten it and driven off, only to find it still there and its contents intact when he returned in panic half an hour later.

'You'd better not put that in your article,' Burton told me. 'We don't want to hurt poor old Ivor's feelings.'

'It's okay,' she said, sending me another bolt from those eyes. 'We can trust him. He's kosher.'

Like Godfrey's in Cap Ferrat, it had been 'quite an evening' – but it was not nearly over yet. At midnight, she stood up, took her mink from the back of her chair and said 'Come on, Dicon. Remember we have to leave for Paris early in the morning.'

'A swift nightcap,' Burton said. 'One brandy.'

'One brandy then. But make sure it's only one.' He kissed her hand and, like the sudden extinguishing of an ArcLight she was gone.

Most of the others at the table also retired to bed, so it was a group of only three nightcap-seekers that followed Burton from the restaurant and into the huge atrium with its serried bedroom galleries which by now was almost deserted.

There was his close friend Brook Williams, the actor son of playwright Emlyn Williams, whom he insisted on having in all his films, so was likewise costumed in Wehrmacht field grey. There was a young assistant director from the film unit, who'd been detailed to act as his gofer that evening. And there was me, expecting at any moment to be noticed and firmly excluded.

It didn't happen; Burton chose a circle of high-backed brocade armchairs at the foot of the staircase to the galleries and I slipped into the one next to his.

The 'one brandy' was a round of large Remy-Martins; and they kept coming for the next two hours, lubricating a stream of hilarious anecdotes from Burton about Noel Coward, 'Larry' Olivier and 'Johnny' Gielgud, each with its own dead-on impersonation, almost all of them beginning nostalgically, 'When I was on Broadway, playing Hamlet...'

He was still going strong at 2 am, by which time all hotel staff seemed to have disappeared from the atrium and the lobby beyond. I'd been unable to avoid getting very drunk myself, and so observed what now unfolded with the slowed-down comprehension and reactions of a sleepwalker.

I became aware that someone had joined our circle uninvited and was seated awkwardly on a brocade footstool, talking to or, rather, at Burton. It was a pudgy, middle-aged man wearing a green Alpine with a feather and clutching in both arms a raincoat with many loops, buckles and toggles.

The assistant director, Brook Williams and finally Burton himself told him he was intruding, but he was completely unabashed, introducing himself as Jim Toal (it sounded like), an American expatriate with an Austrian wife, living in Salzburg. He was a great admirer of Mr Burton's movies but, more than that, felt a special kinship between them.

'My ancestors were Welsh, born and bred in the dear, bonny Vale of Neath,' he explained. 'That means, I'm every bit as much a *Selt* as you.'

'No,' Burton replied without a beat, 'I am a Selt. You are a Sunt.'

I wasn't sure if the man even heard because at the same moment Brook Williams said something very much less subtle which caused him to lunge behind Williams's chair and try to put him in a headlock. Burton jumped up, whereupon the man thrust a hand inside his over-embellished raincoat and brought out something which, to my fuddled senses, looked altogether too big, black and lumpy to be a handgun – but was.

A few minutes earlier, Burton had been declaiming like a bard at an Eisteddfod; now his accent changed to that of a gangster in the James Cagney mould. 'Don't mess with me baby!' he bellowed. 'Either use that rod or stick it up your jacksy!'

Nazi officer and Alpine feathered hat faced each other in a surreal tableau of which the third member was the young assistant director. He was not much older than me and this evening must have promised to be an undemanding one of fetching Burton's cigarettes and keeping his glass topped up. Now the main asset of a £6 million film seemed in imminent danger of getting shot while in his care.

His face a mask of unutterable horror, he sank to his knees before the man, literally praying: 'Please … please …*please* put the gun away.'

Despite the amount he'd drunk, the asset was behaving with considerable restraint. When attempts to provoke him verbally failed, the man cuffed him across one cheek. 'Doesn't matter what you do, love,' Burton said. 'I won't hit you.'

At this point, my gaze wandered dreamily away from the fracas and up its immense backdrop of bedroom-galleries. Near the top I noticed a flicker of bright pink, descending rapidly gallery by gallery. I'd identified it by the time it was halfway down but for everyone else, who came around the final curve of stairs to ground-level was a complete surprise. The pink was a frilly chiffon nightdress around which she clutched an old black leather coat. Her hair was a crumpled mess, her face scrubbed clean of makeup, her feet bare, her violet eyes ablaze.

'Richard,' she hissed, 'Your voice is echoing all *over* this hotel!' Just roused from sleep and furious as she was, the import of the scene was lost on her.

The man stared at her in stupefaction for a moment, then stuffed the gun away and held out a hand. 'Oh,' he gasped. 'This is such a pleasure. I had no idea…'

'I'm sure you didn't,' she snapped, then dismissed him as though he was just another annoying fan. 'Richard, you just come to bed this *minute.*'

Burton, for his part, reacted not as one whose life might just have been saved but as if unconscionably interrupted. 'Aah, get out,' he snarled, waving an obergruppenfuhrer's field-grey arm.

'Get out yourself,' she snarled back. 'Do you think this is any way to behave, you big palooka?'

He broke into a torrent of Welsh, its meaning plainly highly uncomplimentary; she answered also in Welsh with equal fluency and pith while the gunslinger looked from one to the other, utterly dumbstruck.

Eventually she returned to English. 'Either come now or don't bother to come at all.' With that, she turned on her bare heel and stomped up the stairs again, still totally unaware of the presence of a firearm.

The man stared for a few moments at the red carpet she had trodden as if unsure whether he should have asked for an autograph or a ransom. Then, unbelievably, he went through the rigmarole of dragging out his big, lumpy gun all over again and sat the four of us in a row on a tapestry-covered stool with our hands up, changing our positions several times before he was satisfied.

The assistant director renewed his tearful prayers to put the gun down; Burton said nothing further, but sang *The Men of Harlech* under his breath:

Ever they shall rue the day
They ventured o'er the border

Here the drama fizzled out in anti-climax that was almost disappointing. The man announced he needed the toilet and ordered us not to move while he was gone. The assistant director had to point him in the right direction, Burton mischievously adding 'It says Damen on the door.' Then the four of us bolted into separate lifts.

When I awoke under the avalanche of white quilt with a Burton-sized hangover, I seriously wondered whether I'd dreamed the whole thing. The hotel turned out to know nothing of what had happened in its atrium nor to have heard of an American expatriate living locally named anything like Jim Toal. Recalling the ungainly black shape in his hand, I thought perhaps it had been only a replica or toy.

At noon, I was in the lobby to see the Burtons depart for Paris with a huge retinue of secretaries, hairdressers and makeup people which until then had been completely hidden. The couple were obviously reconciled and I half-expected a telling-off from Mrs Burton for helping to lead her husband astray but as they passed, she darted over and kissed me on the cheek.

Behind her, Burton caught my eye and I realised this was no time to bring up the subject of men really waving guns behind the scenes of a film about men waving guns. However, he gave me a wink and resolved that lingering doubt.

'It was the real thing,' he murmured. 'It was a Webley four five-five.'

The immediate question was what to do with the scoop that had fallen into my lap. The newspaper reporter in me wanted to phone it straight to the *Sunday Times's* Newsdesk for use that weekend: 'BURTONS FACE MYSTERY GUNMAN IN MOZART CITY'. On the other hand, it was a God-given intro to my profile - but that way, wouldn't get into print for at least five weeks, during which it might well leak out somewhere else. I decided to take the risk and sit on it.

So, I returned to the *Magazine* in triumph, or so I thought; as blissfully unaware of the political situation the profile had created as its subject had been of the pistol pointed at her spouse.

In the flurry of my departure, I'd never stopped to think that senior executives regarded as experts on the cinema might reasonably have expected to do the interview and write the piece and must have taken it very hard when the assignment was awarded to such a pipsqueak. Even now I still didn't get why none of those usually avid cineastes showed the slightest interest in the new information about Taylor and Burton I had gleaned without asking, mostly over dinner at the Osterriechischer Hof.

Godfrey was agog to hear all about it of course, and Dick Adler and Mrs Susan Raven up to a point, and Nick and Brenda at lunchtime in The Lamb. But whenever I tried to share my insights anywhere west of Godfrey's office – the domain of Peter Crookston, Meriel McCooey, Francis Wyndham and the art department – I felt like a snake-oil salesman with a particularly unpersuasive line in patter.

Laughably mystified, I consulted Dick: 'Don't you think it's peculiar that Peter and that lot don't like me to talk about it?'

'Then don't,' he said. 'This business is full of people who talk about their stories so much, they have nothing left to put on the page. Write it.'

I worked on it for five days, refusing all his invitations to multi-stop lunches in Soho, staying so late that Thomson House's only security – a nightwatchman with a torch – regularly looked in on me during his rounds.

I started with Burton in his Nazi uniform, Jim Toal and the gun, then welded together the numerous files from my superiors, including Godfrey, who turned out to have been my researchers. The pre-ordained length was 5,000 words, which in those days had to be counted without electronic aid, and I ended with 5,000 exactly.

The day after handing it in, I was summoned by Godfrey and saw the thirty clipped-together sheets disfiguring that normally virginal space, his desk. 'I've read this with some admiration, dear boy,' he said. 'But we'd better see what Francis thinks.'

'Great,' Francis said - and this time seemed to mean it, for he went further. 'I liked what her mother said about her being tidier since she met Burton.'

'About her emptying ashtrays?' I said.

'Yes. *Awfully* good.'

Believing myself home and dry, I sent a cheery memo to Peter Crookston, suggesting a couple of ideas for my next job. Back came an acid reply, beginning 'If you have nothing to do, you might try to improve your Elizabeth Taylor piece…'

At the time, I happened to be dating Jackie Addison, the secretary who worked jointly for George Perry and Francis, though her duties consisted mainly of typing George's *Penguin Book of Comics*. She told me Francis had tried to kill the profile because 'the quotes don't add up to anything', but too much had been invested in it and the Advertising Department were already working on a promotional campaign.

Despite the overwhelmingly positive tone of what I'd written, I had to undergo several lengthy interrogations by Mr Calderan at Theodore Goddard, largely consisting of the question 'Did he (or she) really say that?' Although neither of the simultaneous writs I'd previously generated had come to anything, he still plainly regarded me as 'libel-prone' and each of his eyebrows went up and down as though on bouncy castles at my replies.

In the end, that bravura opening at 2am in the Osterriechischer

Hof's atrium was watered down almost to extinction for fear that 'Jim Toal' might see it and sue.

The issue itself was trailed by a television commercial, in those days a rarity for Sunday colour supplements. 'She loves hot dogs,' a plummy voice intoned, 'and she can eat five of them at a sitting...' By then, any pleasure or pride I might have felt had been killed stone-dead by the stilettos crowding between my shoulderblades.

Godfrey's headline 'Portrait of a Woman' had all his thin-man's elegance. But below it, I didn't really have a byline at all, just a mention in the long list of photographers, picture agencies and archives that had supplied illustrations. And the cover and whole page after page inside were sickly-coloured 'glamour' shots from 1950s film magazines like *Picture Show* and *Photoplay*, an orgy of camp that was an affront to the most real and vital person I'd ever met.

I received little reade feedback afterwards, although there was a letter from the makers of Polo mints, which I'd mentioned in the piece, wondering not very hopefully if she'd do an advertisement for them.

Cynics, of whom I'm usually in the vanguard, might say the Burtons were just actors, unable to resist putting on a show even for a gang of screen Nazis and a 24-year-old journalistic nobody. Or else that I was so plainly out of my depth that they felt sorry for me.

Either may be true. I only know I fell utterly in love with her and, less predictably, the all too familiar drinking and hellraising notwithstanding, found myself wishing he was my dad.

There was one more memory to lay away in what Scott Fitzgerald called 'the most pleasant lavender of the past.' Just before the piece came out, I had to phone one of her secretaries in Gstaad to check that the title of her next film really was just *Boom*.

As I spoke to the secretary, I sensed that both of them were in the room with her. The great gulf between us was back; I simply did my fact-check and got the answer but then as she rang off, she said 'Elizabeth and Richard send their love.'

*   *   *

13

Keep it up, old top

After that gourmandising of space in the *Magazine* – 5,000 words each for Elizabeth Taylor and Route 66 – I found myself back on austerity rations as meagre as I'd ever known. For the rest of 1968, I was to get little of any significance into Plantin type, although a respectable amount into other, lesser fonts.

Only one assignment, from Derek Jewell, had any real meat to it. As my contribution to his Alamein and the Desert War series, I went to Cheshire to meet some former Eighth Army sappers responsible for clearing the land mines which the Germans, always ingenious toymakers, had planted in the Libyan and Egypt deserts; around a million all told. On my journey, I passed through Liverpool and caught my first, brief glimpse of its neoclassical city centre, little dreaming how much time I would spend there one day and how I'd grow to love it.

Across the Mersey in Wallasey, I hosted a pub reunion for survivors of a unit recruited from the local rugby club whose commanders at first nicknamed them 'the Intelligent Bad Element' for their middle-class bolshiness but who made good, triumphantly, in the Battle of El Alamein.

Even that fierce, pitiless struggle in hellish heat had its farcical moments. One of them recalled how their convoy had stopped for a meal in a seemingly quiet bit of desert when a Stuka dive-bomber swooped out of the sun, spitting bullets. Caught without a helmet, he clapped a metal dish onto his head for protection, forgetting that it was full of warmed-up rice pudding.

Yet, try as I might, I still hadn't managed to broach the charmed circle of Peter Crookston writers whose work always flew into the *Magazine*: Richard West on Greece's new military dictatorship, Nicholas Woolaston on the Bihar famine, John Mortimer on the celebrated interrees at Highgate Cemetery, Norman Harris on the coming Olympics in Mexico City, Brigid Brophy on Mickey Mouse, Pauline Peters's satires of bourgeois rituals like cocktail parties and christenings (her own baby's in fact; thanks, Mum.)

Peter had recently brought in an old colleague of his at the *Daily Express* named Bill Cater, said to be a rewrite-man par excellence. Small and chainsmoking, with thick bifocal glasses, he worked from a small desk in Peter's room, his strongly implied role to sort out the over-hasty and immature efforts of people like me.

Derek's grand plan to take Viscount Montgomery back to Egypt to launch Alamein and the Desert War came off despite the minefields involved, both diplomatic and literal. The party also comprised C.D. Hamilton, Michael Rand and two photographers, Ian Yeomans and Don McCullin, the latter after his time in Vietnam with a near-as-dammit army haircut - yet Monty still objected to his sideburns.

The series afterwards came out as a paperback book, including my piece on the Wallasey sappers. Then, unfortunately, a British general it said had been responsible for the deaths of thousands of his men turned out not to have been, and the paperback was withdrawn, never to reappear.

Under Lord Thomson's benign rule, no blame whatsoever attached to Derek, who soon afterwards was promoted to a management post in the newly constituted Times Newspapers company. He'd been a huge presence on the *Magazine* with his many enthusiasms, white socks and 'sweeties'; now it was rather shocking to see him consigned to outer darkness like one of Stalin's Politbureau after a purge. In his new management role, he evidently showed just as much energy and enthusiasm yet when his name was mentioned at Ideas Meetings, it was always with derision, Godfrey alluding to him as 'Mighty D.J.'

There was another change in the *Magazine's* top echelon when Mark Boxer, its founding editor, for so long the Pretender to Godfrey's throne, became a part of it again. Not with any definite title that might suggest being subordinate to Godfrey but simply as Mark Boxer, the name a role in itself, conveying all his beauty and elegance, his superstardom at Cambridge, his social ambitions, his bias toward visuals rather than words, usually at the words' expense, his discontentment, fastidiousness, superiority and unproductivity.

He'd given up running the paper's Review front and for some time had been occupied solely by the cartoon he drew every day in the new-look Thomson daily *Times* under the nom-de-plume 'Marc'. Compared with the cartooning talent of that era – Bill Tidy, Michael Heath, Ralph Steadman and, of course, Gerald Scarfe – I thought them meagre of both line and wit, but they had their loyal following in intellectual north London.

He came to the *Magazine* ostensibly to run a new section called Design for Living after the Noel Coward play and with a similarly precious approach to domestic décor. The actual work was done by Maggie Angeloglou, wife of the former picture editor Christopher, a sweet-natured woman with the old-fashioned female habit of wearing a hat at work.

The first task Mark gave her was to design an entire flat whose walls and furniture the reader could cut out and assemble in three dimensions with the tabs provided like a paper doll's house. The art department hated it but still had to lay it out; David King's revenge was to put Maggie's byline into type of almost Hollywood sign proportions to make clear that no one else had had anything to do with it.

Soon tiring of Design For Living, Mark formed an alliance with George Perry and those two notable products of Cambridge University began putting together a special issue on the BBC which seemed to involve more portentous meetings – some at a rented villa in Tuscany – than the setting-up of the Corporation itself.

Most of his time, however, was spent simply being Mark Boxer; sitting at ideas meetings, nibbling a celery-stalk and wincing at every idea as if it caused him actual physical pain. Most afternoons found him in Meriel McCooey's office, playing bridge with Francis Wyndham and various partners from their mutual acquaintanceship.

He brought with him a snobbery which, for all the *Magazine's* manifold other vices, had never existed previously. Now whenever a party took place in the concourse, there would be a pointedly separate and exclusive one with Mark and Francis and their circle in Meriel McCooey's 's office and the subtle one-upmanship of whisky instead of Champagne.

Yet Godfrey, against all the evidence, persisted in regarding us as one big happy family. That Spring, the various warring factions trooped up to the Roof Studio for a school-type group photograph around our mirthful editor holding a rugby ball with '1968' chalked on it.

The line-up included Lord Snowdon, who inevitably arrived rather late. We'd been warned in advance no longer to call him 'Tony' – which few of us did anyway – but 'Trendy Snowy'.

The early summer was my nadir on the *Magazine*, deprived of the work Derek Jewell had always given me but with no other patron in the executive tier to take his place, and increasingly pulled more towards the newspaper.

The *Northern Echo's* former arts editor, John Whitley, had recently joined J.W. Lambert's literary department (filling the vacancy I'd so grandly turned down with more distinction than I could ever have given it). John regularly gave me a pile of new novels on which to write unsigned 'short reports' and once let me do the main new fiction review, which meant my byline appearing on the same page as the great Cyril Connolly's.

A bookshop called Gastons in Chancery Lane bought review copies for half their marked price. But I'd never before been able to accumulate books, so kept every one, savouring the shiny, gluey aroma of even the most unreadable.

Occasionally, I stood in for Derek in the Pop/Jazz column he was continuing from his new executive heights. It was primarily about jazz, usually a review of the current attraction at Ronnie Scott's club in Frith Street. Not letting my complete ignorance of the subject stand in my way, I pontificated on the techniques of American legends like the drummer Buddy Rich, the (male) trumpeter Ruby Braff and Rasthaan Roland Kirk, who played three saxophones at once, all superbly.

I finally got back into the *Magazine* with a piece indicative of how desperate I'd become. Its subject were the young female novelists currently in the news for writing about sex with the same candour as men and, often, going to new extremes. My theme, prescribed by a chuckling Godfrey, was the non-literary spell they had supposedly cast over middle-aged London publishers like the self-described 'Nijinski of Cunnilingus', George Weidenfeld.

I interviewed four, including Jackie Collins, younger sister of the actress Joan, and Terry O'Neill photographed each one spectacularly mini-skirted and kinky-booted. I liked them all but stuck the knife impartially into them as required. The piece's working title had been 'Reading Between the Loins', but Godfrey changed it to the equally blush-making 'Four Pretty Faces, Four Slim Volumes'.

This ignoble episode made me aware for the first time of literary agents and the fortunes a novel could earn from the sale of its paperback, book club and sometimes even film rights. Here yet again Dick Adler had useful knowledge to impart, for a close friend of his wife Jane was Pat Kavanagh of the A.D. Peters agency, whose youthful chairman I'd often heard the normally unimpressionable Brenda Jones call 'beady-eyed Michael Sissons'.

Although Dick hadn't yet tried a novel, he'd often considered it, encouraged by his many famous friends in the profession. 'Richard Condon always says the most difficult part are the first hundred pages … after that you can settle back and enjoy it,' he told me. 'And according to Kingsley Amis, you only need to write one page a day and after 365 days, you have a book.'

So for the second time, at my big green office typewriter, I set about the task despite having no more idea how it was done than when I'd tried it for Anthony Blond.

Its starting point was a dreadful Christmas Day when I'd been staying with my father and Joan, and we were invited by the landlord of the one the pubs where his fruit-machines resided to have lunch after closing-time. By then, however, the landlord and his girlfriend were blind drunk and lunch was forgotten amid a ferocious row in which they pelted each other with the gifts they'd exchanged earlier.

I had no idea what was to happen after that but, as in the 'Blond fragment', vaguely planned that its hero would be overweight, as I'd thought myself to be since the age of about ten, and an unhappily miscast end-of-pier showman.

Dick asked if he could read it and I gave him the typescript, half-afraid of what such an aficionado of F. Scott Fitzgerald would say; already imagining the circumlocutions he might employ to tell me I'd been wasting my time and shouldn't waste any more. The next day, I found it on my desk, his verdict on the first page in the handwriting all Americans seem to share: 'Terrific!'

That full-hearted encouragement was typical of him and, typically, came when his frustrations at the *Magazine* were far worse than mine. The problem was that his main area of expertise was films and it already had two cinema experts in George Perry and Francis Wyndham, one dealing with the mainstream Alfred Hitchcocky side, the other with anything needing subtitles. But that hardly explained the concerted effort to freeze him out, to which even Godfrey - who'd brought him in in the first place – seemed to become a party.

On his arrival, he'd been given the green light for two profiles, one of the actor and raconteur Peter Ustinov, the other of the Hollywood perennial Burt Lancaster. The Ustinov piece came back from Godfrey with a note saying it 'hadn't got to the heart of the man' and making clear that there would be no second chance; the Lancaster was not even acknowledged.

As to who was plying the knife, there could be little doubt. George, although self-important, was not malevolent whereas Francis exuded almost ectoplasmic disdain for Dick - or 'Ardler', as he pronounced it with an audible sneer. After reading the office copy of Variety, in a charade of camaraderie, he'd bring it to our room because 'Ardler likes to look at it', somehow making that seem the most futile of exercises.

Dick bore all these snubs and slights with stoicism, never harbouring the smallest resentment of my own fleeting appearances in the *Magazine*, hugely proud that his now wife Jane Wilson, had managed to sell a piece to *Esquire* in the U.S. 'The trouble is that when Godfrey and I met, we were both editors of magazines,' he reflected. 'It's too big a jump that now I'm just another taxi for hire.'

I saw him boil over only once, when the *Magazine* ran a lengthy piece by its intellectual cineaste about a French film actress of whom most of its readers would never have heard. 'Why didn't my Burt Lancaster interview go in?' he fumed. 'It's gotta be better than that boring thing about Anouk Aimee that Francis wrote between jerk-offs.'

But by the end of the summer, he'd had enough and decided to return to New York and start a family with what Jane, in her demure English rose way, called 'a fiesta of fucking.'

We said goodbye over dinner round the corner from my cocktail-bar bedsitter in Scarsdale Villas and afterwards Dick sang and danced *'Singin' In the Rain'* down Marloes Road like a pear-shaped Gene Kelly. His parting shot was 'Keep on with that novel.'

Life seemed empty for a long time afterwards, even if my diary wasn't. The 'permissive' Sixties came to a head with the abolition of theatre censorship, for 200 years exercised by an arcane official called the Lord Chamberlain. Its end was celebrated by the opening of an American 'tribal rock' musical called *Hair*, which put naked genitalia on the West End stage for the very first time and used the word 'fuck' almost as freely as David King.

I reviewed it on its opening night for the paper's arts pages. taking along my sister Tracey, now aged 14. Afterwards, I received a stern reproof from my father which lives in my memory as the first time his disapproval didn't cut me to the heart.

When Louis Armstrong, the greatest jazz musician of all time, paid his last visit to Britain, to appear at Batley Variety Club in Yorkshire, John

Whitley sent me there, supposedly only to describe the performance. But I happened to run into the jazz singer Salena Jones, whom I'd reviewed kindly at Ronnie Scott's; she grabbed my hand and pulled me backstage to meet 'Pops'.

The trumpet's towering genius was a tiny man, reduced still further by extensive dieting with the aid of a laxative called Swiss Kriss. He gave me a small packet to try and a picture postcard of himself framed by a keyhole shape sitting on the toilet.

My only profile in those months wasn't written for the *Magazine* but for *Argosy*, following on from the several short stories of mine they'd published. The subject was John Betjeman, whose *Collected Poems* had been the sixth form prize with which I'd left school not to go to university, and whose secretary, Lee Sturgeon, I was currently seeing.

Thanks to Lee, I spent an unsurpassable afternoon with Betjeman at his little Dickensian house in Cloth Fair, off the old Smithfield meat market, and walking around nearby Charterhouse Square. He urged me to read George and Weedon Grossmith's *The Diary of a Nobody* as he said he did every day of his life.

After the profile appeared in what he called 'dear old *Argosy*', he sent me a handwritten thankyou letter, signing off with a Betjemanesque flourish that was good advice to any journalist but particularly one struggling on the *Sunday Times Magazine* - 'keep it up, old top.'

Harry Evans had by now been editor of the *Sunday Times* for a year, and galvanised a product hitherto thought to be unimprovable.

In his first weeks in the chair, the paper had exposed Kim Philby as the long-sought 'Third Man' in the ring of Cambridge-educated spies recruited by Communist Russia (so very British that even to betray your country you had to have been at Cambridge.)

The story was equally an expose of incompetence and complacency in the security services which had allowed Philby to escape detection for so long. This had put Harry at risk of prosecution and possible imprisonment under the Official Secrets Act but, with Lord Thomson's unwavering support, he'd refused to be cowed and the government had backed down.

Other triumphs quickly followed: the unrivalled coverage of the Arab-Israeli Six Day War in a 16-page 'briefing'; the Insight team's investigation of 'the sad truth about fun furs.'

All this of course was of purely academic interest to the *Magazine*, which carried on exactly as before, its advertising revenues underwriting the paper's costly investigations, and answerable to no one but Lord Thomson via C.D. Hamilton. Or, rather, not answerable: the only censorship for months had been over the cover of the Female Form issue, a full-frontal nude torso in soft burnished gold which, on CDH's orders, had been enveloped in a white bodystocking.

Yet, although I was on the *Magazine*, I still saw myself as essentially Harry's man. I smiled inwardly at the so familiar reports of his tearing energy and complete absence of grandeur, for even as editor he'd take his turn on the subs' back bench or pound out the final version of a story on his battered portable. I believed his eye was on me and felt vaguely spurned each time he signed up some new star columnist or foreign correspondent.

Often it seemed to slip his mind that he had no dominion over the *Magazine* and he'd send down ideas that had popped into his mind even amid the pressures of running the paper. These invariably fell into the 'reader-service' category and required illustration by maps, charts or graphs or sometimes all of them.

When Godfrey read his memos aloud at Ideas Meetings, there were pitying smiles, if not outright guffaws at this failure to understand the *Magazine's* special alchemy, and the notion of its concerning itself with anything so mundane as 'reader-service', which always made me deeply uncomfortable, even when I half-agreed.

Secure in his autonomy, Godfrey sent back the unanimous thumbs-downs without taking too much trouble to be tactful. 'Please compose a vibrantly appreciative but heartbrokenly regretful reply,' he would tell Sheila, 'of which the underlying sentiment is "Piss off."'

Despite Harry's coups with Philby and fun furs, nothing competed in reader-appeal with Francis Chichester's solo world circumnavigation and triumphal homecoming to Plymouth to be knighted by the Queen on Plymouth Hoe, the very spot where his Elizabethan namesake, Sir Francis Drake, had finished a game of bowls before trouncing the Spanish Armada.

Hence in the summer of 1968, the paper announced it was staging a long-distance sailing epic to surpass even Chichester's. This was a solo round-the-world race without Gipsy Moth IV's midway stop-off in Australia. There would be two prizes: a trophy named the Golden Globe for the first nonstop circumnavigation and £5,000, for the fastest time. Chichester, the chairman of the judges, dubbed it 'the Everest of the sea.'

Back then, health and safety considerations seldom got in the way of anything. There was no vetting of the entrants for their competence afloat, nor of the craft in which they might have to battle 50-foot waves off Cape Horn. They could start from any UK port they chose, any time between June 1st and October 11th.

So underemployed was I on the *Magazine* by that time, I'd begun doing pieces for the paper's Newsdesk on Fridays and Saturdays. I was thus around the fifth floor when Harry needed someone to profile each of the Golden Globe race's 11 competitors as they were announced. He seemed to remember my coverage of Chichester as a success and made me in effect the *Sunday Times's* round-the-world sailing correspondent.

All the Golden Globe's entrants were men - the idea of a female long-distance sailor then being unthinkable - and ten of them seemed well-suited to their colossal ordeal. These were an Australian whose very name, Tahiti Bill Howell, seemed to prophesy an easy win; two former Royal Navy commanders, Nigel Tetley and Bill King, the latter twice-winner of the D.S.O; three highly experienced French single-handers, Bernard Moitessier, Loick Fougeron and Yves Wallerand; one Italian ditto, Alex Carrozzo; Merchant Navy officer Robin Knox-Johnston; and SAS captain John Ridgeway and sergeant Chay Blyth who had together rowed across the Atlantic the previous year. The odd-mariner-out was an electronics engineer named Donald Crowhurst from Devonshire, who had entered purely to publicise a marine direction-finder he had invented called the Navicator.

On my pre-race interviews, I was usually accompanied by the *Sunday Times* photographer Michael Ward. Tall and extraordinarily handsome, Ward had formerly been an actor, specialising in junior naval lieutenants in black-and-white British war films, usually with a single line of dialogue such as 'Enemy bearing green-one-o, Sir.'

He still kept up that persona, calling every reporter he worked with 'Number One' - naval slang for a first lieutenant which was a constant reminder of my own bizarre miscasting. He wore a bushy beard and a Panama hat, and we drove to see our lone sailors in his vintage Rolls-Royce. As we went through one Devon village, children threw stones at us.

The fact that the *Sunday Times* was staging the race didn't stop contestants from making deals with rival papers for the exclusive rights to their stories. The *Daily* and *Sunday Express* jointly signed up Bill King (at 58, the closest in age to Chichester), the *Sunday People* grabbed John Ridgeway and the *Sunday Mirror*, Robin Knox-Johnston. When we arrived in Falmouth harbour, where Knox-Johnston was berthed, I narrowly escaped being thrown into the water by his *Mirror* minders.

The writer who'd confused 'spinnaker' with 'catheter' waxed omniscient both about the seafarers and their craft. The ex-naval commander, Nigel Tetley, I thought, had a touch of Jack Hawkins portraying the rugged, uncomplicated Captain Ericson in *The Cruel Sea*. After a brief, crackly phone conversation in schoolboy French with Bernard Moitessier aboard his ketch Joshua in Toulon, I decided he possessed a Zen-like stoicism that would arm him against his months of solitude.

Out of all of them, my only real empathy was with Donald Crowhurst, the weekend sailor from Devon whose only sponsor was a local caravan-dealer and for whom the race was a last desperate gamble to save his ailing electronics company.

I visited 35-year-old Crowhurst at the Gothic-style house he had mortgaged to build his trimaran, Teignmouth Electron, and met his wife, Clare, and four small children. After dinner, he drove me to Teignmouth station, still talking excitedly about the adventure in front of him. I remember thinking what a nice guy he was and the intro forming in my head: 'Donald Crowhurst is as normal as English roast beef...'

With similar perspicacity, the entrant I rated lowest was Robin Knox-Johnston. Snootily I recorded how even in harbour his old teak ketch, Suhaili, seemed barely able to stay afloat and that he was preparing to sail with several unreturned library books on his cabin table.

None of the race's most hotly-tipped names lived up to expectations, least of all its supposed shoo-in winner, Tahiti Bill Howell, who didn't even manage to start. Before long, storms or boat trouble or both had forced everyone to drop out but Knox-Johnston and Crowhurst.

Nothing had been heard from Crowhurst for three months, but then he suddenly broke radio silence to say that Teignmouth Electron had girdled the globe at an amazing rate, was just rounding the tip of South America and might win the £5,000 prize for fastest time.

It was all a fantasy: his outbound journey had come to a stop in the South Atlantic, where he loitered for several months, radioing fictitious reports of his winged onward progress, at one point going ashore for repairs in Argentina. His plan was to slip in behind the race's leaders as they returned on the final leg back to Britain.

He'd apparently calculated that being a runner-up would still win publicity for his invention and solve his financial problems but mean nobody would look too closely into the details of his voyage. This strategy capsized when only he and Knox-Johnston were left in the race and there was even a possibility he might be named the winner.

Back in his home port of Teignmouth, preparations began for a civic welcome at which 100,000 people were expected. Then Teignmouth Electron was found drifting in the South Atlantic, with no sign of Crowhurst. He had evidently drowned himself rather than face exposure as a fraud.

So Robin Knox-Johnston, in the shabby old ketch I had mocked, won both Golden Globe awards and became the new Chichester, knighted in his turn and a national treasure to this day. He still recalls with distaste the long-haired, flamboyantly-attired Sunday Times man who interviewed him before his departure in a state of utter maritime ignorance, then wrote that he hadn't a prayer.

The race would have two other casualties, each further underlining how ludicrously wrong I'd got everything. Bernard Moitessier, the Frenchman in whom I discerned Zen-like stoicism, at one point threatened to beat Knox-Johnston back to Britain but then suffered a breakdown and, instead, decided to keep on going for a second circumnavigation.

And Nigel Tetley, who had also looked like a winner until his trimaran broke up and sank, proved not quite the uncomplicated old seadog I'd portrayed. Three years later, he was found hanging from a tree wearing women's lingerie.

All through all that almost monotonously sunny summer, Grandma Norman was dying of cancer. I never knew exactly which kind she had. In those days, people didn't specify; they were regarded as all one, all irreversible. She was admitted to the Radcliffe Infirmary in Oxford, but soon sent home and not offered any further treatment.

From then on, every time I went to see her, she'd give me something from the ramshackle household that had followed her around for the past 50 years, from Clapham Old Town down to the Isle of Wight and finally to the little sideways house in Lambourne with the grocer's shop that had tried so hard to take the Kiosk's place.

She gave me souvenirs of Grandpa Norman's 19th century seafaring, a fossilised seahorse and sea cow, a pair of elephant's tusks, polished and strung-together, and the saw from a sawfish. She gave me a tattered pink copy of the *British Gazette*, the propaganda sheet produced by the Stanley Baldwin government during the 1926 General Strike, a brass gas lamp with a pink china shade, a Toby jug advertising Charrington's beer and the wooden kitchen chair that I'm sitting in at this moment.

The time soon came when she could no longer look after herself and had to move in with my father and Joan in Hungerford. Before she left the sideways house, she had the enamel sign for Lyons Tea (the one with the thermometer, saying 'Degrees Better') unscrewed from the wall outside to give to me because I'd always liked it. No matter that the town's racehorse trainers and jockeys had used it to check the temperature for generations past.

She spent her last days in the 'overflow' cottage next to my father's, lying in the huge half-tester brass bedstead that had been in her family for around 150 years. He looked after her with the same tenderness he had through all her years of robust, seaside rock-peddling health. Joan – whose existence she had only recently come to acknowledge – was very kind to her.

I'd go and sit with her whenever I could get away from solo round-the-world yachtsmen. One afternoon, she took my hand and whispered 'You know, Phil, I'm so proud of you'- the first time anyone in my family, had ever said such a thing. 'When you were a little boy, I always somehow knew that you'd travel.'

'It's all because of you, really,' I told her. 'That article I wrote about you.'

'About me, sitting in bed at Five Castle Street, having a glass o' gin? Whyever would anyone have been interested in that?'

'Everyone was.'

In the final week, she fell into a coma, my father and I sitting on either side of the bed's foot-posts, tortured by the loud, stertorous breathing. 'If it wasn't for this, she could have gone on for years,' he said. 'It's such a foul disease.'

When I left that afternoon, I knew I'd never see her again. I squeezed her hand, kissed her on the brow and said, 'I'll never forget you.'

She'd wanted to be buried back in Ryde so as to be with Uncle Phil, the awful firstborn she'd always preferred despite all her younger son's solicitude. I had to be in Falmouth that day, interviewing Robin Knox-Johnston, but my mother made the journey to the island for a ceremony that ended at Ryde Pierhead, now shorn of its Pavilion but still with its old power to create squalor and indignity.

The closest to a wake was held in its railway station buffet and, at my father's instigation, turned into a game of poker. Drunk as he was, he lost heavily to my mother and she boarded her ferry with a purse full of his IOUs. Long experience gave her little hope of their ever being honoured.

*   *   *

14

We've hit the button first time

In 1969, my position on the *Magazine* finally seemed to stabilise. That's to say, I began to get pieces into it on a fairly regular basis and be visited less often by the fear of being found out and instantly sent back whence I had come.

Mainly, this was thanks to Peter Crookston's departure to the only job conceivably more desirable than *Sunday Times Magazine* features editor. He had gone to edit *Nova*, a high-glamour glossy with a feminine bias, although by no means aimed only at women, which used many of the same designers, writers, photographers and illustrators.

I'd never stopped wanting to win Peter over but had more or less given up after suggesting a profile of the Latin-American bandleader Edmundo Ros, a subject that positively cha-cha-cha-ed with period charm, and receiving the tetchy response, 'No, no, no … think *modern*.' Then, soon after he arrived at Nova, it carried an Edmundo Ros profile by one of his regular *Magazine* writers, Arthur Hopcraft. I sent him an acid note about it, certain that our days as colleagues were over.

This last year of the decade had done so much to shape the *Magazine's* fortunes to an all-time high. Its issues swelled to enormous size, sometimes 72-pagers; advertisers stood in line more eagerly than ever for the privilege of appearing in them, the vast majority rejected and sent away, sobbing piteously.

But in an otherwise beatific outlook there was a cloud, small enough in the overall scheme of things but vexing in its stubborn annual reappearance - the hiatus in both advertising and reader attention during the holiday months of June, July and August.

Recently, Godfrey had varied the Ideas Lunches in his office with an ideas breakfast at the exclusive Connaught Hotel in Carlos Place: not the frugal coffee 'n' croissant of modern 'working breakfasts' but fleets of silver chafing-dishes offering eggs every way, bacon, sausages, kidneys, sauté potatoes, tomatoes and black pudding, plus omelettes, hams of several nations, porridge with fresh cream, sugar or salt, kippers, haddock and kedgeree.

All the young rips partook heavily except Francis Wyndham, that maestro of belittlement: 'I think I'll just have a China tea,' he said, 'and a yoghurt.'

Ideas breakfasts at the Connaught were now a regular fixture; and at the most recent, Godfrey had come up with a possible remedy for the summer advertising dip he'd thought of, appropriately, while in his bath.

This was a multi-part series called the 1,000 Makers of the 20th Century that readers could cut out week by week and insert into a binder to form a permanent work of reference. It would contain 200-word biographies of the century's most significant names in everything from politics to medicine, even mass murder, by leading experts in those fields. Packaged in the *Magazine's* inimitable way, there was a chance it might hold our readers' attention even on holiday when ordinarily they sought no reading matter but giant pornographic paperbacks stained with Ambre Solaire.

Deciding on the 1,000 names, commissioning the potted biographies and finding illustrations would have to be done in a great hurry if the series were to start at the beginning of June, and call for something normally alien to the *Magazine*: teamwork. Nonetheless, even Michael Rand liked it.

The young rips had lately increased by a brace. Arriving early at the office one morning, I was greeted by a tall, rather stooping stranger with an unmistakably aristocratic air and offered a large, cold hand to shake under the misapprehension that I was a sub-editor about to deal with a piece of his copy, so in need of diplomatic handling.

Like Mick Jagger's co-star in *Performance*, his name was James Fox and he was, if anything, even more classically good-looking. But this James Fox was more than an actor: he was an Astor - or, anyway, a member of the near-mythic Anglo-American family who'd once owned *The Times* as well as building the Waldorf-Astoria in New York.

As the best-connected person in the office, and an Old Etonian, it was somehow inevitable that he'd be the only one to talk like a hippie; he never departed but 'split', never spent money but 'bread', never got upset but 'freaked out' and described any misfortune from an upset stomach to the then current genocide in Biafra as 'a bad scene.' A mellifluous voice with a slight stutter and a rather vague, dreamy manner gave this a charm it might otherwise have lacked.

Two years my junior, he'd somehow missed Oxford or Cambridge and been in South Africa, working for the 'black' magazine *Drum*. With him he brought a clutch of as-yet-unpublished pieces which instantly flew into Plantin like so many guided missiles. No prizes for guessing whose hand worked the joystick; he was clearly one of those young writers I'd heard so much about whom Francis Wyndham delighted to encourage and nurture.

Although he never mentioned his exalted family background, it had clearly been no great hindrance to joining the *Magazine*. The forthright Brenda Jones even took Godfrey to task about it – so she told Nick Mason and me later – when she took a layout in to be signed. 'But he's so *beautiful*,' Godfrey said. I said, 'Godfrey, *you're* not supposed to notice that.'

The second arrival was Robert Lacey, one of the runners-up in the *Magazine's* writers contest who'd since been freelancing and working for another Thomson acquisition, the historic monthly *Illustrated London News*. Robert was both a young rip to delight Godfrey's heart and a prodigious worker; he threw himself into the 1,000 Makers of the 20th Century with such effect that he ended up virtually running it and being made an assistant editor.

That made me wonder if I'd be better advised to become an editor, too, so I took over the section of the 1,000 Makers known as Odds and Sods, containing such unclassifiable and wildly incompatible names as the strong man Charles Atlas, the First World War secret agent Mata Hari, the gangster Al Capone and the foot-care pioneer Dr. William Scholl.

To do 200 words on Mata Hari for the standard £25 fee, I telephoned Barbara Cartland, the romantic novelist who dictated roughly one 'bodice-ripper' per week from a pink boudoir in her 10-bedroom stately home and negated the jeers of literary critics by selling around 750 million copies worldwide.

'Certainly, old chap,' she said. 'What's your deadline?'

Her copy arrived in gold covers tied together by silver ribbon. It was exactly to length and word-perfect.

By now, I had abandoned any semblance of formal dress, not only at the office but on assignments, too. My typical outfit was a three-quarter-length belted black leather coat with Beau Brummel lapels from Just Men in the King's Road – its honeyed aroma comes back as I write – accompanied by hipster trousers whose many-coloured check even Rupert Bear's friends in Nutwood Forest might have considered *de trop*.

My tireless quest for ever-higher Chelsea boots had ended with a pair rising halfway up my calves but disfigured by three effete-looking cloth-covered buttons at each ankle. I managed to prise off their tops but the sharp spikes that had secured them were immovable, sticking out horizontally like the swords on Queen Boadicea's chariot wheels. I was conscious of having somewhat the same effect whenever I walked through a crowded room.

Since the end of 1968, I had been living with someone I'll call G who was far above what I considered my usual level of girlfriend. When we'd first met, for some insane reason, I'd told her I was her age, 24, rather than 25, meaning that throughout our relationship I'd have to remember to adjust my backstory accordingly, saying for instance that when King George VI died in 1952, I'd been eight not nine, or when the Beatles released *I Wanna Hold Your Hand* in 1963, I'd been 19, not 20 …

Settled as I was in my little cocktail-bar bedsit in Scarsdale Villas, I hadn't visualised us living together. G had forced the issue by giving up her flatlet in Queens Park without warning and arriving on my doorstep – or, rather, window-step – with all her belongings. I didn't feel coerced, just incredibly flattered that someone like that should want to be with me.

The cocktail bar's cohabitational facilities being severely limited, we began the dreary search for a furnished flat in the only endurable areas, Kensington and Notting Hill. Then an unlikely saviour emerged: it turned out that Mrs Susan Raven wanted to rent out the lower part of her large house in Elgin Crescent, just off Ladbroke Grove. The accommodation was one large and pleasant ground-floor space with a modern open-plan kitchen, and a winding stair down to a two-bedroom basement. Holland Park tube station was only five minutes' walk away and Portobello Market just around the corner.

Although Mrs Raven was living above us, we were hardly aware of her, apart from the front door's almighty crashes as she came and went. G remarked how, despite her strident manner, she was always prettily dressed and meticulously made up. As I soon learned from Brenda, she was having an affair with a much younger man, one of the so-called 'Australian Mafia' who largely staffed the paper's Insight team.

The main bedroom's ceiling was of sufficient height for Grandma Norman's brass bed, which she'd left to me as promised. My father somehow arranged for it to be brought up from Hungerford with a lorryload of cabbages bound for Covent Garden Market and the driver and his mate assembled it for me: the seven-foot headposts with swinging testers, or curtain-rods, and the solid black iron frame and underlay like medieval chainmail.

What I hadn't taken into account was the featherbed that came with it, an enormous, sepia-spotted mass that took two people to make and, moreover, bore numerous ancient stains marking the sometimes-troubled entries into the world and departure from it of Grandma Norman's forebears over a century and a half.

With G's wholehearted agreement, I decided to get rid of it but couldn't think how until a film director friend named Stephen Weeks thought it might make a bed for his cats. It took Stephen about 20 minutes to get it into the back of a taxi and when, after an equally strenuous battle he got it inside his house, the cats refused to go near it.

Stuck with the heaving, almost hostile mass, he thought it might be easier to dispose of if reduced in size – so he cut it open. Set free after 150 years, the feathers had an almost daemonic energy and their whirling blizzard filled the place for weeks afterwards. Long after he thought they'd finally been dispersed, he'd open a cupboard or drawer and another little squadron would rush out.

It was at Mrs Raven's open-plan kitchen table that I pressed ahead with my novel. The seaside pier motif permeated it, even to the title. One of my father's stranger slot-machines in the Pavilion, supposedly built by Polish prisoners-of-war, was housed in a cabinet made of gunmetal and named 'See Him Sweat'. Behind its glass was a miniature castle; when you inserted a penny, the gates opened to reveal Hitler in Hell, seated on a chamber pot, flanked by leering devils and with a paper turd on a thread dangling underneath him.

'See Him Sweat' perfectly described the state of my uncomfortable, overweight alter ego, just as it once had the real me in those hellish childhood summers at the Pavilion when I was always too hot and had no escape and using its backstage doorless WC was an ordeal not to be undertaken lightly.

All the other characters were based on people I'd known in Ryde, often with names barely changed. 'Moorman', the one assigned to my hapless hero belonged to the school classmate who came immediately before me in the register. There was also an appearance, under her real Christian name, by the 'County' girlfriend I'd had in Cambridge; the one from whom I'd so heartlessly fled to the North-East, the *Northern Echo* and Harry Evans.

At about the book's halfway point – so far as I could tell, since I was working to no kind of plan – I followed Dick Adler's advice and sent the opening chapters to his wife Jane's friend, Pat Kavanagh, at the A.D. Peters agency. I'd met Pat only once with Dick and Jane, and been rather intimidated by her fierce-cheekboned beauty, but she wrote back immediately that she was passing them on to her colleague, Brenda's 'beady-eyed' Michael Sissons.

That same week, she phoned me. 'Michael wants to take you on,' she said. 'He says you made him laugh even though he had a hangover.'

I met with both of them at the A.D. Peters offices, a Georgian house in Buckingham Street, just off the Strand. Sissons, only half a dozen years my senior, was tall, pink-faced, hesitant of speech and not noticeably beady-eyed. But, between lengthy pauses, he corroborated that I had, indeed, made him laugh and that one of London's top literary agents wanted me as a client.

The fair copy was typed by Godfrey's secretary, Sheila. Contrary to office custom in such circumstances, I paid her for the hours but not for all the correcting and subtle editing she did along the way.

A month later, Michel Sissons sent me a letter beginning 'I'm delighted to say we've hit the button first time…' Charles Pick of William Heinemann wanted to publish *See Him Sweat* and was offering a £350 advance against royalties. 'He feels the manuscript still needs some editorial work [he wasn't kidding] but he's promised to do everything possible to give your book a good send-off.'

In those pre-conglomerate days, British publishers were all small independent firms, in several cases still headed by the men – always men – who had founded them, like Hamish Hamilton and Andre Deutsch. They literally were publishing 'houses', their elegant premises scattered through Bloomsbury, Covent Garden and Mayfair.

Charles Pick was a perfect example of the old-school 'gentleman publisher', late 50s, avuncular and palpably without any of the corporate cares that would burden his 21st century successors.

He took me to lunch at the Savile Club, the traditional home of old-school writers and artists and told me that *See Him Sweat* had reminded him of Patrick Hamilton, a name I'd never heard before. At his urging, I went away and read Hamilton's undervalued comic novels of London pub life in the 1930s, like *Hangover Square* and *20,000 Streets Under the Sky*, with their wonderful ear for the affectations and nervous tics of English conversation, especially in drink. That I instantly recognised the pubs and the conversations didn't curtail my pleasure.

'The only thing I didn't like,' Charles Pick said, 'was the title. Better not to have the word "sweat" in it.' Since See Him Perspire didn't have quite the same ring, I agreed to think of an alternative.

All this was contrary to anything I'd ever read or heard about becoming a novelist … the years of solitary labour … the poverty and self-denial … the humiliating hawking-around … the rejection-slips papering the wall …

I'd written what I knew in my heart was a piece of crap, yet 'hit the button first time.' Those were the Sixties for you.

My main preoccupation in the spring of '69, was getting back to America. Only this time with no ready-made subjects like Route 66, I'd have to think of them myself.

The first all but semaphored from my 'Odds and Sods' section of the 1,000 Makers of the 20th Century. This was Charles Atlas, whose mail-order bodybuilding course, guaranteed to turn 'seven-stone weaklings' into physical specimens as perfect as himself, had spread from the U.S, around the world and even to the Isle of Wight, where I and several schoolfriends had followed it, but without noticeable benefit.

There clearly was a real person named Charles Atlas even though the photographs that came with the course suggested his title as 'the World's Most Perfectly-Developed Man' had been awarded a good bit of the century ago. I found a phone number for his organisation in New York and learned that he'd now retired and was living in Palm Beach, Florida.

The idea of trying to interview P.G. Wodehouse in his long-time American home was slower to form. Since Grandad Bassill had got me reading him when I was about 10, I'd never seen a photograph of Wodehouse other than the vague, bald, beaming mugshot on the back of his Penguin editions. The sheer enormity of his oeuvre, more than 100 titles featuring Bertie Wooster and Jeeves, Lord Emsworth,

Psmith, Mr Mulliner, Stanley Featherstone Ukridge and a dozen more immortal creations, suggested somebody who must long since have worked himself to death.

But no: Wodehouse was alive, in his late 80s, still turning out a book a year for his original British publishers, Herbert Jenkins, lately renamed Barrie & Jenkins. Indeed, his latest, *Do Butlers Burgle Banks*?, was due in September.

Diligent burrowing in the Morgue revealed him to be a rarity in English letters: a hugely popular and highly-paid novelist, yet lauded by critics and acknowledged 'the Master' by fellow writers as diverse as Evelyn Waugh and George Orwell. Often overlooked, too, was his parallel career as a lyricist for musical comedies between the wars, partnering composers like George Gershwin and Jerome Kern, when he might have four shows at once running in the West End and on Broadway.

One dark chapter marred this tale of steadily accreting fame and wealth. During the Second World War, Wodehouse had been vilified as a traitor for making radio broadcasts from Nazi Germany while in internment there. The broadcasts had been to his readers in America, which hadn't yet entered the war, and actually had been subtly anti-German. He'd later been officially exonerated of any collaboration, yet still some of the mud had stuck. It explained why this maestro of British dottiness had never returned to Britain nor received any public honour.

My omniscient *Magazine* friend Nick Mason was the *real* Wodehousian; he knew what 'P.G' stood for (Pelham Grenville, 'Plum' for short) and that Ukridge was pronounced 'Yewkridge'. Unlike me, he'd read the stories about public-school life with which Wodehouse's career had begun before the Great War. 'There's one very good one called A Prefect's Uncle, about a blood who discovers this kid in the lowest form is technically his uncle. It's like *Vice-Versa*, but funnier.'

The Long Island address for Wodehouse that his publishers gave me seemed hardly sufficient: just the name Remsenberg and a zipcode. Nonethless, I wrote and asked him for an interview, disingenuously beginning 'Dear Mr Wodehouse, I have read every one of your books but A Prefect's Uncle…'

Two weeks later came a reply, evidently typed by Wodehouse himself:

Remsenberg
New York 11960

Dear Mr Norman

That's fine. I will look forward to giving you lunch any day after your arrival. The slight catch is that our maid comes only on Monday, Wednesday and Saturday and on the other days, we go to the inn at Westhampton Beach about six miles from here. If you come by train, the station is Speonk and we would meet you there.

Do you really want A Prefect's Uncle? It is a pretty bad book. But I can give you a copy.

Yours sincerely

P.G. Wodehouse

The third pretext to take me across the Atlantic was simply one to bring me back by a pleasanter method than flying. The Cunard company had just introduced a brand-new liner, the Queen Elizabeth the Second, or QE2, to replace its stately old Queen Mary and Queen Elizabeth whose dim silhouettes I'd so often seen passing the end of Ryde Pier en route to and from Southampton.

I'd had a fantasy about making such a trip ever since reading Wodehouse's The Luck of the Bodkins, particularly the moment when Monty Bodkin arrives in his stateroom aboard the SS Atlantic to find HI SWEETIE written in lipstick on the dressing-table mirror.

By now, I'd learned to wait until almost the end of ideas meetings before suggesting something; it was less likely to be shot down with everyone stuffed full of food, half-drunk and starting to stumble back to their desks.

At the next such opportunity, I suggested I should return from America on the QE2 as the five days at sea would give me time to reflect on the material I'd gathered. Francis had already left the room, no one else seemed to hear and Godfrey just nodded through wreaths of cigar-smoke. 'Very well, dear boy. You can write us an Atlantic Notebook.'

And, in order to have access to every part of the ship, wouldn't it be only sensible for me to go first class?

'You're probably right, dear boy. Ask Sheila to make the arrangements.'

Now that the *Sunday Times* and *The Times* were both owned by Lord Thomson, they shared a New York office, high above Lexington Avenue, that was almost a pantomime of Britishness. There were framed photographs of the Queen and Winston Churchill on the walls, a grandfather clock with a Westminster chime like Big Ben's, and an African American doorman in a dark blue uniform with 'The Times of London' in gold around his peaked cap. In overall charge was a man named Bob Ducas, himself a Wodehousian parody with a drooping blond forelock and haw-hawing voice; all he lacked was a monocle.

Dick and Jane Adler had settled in Greenwich Village, he vastly tickled that their apartment was actually located on Jane Street. Seemingly with no trouble at all, he'd become deputy entertainment editor of *Life* magazine, still the world's greatest vehicle for photojournalism despite all the latter competition from 200 Gray's Inn Road.

His job mainly seemed to consist of sitting in air-conditioned screening rooms furnished with just a handful of deep plush armchairs, watching new films reflecting the seismic changes afoot in Hollywood; on successive evenings, I went with him to see *Easy Rider*, *Midnight Cowboy*, *Butch Cassidy and the Sundance Kid* and *True Grit*.

He was delighted to hear about my novel ('Here's to Charles for picking *See Him Sweat*, or whatever the fuck it winds up being called') and, typically, bore Godfrey no grudge for the way he'd been treated at the *Magazine*. 'I'll just say what Bob Dylan does in *Don't Think Twice, It's All Right* … you just wasted my precious time.'

I flew to Palm Beach by shuttle plane – in those easygoing days, they used io hang around at airports, waiting for the small quorum of passengers required to depart – and talked to Charles Atlas at his apartment in a beachside condominium. Although now 76, burned almost black by the sun and with more lines than a Dürer etching, he was still in magnificent shape, all the more noticeable among the men of that retirement community with their coffee-coloured straw hats, Bermuda shorts and pet poodles. In the background was a silent younger woman he introduced with old-world formality as 'Miss Lucas'.

For five straight hours, he told me his life story in an accent hovering between Little Italy and the Bronx; how, born Angelo Siciliano, he'd been the original 'seven-stone weakling', how he'd developed his Dynamic Tension bodybuilding system by watching the lions and tigers at the Bronx Zoo stretch themselves in their cages, then returned as Charles Atlas to sort out the beach bully who'd once contemptuously kicked sand in his face.

In the 1920s, he'd acquired a worrying fitness disciple in Al Capone, who considered him a Sicilian blood-brother and once offered him a Mafia credit card that would have meant he never had to pay for anything again. He refused it, but then another time, when he had the flu, Capone had shown up 'in a fifty-dollar hat, with sackful of Aspro and Milk of Magnesia'.

His physique had always been a magnet to women and still was, much to his embarrassment: only recently, at a cocktail party in Miami, two women had taken him aside and suggested a threesome. '"But, ladies, *please*," I told them, "I am *seventy-six years old*."'

A week later, a bus set me down in the village of Remsenberg, deep in the Long Island forests, where P.G. Wodehouse, his wife, Bunny, and an old black Labrador with a grey muzzle were waiting for me at the roadside.

The face was as smudgily benign as on the backs of all those Penguin books; what I hadn't expected was height. Wodehouse at 87 still stood well over six feet, He wore a flowered shirt, heavy brogue shoes and a cavernous tweed jacket he himself might have likened to 'something run up by Omar the Tentmaker.' His voice had a fruity timbre peculiar to middle-class Englishmen born before 1900; like that of Lord Emsworth's butler, Beach, it was 'like good, sound port, made audible.'

Bunny Wodehouse, a little, skittery woman of 84, drove us to Westhampton Beach for lunch in a big American sedan which partly owed its impetus to hitting, then bouncing off the kerbs. At Nick Mason's suggestion, I'd brought Wodehouse a copy of W.S. Gilbert's nonsense verses, *The Bab Ballads*, one of his earliest comic inspirations - and the foundation for a strain of pure English silliness that led on to the Goons and Monty Python. 'Oh, I say,' he beamed as if it was a Shakespeare First Folio, '*thanks*!'

With lunch came the revelation that he wasn't very funny or even especially articulate: that ability to make the English language turn back-somersaults existed only on the page. Oddly enough, he said the same about W.S. Gilbert, whom he'd met at a lunch-party in 1900. 'I always thought Gilbert was rather a small joke man. He used to pretend there was a certain wasp that always followed him around while he played croquet.'

After lunch, Bunny drove us slowly and reboundingly to a home for stray cats called the Bide-A-Wee that she and 'Plummy' financed. The big, slow man scooped up a tiny kitten, shutting his eyes in rapture as its paw clubbed his freckled head. He'd never had children, although when he married Bunny, she already had a daughter, Leonora, whom he came to adore as if she was his own. She had died tragically after a routine surgical procedure halfway through the War, while he was in a Nazi internment-camp.

The Wodehouses' home since 1952 was a modest two-storey house at the end of a grass track named Basket Neck Lane. Two further dogs and three cats greeted our arrival. The man synonymous with majestic butlers, gliding 'gentleman's gentlemen' and officious private secretaries nowadays had no domestic staff but a local woman who came in to clean and cook three days a week and possessed little in the way of stately-home formality. 'When she brings in our lunch,' Bunny told me, 'she says "If you want anything else, just holler."'

Bunny went upstairs to rest and I followed Wodehouse into the little book-lined room off the garden where he worked and, apparently, slept alone. It was sparsely furnished with a table, a chair, a dish of pipes, an ancient Royal typewriter and the manuscript-in-progress of his one hundred-and-somethingth book, *A Pelican At Blandings*. In an alcove was a child-size bed with a yellow counterpane. It might have been a study at his beloved alma mater, Dulwich College.

I asked if what he wrote ever made him laugh as it did so many millions of others. 'Not really,' he said. 'When you're alone, you never do much laughing.' Then he remembered something that I'd forgotten, peered along the bookshelves, took down a copy of his school story, *A Prefect's Uncle* and wrote in it 'To Philip Norman, all the best from P.G. Wodehouse.'

Back in the main house, where our formal interview was to take place, he settled himself into an armchair with a black cat on his lap and began filling his pipe with the remnants of cheap American cigars. Things did not exactly go with a swing: his answers were mainly 'Yes' or 'No', with an occasional 'Oh, *really*.' Before long, I saw his eyelids start to droop. His only moment of animation was provided by the lawn outside the window. 'Ooh, look!' he exclaimed. 'A pheasant!'

All too soon, Bunny reappeared, carrying an overladen tea-tray in a manner reminiscent of her car driving. Tea over, she shooed Wodehouse upstairs to the TV set in her boudoir where he always watched a dire American soap opera called *The Edge of Night*. 'I'm afraid you'll have to go,' she told me, 'because Plummie has to have his sleep and then we've got people coming for dinner.'

When I made my face fall as if from the top of Beachy Head, she relented. 'All right then, you can stay if you'll decant the wine.'

She took me into the kitchen, pointed to two bottles of Mateus rose and cut-glass decanter on the table, then disappeared again. I knew enough about wine to know that one didn't normally decant the sparkling kind but felt I should keep my side of the bargain. So, I poured both bottles into the decanter through a sieve, thereby removing most of the sparkle.

The people coming to dinner were Guy Bolton, Wodehouse's old musical collaborator, and his wife, Virginia, who lived only at the other end of Basket Neck Lane. Beforehand, Bunny served dry Martinis with the aid of a patent glass-froster that also frosted everyone in the vicinity. When Wodehouse received his frosting, he seized her wrist, kissed it and said adoringly 'Bunny – you're *crazy*!' Fortunately, no one seemed to notice the unsparkling Mateus.

I had expected an evening of wonderful theatrical gossip from the era of George Gershwin, 'Flo' Ziegfeld and 'Jerry' Kern but instead the talk revolved mainly around Virginia Bolton's first husband, who had discovered the silent-movie wonder dog Rin Tin Tin. Wodehouse in his heyday had earned more than any writer alive, yet clearly felt envious of the talented canine. 'That dog was on $6,000 a week,' he marvelled, 'in *1923*!'

'*And* a percentage of the gross,' Virginia added.

A few days later, I returned to Remsenberg with the New York photographer Carl Fischer whom the *Magazine* had hired to take Wodehouse's portrait (and whom nothing could dissuade from calling him 'Mr Woadhouse').

Again, I found myself with Wodehouse in his little garden room and again he took a book from his shelves, signed it and gave it to me. It was one of his earliest, *The Swoop*, published as an early paperback in 1909; the story of a Boy Scout named Clarence Chugwater who saves England from a German invasion nobody else has noticed because they're all watching cricket.

In its pristine condition and signed, it's since been valued at £2,000-plus. Robert McCrum's authorised biography of Wodehouse in 2004 revealed that it was the only copy he'd had, and this impulsive generosity left him with nothing but a grimy photostat.

When I was shown to my First-Class stateroom on the QE2, I found no HI SWEETIE in lipstick on the mirror like Monty Bodkin. Instead, there was a 'sailing gift' of 25 Montecruz cigars, America's home-grown substitute for forbidden Cuban Montecristos. The card read 'Happy crossing from Plum and Bunny Wodehouse.'

* * *

15

The Beatles are the biggest bastards in the world

For people like me, the generation on whom the 1960s had lavished such unexpected blessings, it came as a shock halfway through 1969 to realise how horribly fast they were running out. Even worse was the likelihood that their greatest blessing of all might come to an end along with them.

Throughout our late teens and early twenties, the Beatles had been a vital element of life with their inimitable style, charm and wit and the breathtaking, breakneck evolution of their music. Now suddenly we had to contemplate a world without them; a prospect as bleak as if the sun itself were to stop shining because of irreconcilable creative differences with the Solar System.

In the crazed Beatlemania years, the four could not have been closer; it was the only way to survive. But since the death of their all-protecting manager, Brian Epstein, in 1967, there had been growing friction between John Lennon and Paul McCartney, whose songwriting partnership ('vinegar and virgin olive oil', according to their producer George Martin) had lifted them into the realm of genius.

Modern pop stars who gripe about loss of privacy and media-intrusion cannot conceive the extent to which the Beatles were considered the property of their fans, the press and the public in general. Never was this more oppressively on show than in the fast-disappearing Sixties, when Lennon and McCartney each found a partner to replace the other.

Lennon, true to form, caused the greater outcry by leaving his wife and young son, starting an affair with a Japanese-American performance artist, six years older, named Yoko Ono and becoming involved in her wacky conceptual art stunts to the apparent total loss of his famous whipcrack humour. But the formerly PR-conscious McCartney was also felt to have failed the nation by not marrying the gracious young British actress Jane Asher and instead choosing Linda Eastman, an unsmiling celebrity photographer from New York.

Lennon-McCartney relations seemed to have worsened still further since the Beatles' launch of a multi-faceted business organisation named Apple Corps – pronounced 'core' – its rapid descent into chaos and the hiring of a tough New York entrepreneur named Allen Klein both to manage them and 'rationalise' Apple. That in itself seemed to portend grim new times, for when had the Beatles, or the Sixties for that matter, ever been *rational*?

Everywhere young people gathered – and in 1969 they were gathering in increasing quantities – the same malaise could be felt. The number six on the calendar had become as comfortable as a much-worn pair of crushed velvet flares; the relentlessly advancing seven looked not only unnatural but threatening, like a little bent gallows.

None of which, needless to say, troubled the *Magazine*. With its long forward schedule, it was already preparing for 1970 what it had so peerlessly served up through the Sixties, buoyant on the same oceans of advertising revenue, still free of all constraint as long as the loot kept rolling in.

The 1,000 Makers of the 20th Century, that simple, instantly do-able concept that had transfigured Godfrey in his bath, had been a huge hit from the moment of its launch in June and was continuing to pile on circulation by the hundred thousand for the *Sunday Times* during the summer dog days.

Other Sundays and magazine publishers were feverishly imitating what now were known as 'part-works'. A follow-up series on the history of the cinema had already been initiated by George Perry and under his aegis was daily growing less simple and instantly do-able.

My crossing on the QE2 had been eventful, although not, alas, in any Monty Bodkin-esque way. On this, only its second return voyage, the spanking-new ship broke down just off the Nantucket Light and remained motionless in the Atlantic for two days; if the problem hadn't been fixed, it would have had to be towed ignominiously back to New York – stern first. I filed a story by radio to my new stablemate, *The Times*, which appeared on its front page and for which I later received a payment of £2.

At the office, everything seemed to have been frozen in time like a scene from *A Matter of Life and Death*. Mrs Susan Raven, busily crossing the concourse from right to left when I'd seen it last, was now busily crossing it from left to right. But I'd brought in material that was proof even against Francis Wyndham's lethal apathy and both P.G. Wodehouse and Charles Atlas went in without undue delay.

Wodehouse wrote me a thank you letter and afterwards we corresponded intermittently, he always signing himself 'Plum' as if we were study-mates at Dulwich College. As in his famous correspondence with his real Edwardian school chum, Bill Townend, he described his daily stint at the typewriter as 'plugging along' and 'a ghastly sweat'; even at 87, with a hundred-plus books behind him, it didn't get any easier.

Carl Fischer had produced a stunning colour portrait of Wodehouse in the garden at Remsenberg, although he noted drily, 'Bunny complained of matted hair on my neck.'

Charles Atlas had been photographed in black and white by Diane Arbus, the Art Department presuming him just one more of the American grotesques in which she specialised. 'He was wondrously dense,' sneered the note she sent Michael Rand. But all the malice in her lens couldn't make him look other than terrific.

The piece's appearance flushed out a surprising former student of 'Dynamic Tension'. 'I can't believe you met Charles Atlas,' Harry Evans called out to me one afternoon as he ran through the Thomson House lobby. '*I* took his bodybuilding course when I was at school.' It had to be true, for there was an editor who'd never have sand kicked in his face.

Neither of the *Magazine's* new recruits, James Fox and Robert Lacey, turned out to threaten my position there, such as it was, and I got on fine with them both.

James specialised in long-term investigations which would increasingly tend towards the lifelong. Thanks to his Africa background, he'd been teamed with his fellow Old Etonian, Cyril Connolly on a story that had long fascinated Connolly: the Delves-Broughton murder-trial in British-ruled Kenya during the 1940s, which had uncovered debauchery and lust among its upper crust 'Happy Valley set' The duo were not exactly fast workers and it would eventually reach book form, under James's name only, as *White Mischief* in 1982.

Robert wrote occasional pieces, but did more commissioning and devising theme issues as well as running an early gay magazine called Jeremy from the office; a purely commercial exercise since he had a beautiful girlfriend, soon-to-be wife, the art director Sandi Avrach.

He'd originally intended to be a teacher and his projects often had an educational slant, for instance a series on careers in the top professions, written by notable practitioners. The one on journalism was by Nicholas Tomalin, repeating some of the advice he'd given me when I was on the *Hunts Post* and near desperation in 1963.

It was strange how Tomalin continued to float vaguely in my orbit without our crossing paths again. He was currently co-writing a book about Donald Crowhurst, the Golden Globe yachtsman I had thought 'as normal as English roast beef', who'd drowned himself somewhere off Argentina rather than face exposure as a cheat in the race.

A reorganisation of the *Magazine's* workspaces, surprisingly, turned out to my advantage, putting me with Brenda Jones in a nice little glass-panelled side office enjoying some natural light from the building's internal well. Brenda had recently moved from sub-editing to running the cookery, medical and gardening columnists, respectively Margaret Costa, with her 'steak' puns, Dr Alfred Byrne, known to *Private Eye* as 'Alfred Byrne the Cakes', and Lanning Roper, known to Brenda as 'Groper'.

Compared with Mrs Raven, she was the easiest and quietest of office mates as well as an incisive first reader of everything I wrote. Although omniscient about our colleagues' love lives, she was utterly discreet about her own; I knew only that she had a boyfriend from the Middle East named Fadell who sometimes presented her with large plastic bags full of pistachio nuts she never failed to share with me.

The paper's Atticus office had recently been moved down to the fourth floor and every morning a man with untidy blond hair, a much-creased face and squashy-soled suede shoes would hurry through the *Magazine* concourse on his way there. As he passed our open doorway, his face would give a spasmodic twitch; not for some time did it dawn on me that the twitch was a smile, and he was defying Thomson House protocol by being friendly.

His name was Michael Bateman and he was 'number two' on the half-page still signed by Philip Oakes. He'd just arrived after being fired from the *Daily Mail's* gossip column for the Wodehousian offence of throwing bread rolls during a Lord Mayor's Banquet.

When we got on speaking terms, as we soon did, I discovered he had a voice like the creak of a rusty gate and, in common with so many journalists, was no great listener. I could get in only about five words to every five thousand of his, but somehow it never mattered.

The first time we lunched together at the Blue Lion, he talked so much - mainly about a recent, unsuccessful experiment with wife-swapping – that he completely ignored his salad for about an hour, then picked up the plate and a fork and shovelled it down seemingly with as little appreciation as a hyena mauling an antelope carcass. It was a surprise to learn he considered gossip-columning merely a temporary detour and felt his true vocation to be as a food writer.

I had one thing, at least, to look forward to in 1970: my novel, re-titled *Slip On A Fat Lady* (I know, *I know*!) was to be published by Heinemann. Thanks to Charles Pick, it was also to come out in America under a new imprint, Harper's Magazine Press. Heinemann's lawyers asked me to confirm it was entirely a work of fiction; I did so, then began a second novel of which that would be equally untrue.

*   *   *

In mid-August, Dick Adler phoned from New York with some good news about himself that was to have consequences for me far in the future. He had left his lovely job at Life to edit an entertainment magazine called *Show*, owned by Huntington Hartford, the heir to the A&P supermarkets fortune.

'That's great,' I said. 'I can't wait to tell them at the office. Especially Francis.'

'I thought you could be our London contributing editor, maybe do six long pieces a year and twenty shorter ones.' Without waiting for my answer, he went on, 'How does a thousand dollars each for the longer ones sound? And five hundred for the shorter ones?'

I told him it sounded fine.

'It'd be great to have something by you in my first issue in in January. Why don't you try to find out what's going on with the Beatles at that Apple outfit of theirs?'

At first, I resisted what seemed yet another piece of total miscasting. For the past six years, journalists all over the world had been pumping out millions – maybe billions – of words about the Beatles; Fleet Street teemed with Beatle specialists like Ray Connolly and Maureen Cleave; the *Sunday Times* had its own, naturally superior one in the former Atticus, Hunter Davies, who'd recently written their authorised biography.

My sole, tiny contribution to the genre had been in the *Northern Echo* when they'd appeared at Newcastle City Hall during their last-ever British tour. On such an overcrowded bandwagon, how could there still be room for me?

'You'll do it better,' Dick said simply. 'With it, we could have a portrait of all four Beatles as businessmen, sitting around a boardroom table.'

I decided to do the story for the *Magazine* as well as *Show* since it would carry more weight than a little-known American title. And with that, the usual magic happened: I was at once invited to Apple's headquarters at Three Savile Row to meet the Beatles' press officer, Derek Taylor.

Three Savile Row was at the Regent Street end of that boulevard best-known for bespoke tailors, an elegant 18th century townhouse whose previous owner had been the impresario, Jack Hylton. Below its front steps at either side stood a little knot of female Beatles fans in a permanent state of pre-prepared hysteria. There they waited all day and half the night, whatever the season or weather, in hopes of catching even the briefest glimpse of their darlings arriving or leaving.

Lately, hysteria had turned to anguish with the increasing press reports of turmoil among the Beatles and the advent of Allen Klein, a stocky man with old-fashioned greasy hair who bore a striking resemblance to Barney Rubble in the Flintstones. It was well known that inside the house, as the first phase of his management strategy, Klein was busily firing Apple executives he regarded as useless hangers-on regardless of the fact that some were among the Beatles' closest friends. These doorstep fans were only a few feet away from a drama the whole world was watching, yet still had no idea what was going on.

Security was virtually non-existent: on the doorstep a single, supercilious-looking young doorman in a dove-grey tailcoat; within, a softly lit vestibule and a single receptionist, seated below an oil painting of two lion cubs. As a result, office equipment and furniture had been walking out of the door and Post Office messengers delivering telegrams had been taking the opportunity to strip valuable lead from the roof.

The Beatles did nothing in the usual way and having Derek Taylor as their official mouthpiece was perhaps the best example. On the first floor, I was greeted by a slender, quietly-spoken man, wearing a white turtleneck and a rather old-fashioned toothbrush moustache and seated in a basketwork armchair with an outsize scallop-shaped back. Nobody could have been further from the standard brash music business PR, yet I've never known one more effective or respected, certainly none more loved.

The press department over which he presided, as it were, on the half-shell was a long, high-ceilinged room, kept in permanent twilight with Beatles music at deafening volume, a psychedelic light show speckling one wall and a scatter of ornaments redolent of Sixties second childhood; for example, a water-filled tray into which a row of little plastic storks perpetually dipped their beaks.

Taylor belonged to that rare breed of publicist with no need to whip up interest in their clients. His office was perpetually under siege from media all over the world, via the telephone, telegrams or cables, urgently seeking answers not only about the current situation vis-à-vis Allen Klein and the Beatles but also to questions of eternal interest, such as what was Paul's favourite colour and in which hospital had Ringo had his appendix out as a child.

Concerning the headline topics, Taylor's official line was threefold: that what he called 'the Fabs' were still as united as they'd ever been, that they were all happy with Allen Klein's management and his 'rationalising' of Apple and that, as in Lennon and McCartney's song on the Sgt. Pepper's Lonely Hearts Club Band, 'it's getting better ... a little better every day.'

The room thronged with Beatles correspondents from the national and music press and the hospitality provided for them was lavish even by the standards of that time. A small adjoining room was stacked with cases of whisky and cartons of Benson & Hedges Gold cigarettes along with giveaway albums by the Fabs and their various proteges on the Apple label, and publicity material of unusual tastefulness. Derek Taylor constantly dispensed chilled ebony tumblers of Scotch and Coke, not least to himself.

Favoured visitors were offered 'hash brownies' or spliffs constructed on the lines of the airship R101. There was an emergency procedure in place for flushing all the house's drugs (there being plenty on other floors, too) down the toilets at the least sign of interest from Savile Row's large police station situated just a couple of hundred yards away.

Taylor was sought after for his charm and quixotic humour as much as the access to the Fabs he could grant, and each day held what other eras would have termed a 'salon'. Those having business with him waited on a zigzag line of velvet couches, inching slowly from one to the next. Finally, one reached the moustachioed, chainsmoking figure, leaning on the right arm of the scallop-backed chair that had become split and frayed by all his hours of leaning and talking.

It was here, with senses fumed by Scotch and Coke, that I learned my inexperience in Beatle-scribery wouldn't count against me and that, despite the delicate situation at the Apple house, I was to be given virtually free run of it.

The reasoning was quintessential Derek Taylor. 'I'm amazed that you've interviewed Charles Atlas. I took his course when I was a lad in Hoylake, though you'd never think so now. I believe a couple of the Fabs did, too. So come in and just hang around.'

Over the next six weeks, I was a fly on the wall (although the *Sunday Times Magazine* could hardly be anything so squalid) observing what went on in different parts of the Apple house. Without knowing it, I had a ringside seat at the Beatles' breakup two years before its official date.

Derek called it 'slipping me in' and on my very first morning he slipped me in with John and Yoko, currently at the height of their notoriety. They had recently married, then spent a week-long 'honeymoon' in bed in front of massed camera lenses at the Amsterdam Hilton hotel, not having sex as was expected but wearing pyjamas and proselytising for world peace. They were also preaching their philosophy of 'total communication' or Bag-ism, whereby all prejudice against a person's physical appearance could be eliminated by wearing a paper bag on their head or hiding inside a sack.

Lennon was the Fab most often to be seen at Three Savile Row, although his presence these days had little to do with business or his bandmates. He was merely using it as a headquarters for the peace campaign that had followed the Amsterdam 'Bed-In', and for his and Yoko's conceptual art partnership, Bag Productions. Apple Records were also expected to release the albums they made together, a cause of some glum faces in the marketing department.

I found them sharing a desk in the beautiful front ground-floor office formerly occupied by Ron Kass, the Apple record company boss recently sacked by Allen Klein. Lennon (like all the Beatles, smaller than one expected) now had shoulder length hair and a Biblical beard. Yoko, in a purple robe, was eating brown rice from a wooden bowl. A perspex figure from their half-robotic Plastic Ono Band stood in one corner; the Georgian fireplace displayed a naked pink plastic doll, sole survivor of a whole brood they had recently incinerated with Napalm in the King's Road as a protest against the Vietnam War.

They were already halfway through two months of saturating the media with their antiwar protests, their art 'happenings', above all with themselves as a living peace-slogan. Lennon's rationale was simple: to exploit the press that had so long exploited him as a Beatle. 'For reasons known only to themselves, people print what I say. And I say "Peace."'

Nowadays, rock stars regularly parade their social consciences and receive public honours for it; in 1969, Lennon's campaign was universally derided. Yet still the reporters and film crews couldn't stay away.

The several other new roles he had acquired at Yoko's impetus - painter, collage-maker, left-wing radical - included that of open-all-hours philanthropist. From my seat next to the Plastic Ono robot I watched a stream of visitors come in to ask his support for struggling causes or oppressed minorities from Europe's Romany community to exploited Hispanic workers in the California vineyards to the family of James Hanratty, campaigning to prove his innocence of the notorious A6 Murder for which he'd been hanged in 1962. Nobody was turned away.

It happened that the previous evening, the couple had hired the Institute of Contemporary Arts in The Mall to show some of the experimental films they'd been obsessively making together. Among these was *Self-Portrait*, a 20-minute study of Lennon's penis achieving semi-erection in slow motion. Beside the screen had stood a large white sack containing two people, assumed to be the filmmakers but actually stand-ins, or crouch-ins.

Inevitably, most of the journalists who came into Apple the next day asked if Yoko had felt any misgivings about putting her husband's cock on such public exhibition. She was more concerned about the total absence of reviews or, as she said ingenuously, 'None of the critics would touch it.'

Despite all this evidence to the contrary, Lennon still spoke of the Beatles and himself as one and firmly maintained that Allen Klein had sorted out their finances and pared Apple down to reasonable proportions. Beneath his earnest social concerns and beard, his old caustic wit still glimmered. 'The circus has left town,' he told an interviewer from *Melody Maker*, 'but we still own the site.'

Another day, I was slipped into the attic studio to watch George Harrison being photographed for the German magazine *Bravo*. Halfway through the session, Ringo Starr appeared and started advising the photographer about which kind of lens to use. His needs from Apple were simple, he told me disarmingly. 'It's nice to have a place where the others can do interesting things. And if ever I want a new watch or a new pair of boots, it's a person here who gets them for me.'

Harrison, far more friendly than I expected, chipped in to say Apple had been 'like a rumour that came back to us quite different from what we originally meant. We became a haven for drop-outs – but then, some of our best friends are drop-outs.'

There was one question put to Derek Taylor many times each day, not least by me, which left him uncharacteristically at a loss. Where was the Fab who'd been most active in setting up their business, had named it Apple after a Magritte painting in his art collection, signed up Apple Records' most successful artiste, Mary Hopkin, and chosen, produced and played backup on her international hit single, *Those Were The Days*?

For Paul McCartney, hitherto the most public and accessible Beatle, seemed to have vanished, not only from Three Savile Row but from London. He had fiercely resisted Lennon's unilateral appointment of Allen Klein as the band's manager and, instead, put forward his new father-in-law, the New York showbusiness lawyer Lee Eastman. But Lennon had turned Harrison and Starr in Klein's favour, so destroying the unity that had always been their great strength and making their ultimate break-up inevitable.

Outvoted, marginalised and more hurt than he ever showed, McCartney had taken refuge with the pregnant Linda at his farm in the remote Scottish Highlands. He was to remain there incommunicado for so long that a rumour would go round the world that he was dead.

Amid all these signs of the Beatles' imminent demise, I often thought with a smile of Dick Adler's instruction to get them photographed 'together around a boardroom table.' It recalled his own story of *Life* magazine during the Second World War on learning that King George VI was to conserve fuel like his subjects by taking baths with only five inches of hot water. 'Obtain photo of King in bath,' *Life* cabled its London bureau. 'A rear view will be fine.'

Because of Derek's closeness to the Fabs (Harrison especially) his department still had some of its old free-and-easy pre-Klein atmosphere. Its personnel included a tall, bubble-haired young American named Richard diLello with the designation of 'house hippie' and a silent teenage boy known only as 'Stocky' who sat on top of a filing cabinet for hours at a time, drawing pictures of male genitalia.

Now and again, some late-coming applicant to the Apple Foundation for the Arts would get through the front door and, however talentless, weird or boring, manage to touch the Press Officer's hospitable heart. One afternoon, his telephone buzzed and I heard a female voice say, 'Derek … Adolf Hitler is in Reception.'

'Oh Christ, not that asshole again.' Derek groaned. 'OK, send him up.'

Allen Klein was not based at Three Savile Row: he flew over from New York for two or three days each week, bringing all his filing cabinets with him to prevent any surprise investigation of their contents by fiscal authorities during his absence. As he ran from his limo into the house, he would already be deeply immersed in balance-sheets and so oblivious to the boos and shouts of 'Mafia!' from the picket of fans at either side of the front steps.

The room he used during his visits was situated directly above Derek Taylor's Press Office. From time to time, ominous scuffling noises would come through the ceiling and faces be turned fearfully upward as if at some malign paranormal activity.

I had requested to be 'slipped in' with Klein, too, but Derek said he seldom, if ever, gave interviews. However, to my surprise, he agreed to meet me for a 1pm breakfast in the coffee shop of the Park Lane Hilton, where he always stayed. He did look extraordinarily like Barney Rubble except that the button eyes had a ferocious intensity more suited to a Rembrandt self-portrait.

He told me his aim was simple: 'to make each one of the Beatles so wealthy, they can say "FYU – Fuck you, money!"' To that end, he had just negotiated a whopping new recording deal with their American label, Capitol. The fact that they wouldn't be together long enough to honour it was of minor concern.

The ogre who'd terrorised a houseful of hippies proved to have a salty wit, that I could see would have appealed to John Lennon. At one point, he brought out what was obviously a favourite little homily: 'I'm not a genius, I just work hard.'

'Genius,' I said, all arch and *Sunday Times*, 'has been described as an infinite capacity for taking pains.'

'No,' Klein said, 'that's a masochist.'

I was still hanging around Apple in mid-September when the first copies of the next Beatles album came in.

It was supposed to have been called *Let It Be*, a saying used by Liverpool mothers to calm fractious children that McCartney had turned into a song memorialising his own 'Mother Mary'.

Their self-produced recording sessions, some in the basement studio at Three Savile Row, had been so unproductive and become so acrimonious that they had all walked out - a first for a band always known for their professionalism. Held in abeyance with the tapes was the film footage of the impromptu concert they've given on the roof one raw January day as the bespoke tailors of Savile Row stared upward, mystified by the thunder in the sky.

Then a resurfacing McCartney had gone to George Martin, the great producer they'd driven away in disgust five months earlier, and said they wanted to make a different album, 'the way we used to do it' i.e. happily and with focus. 'If the album's going to be the way it used to be,' Martin told him, 'then all of you have got to be the way you used to be.' Like penitent schoolboys, they gave their word - even John.

The result was *Abbey Road*, named after the leafy north London boulevard where EMI's studios were located, its cover a shot of all four Beatles walking single file over the nearby zebra crossing that aspiring bands would mimic for evermore.

Because of its impulsiveness and simplicity, but overwhelmingly because of George Martin, the album had turned out 'just like they used to be', with no audible sign of the conflict that had jinxed *Let It Be*. For a brief spell, the Beatles' terrible ennui with one another disappeared; their sound was once again newly minted, their harmony as sweet and close as ever, their summons to joy as irresistible.

One evening, after the Scotch and Coke had flowed particularly freely in the Press Office and when the avenue of sofas to his desk had emptied, Derek Taylor gave me a rather different slant on Apple than the general one, first making me swear it would be completely off the record.

He admitted that Three Savile Row had been overrun by con artists and freeloaders but said its extravagances had been insignificant when weighed against the success of its Apple record label under

McCartney, and that Klein was firing executives not for incompetence but standing between him and total control of the Beatles.

In passing, he mentioned how, when even their oldest mates were terminated and appealed to them for support, they suddenly became as unreachable as King Henry VIII after signing one of his wives' death-warrants.

'I love them dearly, but John was so right in what he once said: "the Beatles are the biggest bastards in the world."'

* * *

16

Help Bob Dylan sink the Isle of Wight

The last summer of the Sixties has gone down in history for the first landing on the Moon, but it was also a time when tens of thousands of young people perversely went in the opposite direction and tried to get as close as possible to the Earth.

Since their inauguration in Monterey, California, in 1967, giant open-air pop festivals had been the most visible mark of youth as a nation and culture apart. More than music events, they were celebrations of the hippy ethos of love and peace, its rejection of the consumer society and yearning for a simpler pastoral life, gratified in this case by a remote, if not always beautiful, location and a dearth of proper catering arrangements and toilets.

Posterity tends to mock the 'flower children' for their pot-headed naivete; the impressive fact remains that huge numbers of them managed to congregate for days on end in their often muddy, weather-lashed encampments with unfailing good humour and not the least crime or violence.

Tellingly, both the two biggest festivals took place in the summer of '69, as if to wring the final few drops of joy and optimism from that dear old number six before it went under. One was in a muddy cow-pasture near Woodstock in New York state, the other on the Isle of Wight, headlined by Bob Dylan.

When I saw the latter announcement in *Melody Maker*, it seemed barely believable. Dylan had just emerged from a three-year retirement following a motorcycle accident, unrecognisable as the rasping, sneering electric poet of mid-decade. He'd released a country album, *Nashville Skyline*, singing in a new, mellower voice and actually smiling and doffing a cowboy hat on the cover. It was still impossible to picture him transplanted to the land of seaside rock, thatched cottages and cream teas I knew so well.

Years later, when I got to know the festival's young promoters, the brothers Ronnie and Ray Foulk, I learned how they achieved their stunning coup. Dylan had been expected to appear at the Woodstock festival which was to take place literally on his doorstep. The Foulks diverted him 4000 miles by telling him that one of his favourite poets, Alfred Lord Tennyson, had once lived on the island.

So, I found myself heading back there, ostensibly to write a news piece about the festival for the paper but with hopes of interviewing Dylan for the *Magazine*. Before setting off, I'd sent him a message via his close confidant, the *New York Post* journalist Al Aronowitz, asking him to see me and dropping the names of a few Tennyson poems for good measure.

The old steamship ferry service from Portsmouth Harbour to Ryde Pierhead still survived, just about, and as the outline of my home town grew nearer, with its three church spires and perpendicular hills, I told myself I was simply a reporter on an assignment and not to let the past get to me. All hope of that vanished when I stepped off the gangplank onto the unchanged pierhead concrete and saw the yawning gap where the Pavilion used to stand in all its grim uninvitingness.

The half-mile plank walkway was as dense with shore-bound figures as I remembered in the Fifties bypassing my father's entertainments. But now they were hippies with headbands, ponchos and bedrolls. Coming out of the gates, I managed not to look at the site of Grandma Norman's Kiosk, now occupied merely by a modern kiosk without a shred of personality.

The festival site was at Wootton, a village a few miles east of Ryde, previously best-known for its wide creek and adjacent nudist colony. Somewhere around 150,000 people would eventually make their way there from all over Britain, Europe and America; the most popular message on T-shirts and souvenir buttons was 'Help Bob Dylan sink the Isle of Wight.'

As things turned out, I couldn't get anywhere near Dylan, who was sequestered at a farm in Bembridge seven miles away, sailing in the Solent with his then wife, Sarah, and holding court to reverential relays of British rock VIPs including John Lennon and George Harrison.

I could only be one of the crowd at his appearance on the festival's last night, white-suited and unexpectedly bearded, accompanied by his superb sidemen, the Band. I shared the general disappointment at what seemed a half-hearted performance, not yet realising that with Dylan, as with Forrest Gump's box of chocolates, 'you never know what you're gonna get.'

I returned to work to find a cable from Bob Ducas in the New York office, saying that my message to Dylan had got through and he'd agreed to talk to me. But by then, he was long gone.

I was still living with G in the lower half of Mrs Susan Raven's house in Elgin Crescent, but looking for a flat to buy. I already had enough money for a down payment on something decent thanks to my first $1,000 cheque from Show (it bore the evocative name 'Wells Fargo') and the always substantial residue of my *Magazine* expenses.

G took it for granted that when the right flat came along we'd go on there together, but I was becoming restive; hence the following disgraceful and demeaning episode.

It came about that she needed a minor surgical procedure which meant going into hospital from a Friday to the following Sunday. It further came about that on the Thursday beforehand, the *Magazine* needed one of the agency-provided temporary secretaries who continually passed through it, seldom staying longer than a day or two.

This 'temp', as we dismissively termed them, was sitting in the concourse directly outside my new office with Brenda Jones, wearing a black mini-dress with a white bib and instantly and massively distracting. So, choosing a moment when Brenda was absent and no one else around, I swaggered over, lordly in my white suit and dark green Mr Fish shirt, and invited her out to lunch.

'That would be lovely,' she answered in a clear, patrician voice.

I'll call her Laurie. She was only 21, but seemed older than her years, having already been married and divorced and had a baby daughter. She knew full well what I was about but had a tranquil, unshockable air which, added to the clear patrician voice, and the physicality, went to my head faster than the bottle of Retsina we drank. Plus, she turned out to like P.G. Wodehouse.

Secure in the knowledge that G would be away for the next two days, I suggested we get together outside office hours. She looked me straight in the eye and answered, 'I happen to have a free weekend.'

We arranged the tryst for Saturday evening, with the clear implication it would extend into Sunday when I'd have several hours grace before G's return from hospital.

Laurie and her daughter were living with her parents in Streatham, a vast distance from Notting Hill by public transport, so I gave her Mrs

Raven's address and told her to take a taxi which I'd pay off when she arrived.

'Oughtn't I to give you my parents' phone-number?' she asked. 'Just in case there's any problem.'

'There won't *be* any problem,' I assured her grandly.

On Friday afternoon, I visited G in hospital with a well-rehearsed story that I'd be unable to do so the following evening because of 'work', but it proved unnecessary. 'Good news,' she told me. 'They say I'm fine now and I can come home tomorrow.'

I feigned rapture and we agreed that I'd collect her at noon. That gave me only the evening and a couple of hours on Saturday morning to get in touch with Laurie and put her off, without knowing her phone number or anyone else who might.

Initially, my one hope seemed to be to find the address of the parents in Streatham she was living with, then, hopefully, get their number from Directory Inquiries. I did, at least, know her rather unusual surname and, as she'd recently divorced, there was a chance she might have reverted to her familial one.

I therefore phoned the Streatham police, pretending to be Sunday Times's Insight team in search of a crucial witness to a major financial scandal. They were incredibly helpful, and the duty sergeant checked through the entire register of local electors for any couple of that surname who had someone called Laurie sharing their address. Even widening the search to West Norwood and Crystal Palace turned up no such household.

The simplest solution would have been to take G out on Saturday night, so that Laurie's taxi arrived at a darkened house, but even I could see that someone discharged from hospital only a few hours earlier might not be in a going-out mood. At a different address I could have intercepted the taxi before it reached the house and told Laurie I was suddenly being sent on a foreign assignment. Unfortunately, this being a crescent, there was no knowing from which direction it would come.

Out of ideas, and near despair I phoned Brenda for advice. Amazing friend that she was, she offered to give up her Saturday evening, wait around outside and deal with Laurie for me. But that wouldn't work because a recovering G would most likely be sitting in the big front window of Mrs Raven's living room which had a panoramic view onto the street.

Brenda then astutely suggested I contact the *Sunday Times's* Personnel Manager – as heads of HR used to be called – since he would know which clerical agency had sent Laurie to the *Magazine* and I'd probably be able to reach her by that route.

I got the Personnel Manager's home number from the paper's switchboard and spoke to him just as he arrived back at his house in rural Oxfordshire. I told him Laurie had mistakenly taken home an article of mine she'd been typing and implied that if I didn't retrieve it in the next few hours, the whole future of the *Sunday Times* might be at risk

He said he did have the name and number of the agency whence she had come, but they were on file in his office. In such an emergency, he'd willingly drive all the way back to Thomson House and look them up for me.

Here, finally, scruples kicked in and I said I couldn't possibly ask him to do that. He gave me the names of the two most likely agencies but didn't know if either would be working on a Saturday.

The second agency I tried the next morning was the right one and agreed to ask Laurie to contact me. Minutes before I had to leave for the hospital, that clear patrician voice came on the phone, and I gave her the sudden-foreign-assignment story.

'Oh, what a tangled web we weave,' Brenda observed, 'when first we practise to deceive.'

Next door to Thomson House, a new building of exactly corresponding size had been constructed with remarkable speed to house Lord Thomson's recent acquisition, *The Times*.

In contrast with Thomson House's slanted casements and copper panels, it was of unadorned granite that seemed to exude discontent and disapproval, for the *Times's* staff had not wanted to leave its historic home, New Printing House Square down by the Thames, still less to be physically lumped together with the *Sunday Times* after generations of vehement dissociation from it.

A covered bridge at fifth-floor level spanned the gap between the two buildings but it saw little traffic: there was no co-ordination between the papers and their staffs did not fraternise. Crossing from the highly profitable *Sunday Times* to the chronically loss-making *Times* felt rather like passing through Checkpoint Charlie from Berlin's capitalist and hedonistic western sector to its pinched Communist eastern one.

The main effect of having *The Times* next door was to lessen the traditional hostility between the *Sunday Times* newspaper and the *Magazine*, for both feared its losses would have adverse consequences for them and were in accord in considering it stuffy and boring.

Godfrey, with his usual stylishness, held a series of getting-to-know-you lunches for his young rips and the paper's Insight team, foreign and sports departments and Business News section which passed off cordially enough, although no collaborations with any of them were to follow.

I rather daringly already knew various people on the paper, one of whom – the straw-haired, creaky-voiced Michael Bateman – counted as an actual friend.

Michael had by now taken over Atticus from Philip Oakes and turned into a print version of the rambling, eclectic – but never, for one second, boring – monologues that I already knew so well. In his old place as the column's 'number two' was David Blundy, recruited from the Thomson evening paper at Hemel Hempstead, whose exceptionally long limbs never seemed quite under control as he loped past Brenda's and my office. 'That boy needs a knot tying in him,' she remarked.

Michael turned out to be an enthusiast of my work; something that never failed to surprise me. I had got into the habit of sending *The Guardian* pieces that had no hope of getting into the *Magazine* or the Review section. It always seemed to have acres of spare space and my unsolicited offerings would appear with huge display within a day of two of my sending them.

The latest had been an attack on the as-yet-unsuspected paedophile deejay Jimmy Savile whom at the time I alone seemed to think creepy and sinister. The day it ran, I found the whole broadsheet page on my desk with 'Mean, moody and magnificent!' scrawled across it in Michael's writing.

Once, Brenda joined us for lunch at the Blue Lion and, knowing how fastidious she was, I felt the direst misgivings when Michael turned up reeking of garlic from his previous night's dinner and spent most of the meal talking about a worrying freckle that had appeared on his 'old man'.

It was then I realised that, however garlicky he smelt and whatever he said, he was constitutionally incapable of being offensive. 'He's so *civilised,* isn't he?' Brenda said afterwards.

For me, the end of the Sixties was less a tragedy than a measure of the distance by which life had exceeded my expectations. I'd begun them as a shabby, self-hating teenager for whom the future seemed to hold nothing; I ended them – literally, in December, 1969 - on tour with Eric Clapton.

Like my Apple piece, the Clapton profile was both for Dick Adler at *Show*, to earn another $1,000 Wells Fargo cheque, and for the *Magazine*, to use its power to open doors. There was an awkward moment when this duality became clear at Godfrey's ideas meeting and Mark Boxer demanded haughtily, 'Why are we picking up an article from an American magazine?' Luckily the inquiry went no further apart from Nick Mason's satirical murmur of 'It all goes to *Show*.'

Clapton was photographed by Lord Snowdon, a major departure from his usual harrowing studies of the aged and impoverished. In those days, even peripheral royals like 'Trendy Snowy' knew nothing about rock music and he asked me for a briefing on our subject. I told him that all Clapton's fellow guitar superheroes, from the Who's Pete Townshend to Led Zeppelin's Jimmy Page, regarded him as 'God'.

Snowdon took it literally, hiring the enormous Lyceum ballroom and shooting Clapton with his guitar on the dancefloor among billowing clouds of dry-ice smoke like a T-shirted deity from Wagner's Götterdämmerung.

He had recently walked out of the supergroup Cream and was touring the north of England with a scratch band billed as 'Eric Clapton and Friends'. Two of those Friends were the American husband-and-wife duo Delaney and Bonnie, whose down-home country rock had briefly engaged his capricious attention.

The third was a bearded extra guitarist in a fringed buckskin jacket and black Stetson hat who kept well to the back of the stage, contributing only chords. It was Clapton's best friend, George Harrison, whom he'd invited to join up as a respite from the Beatles' infighting. Most of the audiences had no idea who he was.

As usual, there wasn't a PR or minder in sight; I watched every show from the wings, rode with Clapton and Harrison on the tour bus and ate with them in motorway cafes. I remember the fastidious way Harrison drank soup, tilting the bowl away from him and plying his spoon outwards as used to be taught at young ladies' 'finishing-schools'.

Outside music, Clapton seemed to have no identity of his own; instead, he borrowed those of his fellow musicians, from their lifestyles to their facial hair. Just in the two weeks between the Snowdon photo-shoot and the tour, he went from stubbly clean-shaven to a Zapata moustache and then a bushy beard like his friend George.

When he told me he came from a broken home – in fact I was the first interviewer he ever told – I recognised the symptoms at once. My own broken home had left me with a feeling of utter ineffectuality as the person I was, but I'd found shelter in a trade that allowed me endlessly to hide behind the personae of others. Just as he felt real only with a guitar, I did so only in a byline.

Backstage with Eric Clapton and Friends, there were no orgies with groupies, drink or drugs. They'd all bought little clockwork toys in the shapes of fruit with which they held races on the dressing-room floor, each cheering on his tottering plastic orange or lemon or strawberry as if his life depended on it.

After the performance, they would return to some stuffy northern grand hotel where, the restaurant having closed at around 9.30, an elaborate cold buffet would have been left out for them to help themselves.

One night, Clapton picked up a bowl of coleslaw and emptied it over Harrison's head, triggering a food fight on the scale of a Marx Brothers film. From then on, the demolition of a cold buffet and plastering of one other with salmon mayonnaise and salad and vinaigrette dressing and trifle and whipped cream became a post-show ritual with hotel staff watching aghast, yet too awed by Harrison's Beatleness to protest.

That, for me, sums up the Sixties: a second childhood for the children of the drab, repressed, unhopeful Fifties, with toys and games and freedom unimaginable and the grown-ups powerless to spoil things.

Now it was over.

* * *

Part Four

*   *   *

We Danced On Our Desks

17

Why was everyone passing round a spot remover?

I started the new decade by buying the first real home I'd ever had. It was a basement flat in Westbourne Terrace, one of the endless rows of tall houses with pillared front porches and private service-roads that commemorate west London's enormous Victorian middle class. Paddington station was in Eastbourne Terrace one street over and Hyde Park only five minutes' walk away.

My flat was in a new conversion and would have been well beyond my means but for Lord Thomson's unlimited blue fivers and the periodic $1,000 Wells Fargo cheques from Dick Adler's *Show* magazine. It had two bedrooms and, unusually, two patios, one the bottom of the building's light-well, the other more of a large backyard that gave me as much space outside as in. Over its left-hand wall lived Phil May of the Pretty Things, a band once even more scandalously hairy than the Rolling Stones. On fine evenings, he liked to sit on the wall with one leg dangling on my side, strumming his guitar and singing to the Moon.

I so longed to be living there that I moved in when the floors were still bare concrete and for some time had no furniture but a collection of Victorian lemonade-bottles with glass marble stoppers and Grandma Norman's brass bed, which fitted – though only just – into the larger bedroom, looking onto the light-well.

The Seventies had lost no time in proclaiming that the carnival of the Sixties was well and truly over. Promptly on January 1, it seemed, frumpy maxi-skirts replaced joyous minis, muddy purple and taupe replaced fluorescent pink and lime green, cynicism and gloom replaced euphoria and optimism and Slade were said to have replaced the Beatles.

For the past 10 years in Britain – and I'm not only talking about the young – a constant steady rise in quality of life had been taken for granted. From here on, all that would be thrown into reverse, never to be corrected.

Yet the spirit of the Sixties was not so easily extinguished, least of all in the publication that had always personified it. Until well into this morning-after decade, the *Magazine* was to carry on just as before, still with the dimensions of a small atlas and the thickness of a Sears Roebuck catalogue, its arrogance, self-indulgence and, occasionally, brilliance still unrestrained.

I myself certainly felt no chill draught from the number seven. I had a dream job with limitless prestige and perks to match. I never had to pay for restaurant meals, books, record albums, film, theatre or concert tickets, taxis, stationery or the Havana cigars of which I smoked at least two a day. Stage-side tables at the best clubs, from the Scotch of St James's to Ronnie Scott's, were permanently reserved for me, with free drinks and food taken as read.

I often thought back to my last term in Ryde School's sixth form when we were given a talk by a monk from the Benedictine community at nearby Quarr Abbey. Much to our surprise, he had a shirt with cufflinks under his cowled black robe, a wristwatch and black slip-ons and socks instead of bare toes protruding from sandals. Such things didn't break his vow of poverty, he explained, as they belonged to the abbey and were just lent to him for his forays as its ambassador-cum -PR.

In much the same way, the *Magazine* had provided almost every bit of clothing I possessed, the IBM golfball typewriter I used at home, the wafer-thin gold Omega on my wrist, my white gold Sheaffer pen, my Dunhill cigar cutter, the very alligator wallet, from Smythson of Bond Street, into which I packed its inexhaustible blue fivers.

The feeling of absolute job security was comparable only with that of monks in their cloisters – although there the analogy ended. The past four years had shown me there was nothing I could do that would earn me so much as a disapproving look, or any kind of official telling-off, let alone the sack.

I remained free of any control or supervision; no one ever asked me how a piece was progressing or when I would hand it in or noticed when I gave up on it (as, for example, with the conductor Daniel Barenboim and two giants of 20th century fiction, Anthony Powell and Philip Roth). I arrived at the office and left at whatever hours I pleased;

I could be absent for days at a time without anyone in authority, such as it was, noticing or caring.

Among my male colleagues it was common practice to take an alleged female 'contact' to lunch and spend the afternoon furthering that contact at a nearby hotel, not reappearing at the office until early evening, if at all. Godfrey himself was famously partial to such postprandial play when the prandial part eventually ended and had coined a name for it: 'Nooners'.

I soon acquired the Nooners habit – initially with Laurie, who'd forgiven me my screw-up while I was still living with G – and discovered I had a decided advantage over married colleagues who commuted daily from the suburbs. While they had the bother of finding short-stay love-nests in Soho or around Charlotte Street, my new flat and Grandma Norman's brass bed were only a short cab ride away.

In my whole time on the *Magazine*, I never went on holiday because every day there was like one.

My acquaintanceship on the paper had widened still further when its venerable American woman's editor, Ernestine Carter, retired and Harry Evans replaced ghetto-ised women's pages with a section called *Look!* covering style, fashion and anything else that was hot, edited by the former Atticus, Hunter Davies.

Its star columnist, Jilly Cooper, wrote about sex in the hearty, hockey tones of an Angela Brazil novel and quickly gained an enormous following. Harry took credit for discovering her, but really it had been Godfrey when they sat next to each other at a dinner party, and her debut piece, about having it off in cars, had appeared in the *Magazine*, headlined 'The Car-ma Sutra'.

At Look's 1969 Christmas party, I met Lesley Garner who, at 24, had been recruited from *The Sun* to be a staff writer. We talked all evening, oblivious of the party, emptying a bowl of tangerines between us. After a fraught holiday season of breaking up with G, Lesley and I began a relationship, my first with a fellow journalist.

It was through Lesley that I got to know *Look's* fashion editor, Molly Parkin, a diminutive Welshwoman with the blackest eyes I'd ever seen, for whom the word 'roistering' might have been invented. The Seventies had seen women start to wear hats again; Molly designed and made her own and was never seen without one. Forget today's wispy little 'fascinators' and think Carmen Miranda.

In America, one of the year's bestselling books was a steamy blockbuster entitled *Naked Came the Stranger* by Penelope O'Grady. Actually, it was a hoax by a group of Long Island journalists, each of whom wrote a chapter competing to be the most mindlessly sub-pornographic.

Hunter Davies assembled a team of 17 from the paper and the *Magazine* to create a work on the same principle called I Knew Daisy Smuten – the name an anagram of 'Sunday Times'. Both Lesley and I wrote a chapter and the advance was large enough to give every contributor £400.

The publisher, Lord Weidenfeld, threw us a launch party at his sumptuous Chelsea flat that was covered live by BBC2's *Late Night Line-Up* show. There, for the first and only time, I found myself in the presence of my first journalistic hero, Kenneth Tynan; dressed in a faux-Victorian blazer, he was smoking a joint and thinking up further anagrams of 'Sunday Times.'

When Molly Parkin married her second husband, the artist Patrick Hughes, I was invited to the reception with Lesley. Also present was Mrs Susan Raven, who didn't know Molly but couldn't bear to miss anything, so persuaded Godfrey to bring her along.

As fascinated by sex as ever, and as blissfully naïve, Mrs Raven listened agog while the unblushing bride described the 'dirty knickers' she was taking on her honeymoon and admitted that in oral sex, she was 'a swallower … it's got quite a nice salty taste, actually.' Later, one of the wedding gifts was circulated for mirthful inspection – a large, battery-operated vibrator.

'That was a lovely party of Molly and Patrick's,' Mrs Raven said the next day, 'but one thing I didn't understand. Why was everyone passing round a spot remover?'

Slip On A Fat Lady (which I blush to name again) was published by Heinemann in April. All its characters were people I'd known in Ryde and Huntingdonshire with little or no disguise; luckily, none sued me for libel although I received a stingingly reproachful letter from the former County girlfriend, whose real first name I'd been idiotic enough to use.

To mark, if not celebrate, its publication, I invited Brenda, Nick Mason and Michael Bateman to lunch at Bertorelli's in Charlotte Street (putting it on expenses later as 'Entertaining Contacts'). Over the sambucas, they very sweetly presented me with a framed 18th century print of the Isle of Wight for the otherwise bare white walls of my new flat.

Book reviewers then were much kinder than today, especially about first novels. In the *New Statesman*, Stanley Reynolds said that mine showed 'not just promise but actual achievement', while in the *Sunday Times* my old *Northern Echo* colleague John Whitley charitably called it 'a jolly seaside postcard kind of book, full of gusto and fun.'

My shame over it didn't stop me sending a copy to P.G. Wodehouse, to whom I'd mentioned it during our interview. I'm sure he must have hated its crudity and scatology, yet he sent me a lovely note, saying I could quote him as calling it 'Extremely original and very funny.'

Grandma and Grandad Bassill both died in 1970, within a few months of each other. Gus went first, slipping away with as little fuss as he'd sat in his wheelchair at the kitchen table all these years, dealing himself endless hands of Patience.

Though Ag by now was well into her 80s, she still refused any help in looking after him. I remember seeing her tiny figure sit his poor legless little trunk up in bed to pillow his head as she gave him some medicine and thinking I had never seen such love. Two days later, she phoned me and said simply, 'He's gone, Phil.'

In true Victorian style, he was laid out for a day in the 'best' front sitting room with the cocktail cabinet and Magicoal fire before the undertakers claimed him. He had no other family still living, but Ag's sisters, Lou and Flo, and her brother 'Elf' all came to give their condolences and to each one she murmured. 'D'you want to see him?'

Determined not to let his passing go unnoticed, I did a *Magazine* cover-story about the pre-television age when five cinema newsreels were in ferocious competition and quiet, modest Grandad was Pathe's star cameraman, unrivalled at 'pinching' major sporting events for which rival companies had bought exclusive access.

I recounted his most famous exploit, when arch-rivals British Movietone had the rights to the 1930 Test Match against Australia and he pinched it from an open-cockpit aircraft swooping low overhead. When Movietone put up barrage balloons to block the view, he snuck into the Oval in disguise and cut all their cables – only they didn't blow away as he'd expected but flopped down onto the pitch and halted play just when Don Bradman was on course to score a century.

Without him, Ag spent much of her time watching cricket on television, for she'd always gone with him when he played for the

Pathe team and even learned the intricate business of keeping score. Then cancer came in its usual unspecific form and she, too, had gone.

She'd been as big a character, in her way, as Grandma Norman but utterly real where Grandma Norman had been mostly pure theatre. In my fractured, wandering family, she'd been the only one to give me roots. They were in true Cockney London, the Lambeth Walk on Saturday nights with gas jets flaring, barrel-organs spluttering, the jellied eel and mash shops still open, and her father, my great-grandfather Skitterell, pushing the 'turns' onstage at Gatti's music hall.

Sixty-Three Lynette Avenue was left jointly to my mother and her younger brother, Frank, with whom she'd never got on. They fell out badly over the sale of the house and at Uncle Frank's insistence let it go for £6,000. Not long after, Clapham's old working-class streets were colonised by publishers and television producers – many of whom pronounced it 'Clarm'- and number 63 changed hands again, for £150,000.

In September, I made what had become recognised as my annual trip to America with a portfolio of *Magazine* assignments. As a year earlier, I was allowed to return by sea, in order to have time and space to mull over my material. This time, it was to be on the SS France, the most beautiful and luxurious ship on the transatlantic run: first class, naturally.

My main story was to be the Motown record label, the only real challenger to all-conquering British pop through the Sixties with vocal groups like the Supremes, Martha and the Vandellas and Smokey Robinson and the Miracles. Its name was an abbreviation of 'Motor Town', for its home was Detroit and its gleaming hits rolled off the production line like cars at Chrysler or Ford.

In New York, I'd been booked into the Hotel Commodore, but it proved an unsympathetic barn of a place, my allotted room having only a shower, so Dick Adler got me into the much nicer Warwick (pronounced 'War-wick' as in Dionne) on Sixth Avenue which by now I'd learned, was also known as Avenue of the Americas.

Meals with Dick this trip included a lunch of enormous steaks at a place called the Cattleman's West, designed like a 19th century cattle baron's private railway carriage even though it was embedded in the Rockefeller Center. Also present was Milt Machlin, an old newspaper colleague of his with a similar bone-dry delivery.

Milt was diabetic and during lunch Dick asked him when he'd first realised it. 'It was one time in Paris,' he said, 'when I suddenly noticed my urine tasted sweet.'

On the Motown story, I was to work with an American photographer named Lawrence Schiller, a huge man with a tiny, sleek head who had a knack for gaining exclusive access to major celebrities in widely differing spheres. In the past, these had included Marilyn Monroe; currently they were the singer Barbra Streisand and the hippy mass murderer Charles Manson.

Diana Ross had just left the Supremes and I saw her first live solo appearance in a vast supper room at the Waldorf Astoria, ending with her soon-to-be international number one, *Ain't No Mountain High Enough*. Freed from the Supremes' clockwork movements and matching coiffures, she'd become like a glittering whirlwind, her hair wildly ringletted, neckline plunging, arms stretching up (so I scribbled besottedly in the darkness) 'as if to feel the finish of the stars'.

Afterwards, tête-à-tête in her suite, she told me how she'd grown up in the Detroit 'Projects' with Smokey Robinson for a neighbour and how she and two schoolfriends had pestered Motown's founder, Berry Gordy, for months to give them a recording test. 'The others wanted to give up, but I knew it had to be because my mama's family name was Moten.'

At the party that followed, I also met Marvin Gaye, the 'Sinatra of Motown', and Gladys Knight with two of her backing group (and brothers) the Pips. An unsmiling woman wearing leather hot pants, with her hair in braids, walked in, sat down at the grand piano and started to play Debussey. It was Nina Simone.

Larry Schiller and I flew to Detroit, a city still scarred by its terrible race-riots of three years earlier, its morale not helped by Berry Gordy's decision to move Motown's whole creative side to the West Coast. All that was left was the little wooden house on West Grand Boulevard from which Gordy had started out, now dubbed 'Hitsville USA', and a characterless administrative building, run by his sister, Esther.

Esther Gordy confirmed that her brother really had modelled the company on the Lincoln Mercury factory where he'd once worked, with a nod to the old-time Hollywood studios. All the raw young talent he'd pulled from the Detroit projects had been given classes in elocution and deportment while the auto-plant model extended to a department called Quality Control which inspected the records before they were released. It was thanks to Quality Control that one of Motown's finest singles, Marvin Gaye's *Through the Grapevine* had been held back for two years.

From there we flew to Las Vegas, to see the Supremes make their first appearance with their new lead singer, Jean Terrell. Larry Schiller's memories of his other photographic subjects, past and present, ensured that I was never bored inflight. 'When I met Charlie Manson, the first thing he said to me was, "Have you ever touched a man's penis?" ... Marilyn was covered all over in fine golden hair like an animal. If she was sitting next to you now, she'd only have to look at you to make you come.'

Thence to Los Angeles and the Chateau Marmont on Sunset Boulevard, a strange old Art Deco pile on a high promontory that was half-hotel, half apartment-house. Checking in with Nick Mason at the office, I received some news that dimmed the California sunshine somewhat. 'P. Crookston is returning to the *Magazine*,' he told me.

At Motown's palatial West Coast offices, I was allowed a few moments conversation with Berry Gordy in a room with half a dozen other people looking on, but he was wary and monosyllabic and said nothing worth quoting. Beforehand, Larry Schiller had told me with absolute certainty that Motown was now controlled by the Mafia as part of a general expansion into the music business with black-owned companies and performers the prime targets.

'Look at Sam Cooke and Otis Redding ... and now Jimi Hendrix,' he said. 'Do you really think their deaths were accidents? They were Mob hits for stepping out of line.'

Gordy had always denied the allegation and did so again to me. It was impossible not to notice the other people in the room were all hard-faced white men, but I suppose they could have been just bodyguards.

Currently, all Motown's energies were focused on the Jackson 5, a group of young brothers from Gary, Indiana, whom they were promoting as 'the black Beatles'.

I watched Schiller photograph them on the beach at Malibu. Their 12-year-old lead singer, Michael, had already been recognised as a formidable talent, but that day he was just a cute kid romping in the sand with his brothers in an obviously welcome break from recording and performing.

Who could have imagined that one day soon he would equal the

Beatles on his own and the plastic surgeon's knife remodel that cute kid into the saddest monster since Doctor Frankenstein's?

*   *   *

18

I'll stay out here with you if you'll stay out here with me

In January 1971 I found myself, for the first time ever, in bad odour with Harry Evans over what seemed the most routine of *Magazine* pieces, about the actor Richard Attenborough.

Throughout the Fifties and Sixties, Attenborough had been a staple of British black-and-white films, usually in small character roles as well-meaning schoolteachers or panicky naval ratings. But in 1969, he'd made the transition to directing with *Oh! What a Lovely War*, a hugely successful satirical musical about the senseless 1914-18 bloodbath.

He was of interest now for both starring in and directing *10 Rillington Place*, a portrait of the serial killer John Reginald Halliday Christie, who had strangled six women at that dingy Notting Hill address, walling several of them up in his kitchen and using the thighbone of one to prop up the clothesline. I remembered Richard Burton in Salzburg talking about a 'bad taste musical' he wanted to write about the case; the corpses were to burst through the kitchen wallpaper, singing a song called *Cupboard Love*.

Small and plump, still baby-faced in his late fifties, 'Dickie' Attenborough was geniality itself, but the father of all luvvies. I interviewed him at Pinewood Studios, where he was shooting *10 Rillington Place*, and at his house on Richmond Green, and each time got little beyond a stream of gush about the big-star friends with whom he'd packed the cast of Oh! What A Lovely War, like 'darling Larry Olivier', 'darling Johnny Gielgud' and 'darling Johnny Mills'.

The various fellow actors and directors to whom I talked about him all performed in the same saccharine key. Dickie was a brilliant actor. Dickie was a natural intuitive director. Dickie was a devoted family man. Dickie was a loyal and generous friend. Dickie was a tireless worker for charity. The only touch of astringency came from my former *Magazine* colleague Philip Oakes, now the paper's arts columnist, who'd known him for many years and once made an abortive attempt to ghost-write his autobiography

'One of the reasons I bowed out was that while we were working together, I put on a stone and a half,' Oakes told me. 'There's a good reason why Dickie's family call him Bunter. Whenever we'd go to a movie screening, he'd insist on taking about a hundredweight of warm popcorn.'

There was some comic value, too, in Attenborough's oddly prancing walk, rather like Judy Garland's as Dorothy in *The Wizard of Oz*, and his studied portrayal of a movie tycoon. It was just before Christmas and as we passed through his secretary's office, she'd laid out six possible choices of card in a row so as to take only seconds of his so-very-precious time.

'The Botticelli, I think, angel girl,' he told her as he pranced past.

Nonetheless, I knew that, mainly due to a shortage of good quotes, the piece I wrote was lamentably thin and it ran in the New Year only because the *Magazine* had a sudden black hole to fill. Proof of its tepidity was that no one could think what to headline it until a chuckling Godfrey came up with 'DICKIE DARLING'.

On the following Tuesday, the first day of the paper's working week, Harry sent for me. 'That was a *vicious* piece about Dickie Attenborough,' he said when I was barely through the door. He opened the copy of the *Magazine* on his lectern and begin picking out the guiltiest phrases (as on happier occasions with other examples of my work, he'd picked out the most felicitous.) 'That line about Bunter is a low blow … Is there something intrinsically ridiculous about warm popcorn as opposed to room-temperature popcorn? … And what's so funny about a Botticelli painting on a Christmas card?'

He turned to me, his long-lashed eyes infinitely reproachful. 'I've already had Dickie on the phone this morning,' he added. 'In *tears*.' I forebore to answer that Dickie was an actor, and probably shed tears if his breakfast egg wasn't boiled to his liking.

Later, Godfrey was also summoned and reprimanded about the piece, an unprecedented occurrence. He said nothing to me about it, but I overheard him in Michael Rand's office, describing the encounter with a belligerence I hadn't thought him capable of. '[Harry] said it was a very bad thing for Philip's career. I told him, "*I'll* be the one to decide what's good or bad for Philip's career…"'

Clarification soon came from Philip Oakes, with his one foot in the Attenborough camp. 'Apparently Harry sat next to Dickie at some charity do and found out he'd been in all his favourite war films. Dickie schmoozed him as only Dickie can and now he's Harry's new best friend.'

The effect on the *Magazine* was seismic, for all its normal cliques and rivalries disappeared amid the general outrage at this challenge to its independence. I had the utterly weird sense of my colleagues lining up behind me in solidarity; even Francis Wyndham told me the puny little piece at the centre of the storm had been 'awfully good.'

Meanwhile, the acting profession rose up as one to defend a figure whom it not only loved and revered but who was in a position to offer it a great deal of employment. Letters from household names poured into the paper, eulogising Attenborough and attacking me with a savagery rather different from the usual luvvie mode. There was increasing evidence it hadn't been my piece so much as the 'Dickie Darling' which unleashed the tirade, but Godfrey showed no inclination to share the heat.

Harry's ire did not subside and he ordered that the three most famous complainants should dominate Sunday's Letters to the Editor page without any response from me. Philip Oakes generously wrote his own letter to the editor, defending me as 'a good reporter' but it was rejected.

I told Oakes what a very different Harry this seemed from the fearless *Northern Echo* editor whose letters page had been called Hear All Sides – and who had backed me to the hilt when I was under attack by the Hon. Sec of the Newcastle and District Operatic Society for criticising the price of its souvenir programmes.

'I'm sorry to disillusion you,' he said, 'but underneath that northern puritanism, our Harry is about as starstruck as they come. If one of his staff was threatened with a government D-Notice or an injunction, he'd fight for them until Domesday. But it's a bit different with someone who might get him uninvited to the next drinks party with Dickie, Larry, Johnny and Johnny.'

At the height of the brouhaha, support came from a quarter I could never have imagined. My office phone buzzed and a voice said 'Philip? This is Spine Millington' – the easily-penetrable alias of Spike Milligan. Before I could utter a word he continued headlong:

'I've seen all the fuss over what you wrote about Dickstrain Attenbore. This is just to tell you I bumped into him the other night and he squeezed my arm and said *"Darling!"* I said, "Well, if I'm darling, why don't you fucking employ me?" I've been waiting for years for someone to see through the phony little twat. So well said, lad.'

In April, Heinemann published my second novel, *Plumridge*. As with its predecessor, I was thoroughly ashamed of it by the time it came out and its *dramatis personae* were real people, this time including several of my one-time colleagues on the *Hunts Post*.

I realised I had described the latter rather too well when the cover illustration depicted F.J. Johnson and Jim Nightingale to the life. Even after the artist had added some disguising touches, both remained instantly recognisable. But once again I was lucky: nobody sued.

Auberon Waugh, then at his splenetic height as a literary critic, gave Plumridge a long review in the *Spectator*, half of it ridiculously over-praising the book as 'one of the great reading experiences of the year,' the other half deriding my author-photograph which, he said, made me look like 'a Roman emperor's favourite.' I supposed he must originally have written 'catamite' but been made to change it by the lawyers.

There was also a review in my old paper, the *Cambridge News*, gleefully pointing out the likenesses to my former colleagues on the *Hunts Post*, only fifteen miles away, and deploring my over-use of scatology for comic effect. Or, as their headline put it, EX 'NEWS' MAN'S NOVEL IS OBSESSED BY SMELLS.

I'd been apprehensive about Peter Crookston's return to the *Magazine* after what had been a rather brief tenure as editor of Nova. The reason was never clear but the part that specially rankled was being replaced by a woman, Gillian Cooke, who seemed to have come out of nowhere. It was some solace when *Private Eye* weighed in in his support with a story about 'the girl who hijacked *Nova*' and how she'd introduced herself to Peter's more hard news-oriented team as 'a touch-y, feel-y, smell-y kind of person.'

Not only was Godfrey's warm stall still open but he came back as deputy editor, greatly enlarging his power to reject my ideas. But after the DICKIE DARLING standoff with Harry Evans, he seemed more kindly disposed towards me; indeed, I owed him an assignment which helped take away its lingering sour taste.

In February, Polydor Records offered me a trip to Washington DC for an exclusive interview with 'the Godfather of Soul', James Brown Godfrey was away so I had to ask Peter, who told me without hesitation to go ahead. It later transpired he'd thought I meant the black actor Jim Brown.

Since I'd seen the Godfather of Soul perform on my first visit to New York, he had amassed an enormous fortune, buying strings of radio stations and fast food restaurants to add to his earnings from recording and touring. Following the assassination of Dr Martin Luther King, he had become black America's most influential voice; his pleas for restraint and dignity had substantially defused the terrible race riots of 1968 and brought him the singular honour of dining at the White House with President Lyndon Johnson.

Washington was under thick snow when I arrived and the 'James Brown Revue' was playing Loew's theater in the downtown section whose decay and deprivation were only spitting distance from the seats of government. Queues stretched around the block, their breath steaming from the sauerkraut relish on their hot dogs, but there was only minimal policing. In law-and-order terms, Brown's presence anywhere was reckoned the equivalent of a hundred police.

Brown had apparently not been told I was coming and kept me waiting for around 72 hours. Seated on a chair in the wings, I watched his show over and over – the bursting onto the stage without need of a warm-up act, the travelating on one leg and bouncing in and out of the splits, the finale of the simulated seizure and envelopment in a cloak, the Lourdes-like instant recovery and boogieing back into the spotlight.

At one point, lulled by the thundering bass of *(Get Up) I Feel Like Being a Sex Machine*, I nodded off and dreamed that Brown was standing in front of me, then awoke to find he really was. That seemed to break the ice and he told me to come to his suite at the Sonesta Hotel the next afternoon.

There I discovered that the self-proclaimed Sex Machine had a wife, an unassuming woman who always accompanied him on tour but preferred to stay in the background. As we talked, she prepared him for the evening's show, soaking his feet in wastepaper bins full of warm water and salts, reshaping his pompadour and tweezering hairs out of his nose and ears like a medieval squire readying a knight for the lists.

As he sat there, perfectly unselfconscious, he told me the stroke-and-cloak routine at the end of his act was not all pantomime; he actually had a serious heart condition and could die in mid-performance at any moment (though, in fact, he kept going until 2006).

Michael Rand 'liked it' and commissioned a cover by the great American caricaturist David Levine. The people at Polydor told me later that Brown carried his copy of the *Magazine* around for weeks.

Of all the *Magazine's* many blind spots, the most glaring to 21st eyes was its complete indifference to royalty. This was long before the Royal Family turned into a soap opera surpassing any on TV and it wasn't wholly without reason that we wrote them off *en bloc* as irredeemably boring.

In 1969, when the Queen had invested the 20-year-old Prince Charles as Prince of Wales, a small group of journalists were invited to Buckingham Palace to meet him over milky coffee and chocolate biscuits like little gold bars. I went along representing the *Magazine* (on my way to the Beatles' Apple house, as it happened), but wasn't expected to write anything.

The taboo was finally broken by Robert Lacey, the most industrious of Godfrey's assistant editors. Robert persuaded the Palace to allow a group of middle-ranking 'royals' each to be shadowed by a *Magazine* writer and photographer during a typical day's engagements. I was allocated the Queen's first cousin, the Duke of Kent, a major in the Royal Scots Greys, stationed in barracks just outside Edinburgh; the photographer was to be Don McCullin.

I had never worked with McCullin nor even spoken to him on his brief visits to the *Magazine* between covering the perpetual Vietnam War, this year extended to Cambodia. To me, he seemed almost a Hollywood version of a daring photojournalist with his hard-bitten good looks and air of fathomless cool. I wondered what common ground I could possibly find with someone whose life was all about danger, violence, suffering and death?

We boarded the night train to Edinburgh separately and it wasn't until early the next morning in Waverley station that I heard a soft tap on my sleeper door and McCullin came in, wearing olive-green and hung with long-lensed Nikons as if for a jungle patrol with the U.S. Rangers.

'Philip, can I ask you something?' he said, almost shyly. 'I'm really into Victorian illustrated books ... Edmund Dulac, Aubrey Beardsley and that lot. Edinburgh's supposed to have some lovely bookshops in Dundas Street. Would you mind if we got the Duke of Kent over with quite quickly and went over there for a look round?'

I assured him I wouldn't mind a bit.

My annual trip to America that spring was principally to do a story on Country music in its capital, Nashville, Tennessee. There was to be a tie-in with the London arm of CBS Records, which had an enormous Country catalogue: the pick of it would go into a special three-album set called Open Country, to be sold through the *Magazine* by mail order.

Unfortunately, all First Class accommodation on the beautiful S.S.France was sold out, so my return voyage would have to be roughing it in First back on the QE2.

I spent two weeks immersed in what I soon realised was white soul music, the refuge of all those many threatened by rock 'n' roll and R & B, with its cowboy hats and conservative values and sequin-sewn sentimentality and self-pity.

There were in fact two Nashvilles, with a vast gulf between them. One was Music Row, where the record companies basked amid well-watered lawns; the other a tatty 'Strip' to which boys from all over the nation trekked with guitars on their backs, hoping to be discovered just like Elvis (who'd started as a Country singer, 'the Hillbilly Cat'.)

The mark of ultimate stardom was to have started a fast food restaurant chain: Minnie Pearl Chicken, Hank Williams Junior's Barbecue Pit, Roy Rogers Roast Beef, Conway Twitty Twittyburgers.

The photographer assigned to work with me was a small, nervy Welshman named Tony Ray Jones and we got on one another's nerves from the very start. But his work was brilliant. Sadly within a year he was to die from leukemia aged only 31.

As usual, every door was open to 'the London Times'. I interviewed Chet Atkins, the undisputed king of Nashville guitar-pickers, and Loretta Lynn, 'the Coal Miner's Daughter', and Roger Miller at his King of the Road Motel, and 'Little Miss Dynamite' Brenda Lee, and Tex Ritter, 'America's Most Beloved Cowboy', whose bullfrog croak of 'do not forsake me, oh my darlin' had echoed endlessly around Ryde Pier Pavilion's sepulchral penny arcade during the bleakest summers of my childhood.

America was in so many ways a wonderfully open place compared with Britain and Tony and I were able to get permission to visit the Tennessee State Penitentiary to see a Country band some of the inmates had formed. Their lead guitarist, serving three life sentences for murder, was in despair because he'd learned everything that other players on the inside could teach him, and so was at a creative dead end.

On our way in and out, we caught a terrifying glimpse of galleries where huge half-naked men sat with their cell doors wide open, drinking White Lightning out of plastic buckets. The guard accompanying us merely shrugged. 'They know there's nothing more anyone can do to punish 'em,' he said.

Even performers who'd crossed over from the Country charts to the Pop ones to become international stars hardly bothered with personal security and I was allowed to spend an entire evening backstage at the Grand Ol' Opry – real name, the Ryman Auditorium - a little circular building with wooden benches, more like a chapel, that none of them ever got too big for.

On the Opry's stage that night was Hank Snow, Dolly Parton, Lester Flatt and Earl Scruggs and as I stood in the wings, a handsome, suntanned man beside me remarked how much his back ached from raking up leaves at his ranch that afternoon. It was Marty ('El Paso') Robbins.

But the interviewee I sought above all was Johnny Cash. He was the greatest Country star with none of its gaudy trimmings, a monolithic man in black with a voice as deep and simple as the Mississippi that spoke directly for and to the poor, the oppressed and the prison bound. His life was a perfect Country lyric: a wild young manhood of drinking, hellraising and his own short spell behind bars, then finding God and true love together in a fellow singer, June Carter from the hallowed all-female Carter Family.

Cash's mansion, 'House of Cash' was partly open to the public and we caught him there, in an atypical blue denim shirt signing autographs for some rapturous visitors, long enough for Tony to shoot off a couple of rolls. But when I asked for an interview, he said he had to leave town that same day to perform at the Canadian National Exhibition in Toronto.

It occurred to me that if I were to turn up in Toronto as well, he'd hardly be able to refuse me. The advance expenses I'd drawn from the Magazine made a plane ticket from Tennessee no problem whatsoever.

That evening, when I approached his backstage trailer a few minutes before showtime, Cash was standing on its front steps. And his quavery boom of '*Hello,* Philip' told me the gamble had worked.

Inside the trailer, I met his wife, June, a lovely woman with (as I mentally noted) 'a voice full of honey and nuts', and Carl Perkins, a rockabilly genius down on his luck whom Cash was employing as a warm-up act. And one of his many younger admirers, then known only as a songwriter, Kris Kristofferson.

He performed on an open stage and halfway through *Ring of Fire*, right on cue, there was a ferocious rainstorm punctuated by thunder and lighting. 'I'll stay out here with you,' he told the audience, 'if you'll stay out here with me.' As far as I could see, no one moved.

Afterwards, when he'd dried off, he invited me to dinner with just June and himself at their hotel. In repose, the craggy face lost its Mount Rushmore solemnity; he spread his arms wide on the red velvet banquette and grinned with surprisingly small, white teeth. 'I almost lost 'em [the audience] back there,' he admitted. 'For a moment, I couldn't remember the words of any song I'd recorded. Then I grabbed 'em again. I wasn't gonna let young Kristofferson see me bomb.'

June had been meant to join him onstage but the lashing rain on microphones and guitar amps made it too risky. 'I've had shocks, many's the time,' he said, 'and once got laid right out, flat on my back in Baltimore.'

'I was knocked out too, baby,' June reminded him. 'When the Carter Family played concession stands at state fairs, I was knocked flatter 'n a fitter cake.'

When I said I liked his puffy-sleeved black shirts, he said he'd give me one, and immediately sent up to his suite for it. I never wore it – it would have been much too big - but often looked at the label: 'Custom Made for Johnny Cash by Nudie of Hollywood'.

All this may sound like gush not far removed from Dickie Attenborough.

But his combination of strength and gentleness made a deep impression on a 28-year-old who'd never had a male role model and must always subconsciously have been looking for one.

He was the other person after Richard Burton I wished could have been my dad.

I returned home (on the QE2) to find there had been a major drama on the *Magazine* over the film part-work intended to repeat the success of the 1,000 Makers of the 20th Century.

Titled Cinema City, it was a far more ambitious affair than the surprise hit Godfrey had dreamed up in his bath. To launch it, there was to be an exhibition at the Roundhouse in north London with the Queen's cousin, Princess Alexandra, performing the opening ceremony and major actors, directors and screenwriters doing Q&A sessions. As the office's cineaste-in-chief, George Perry had been given charge of both part-work and exhibition, with a huge budget and more than a year in hand to put them together.

All George's *Magazine* projects had an element of wild panic and would at some point find this outsize man flinging himself across the concourse to answer a phone with tendrils of loosened hair whirling around him like a male Medusa.

So now it had transpired that, with Cinema City's first instalment looming, the exhibition at the Roundhouse was not nearly ready. In addition, George had managed to slip a disc and was in a wheelchair, looking like Chief Ironside in the television series. There was little dissension from Brenda Jones's diagnosis of 'a subconscious cop-out'.

A rescue squad led by Brenda had to be sent in to ensure the exhibition would at least open on schedule. Even so, when George conducted Princess Alexandra around it, he had to use a tortuous new tense to account for the many yawning gaps: '…and over here, we had hoped to have had…'

Private Eye gleefully recounted the disaster in full, yet he received not the smallest whisper of censure; instead, C. D. Hamilton sent him a note, commiserating over the *Eye's* 'unkind piece' and telling him not to worry.

'No blame,' decreed the I Ching, but it had nothing on Times Newspapers Ltd.

*   *   *

19

Sketches by Bosnia

I never knew exactly who suggested the *Magazine* should chronicle a day in the life of Sarajevo. Admittedly, it had used that same formula twice already; a mass descent of writers and photographers on Cambridge first, then London's Soho, to produce the sort of behind-the-scenes documentary not yet seen on television. This time, however, it was mainly an excuse for Godfrey to take his young rips on a 'jolly' further afield than any before.

The choice of Sarajevo was never really explained either. Its unalluring claim to fame was having been where the assassination of the Austrian Archduke Franz-Ferdinand in 1914 began the countdown to the Great War. It was now located in Yugoslavia, the amalgam of formerly unstable Balkan states whose age-old ethnic and religious conflicts were firmly held in check by its Communist dictator, Josef Broz Tito.

Mrs Susan Raven called it 'a *rapprochement*', and certainly the four-day trip suspended the *Magazine's* usual factions and feuds and created a spirit of togetherness even stronger than had my Richard Attenborough piece - although, in the end, no less temporarily.

As well as Godfrey, its 18-strong expeditionary force included almost its entire top executive tier of Peter Crookston, George Perry, Meriel McCooey and Robert Lacey; plus the new science editor, Tony Osman; Nick Mason, taking a rare leave of absence from his latter post as production editor; Mrs Raven, Brenda, Bill Cater, me and two photographers, Colin Jones and David Reed. Four others were making their first outings as a young rip: Godfrey's secretary/PA, Sheila McNeile, the regular freelance contributor Peter Gillman, Gilvrie Misstear from the art department and the new sub, Dick Girling.

There were a few abstentions, notably Mark Boxer, Francis Wyndham and Michael Rand, the last of which should have set warning bells pealing before we even started out.

If we weren't taking the project very seriously, the Yugoslav government certainly was. A reception was given in our honour at the Yugoslav Embassy and the Ambassador made a speech, welcoming us in advance to his country and rhapsodising about the benefits to its tourist industry the *Magazine's* coverage would bring. There, too, we had our first taste of slivovitz, a highly potent plum-based spirit drunk throughout the Balkans (as quite a few of us soon would be on it).

Appropriately enough, the journey started with a hiccup: our flight from Heathrow to Belgrade had its takeoff delayed for an hour by a bomb scare – another quickly-established mark of the Seventies. That melted the initial frostiness; during the necessary disembarkation and re-embarkation, those who'd had their knives deepest between each other's shoulderblades in the office yesterday chattered and laughed together like old school chums.

We arrived in Sarajevo to find we were VIPs on a scale to which even *Magazine* people were unused. At the airport, we were greeted by local press and television, and more waited in the plywood-looking lobby of the vast hotel where we were booked. Word quickly went round the group that Godfrey's room - or, probably, suite - number was 701. After that, whenever any of us ordered food or drinks, an almost incantatory cry would be heard of 'Charge it to 701'.

To facilitate our chronicling, the Yugoslav Tourist Authority had provided a fleet of chauffeur-driven cars and a squad of interpreters in a ratio of about one between two. The problem was that, after we'd visited the spot near the Latin Bridge where Princip had opportunistically killed the Archduke and his wife, Sophie Duchess of Hohenberg, after their official limousine lost its way, there was desperately little in Sarajevo to write about, still less photograph.

The city had a football team, a prison, a monastery, a few baroque remnants of the Austro-Hungarian Empire and an unexpected number of mosques, but overall our notional 'day' in its life seemed quite capable of passing without any notable incident. I was often to recall its slumberous quiet during the savage Bosnian wars of the Nineties when it would be besieged for three times longer than Leningrad by the Germans in World War Two.

For us journalistic wastrels in 1971, the Yugoslav tourist people tried to fill the void with a programme of official receptions, banquets and displays of folk-dancing in competitively picturesque traditional dress. Perhaps the most bizarre was the musical Wedding Rite of Upper Macedonia, when the consummation was apparently witnessed by twelve clapping friends.

Godfrey led us with his usual benignity, wearing a hairy grey V-necked jumper that gave him the appearance of a guffawing hearthrug, presiding over vast meals, never jibbing at his exponentially-lengthening hotel tab and, with his usual thin man's adroitness, slipping away to bed before each evening's drinking and carousing got out of hand.

For the flowing, not to say flooding, slivovitz and the distance from home spurred some male members of the group to a young-rippery far beyond the wildest *Magazine* Christmas parties. Two female members heard unwelcome knocks at their hotel room doors after midnight and the beautiful but very proper Gilvrie constantly had to flick away groping fingers like so many marauding tarantulas.

Although we were in a Communist state, the authorities had clearly been ordered to show us special indulgence. George Perry, who went around festooned with Nikon cameras – 'like a one-man Japanese trade fair' Nick Mason observed – unwittingly photographed the exterior of an army barracks but instead of being thrown in jail for spying, was given the mildest of remonstrances.

Venturing into town without our minders one night, Peter Crookston and the photographer Colin Jones came upon a night club seemingly full of beautiful women and boldly entered, only to find themselves amidst a crowd of male cross-dressers; then as they tried to leave, they literally collided with a police raid. But they were simply put into a squad car and driven back to the hotel.

For the first two days, Peter was young rip-in-excelsis, but then over-indulgence and lack of sleep forced him to spend a day comatose on his bed. His role passed naturally to Robert Lacey at a drunken lunch in a mountain restaurant, which ended with a collective skinny-dip in a nearby river and Robert's underpants being tossed into the water and carried away by the current.

He had recently begun his career as a royal biographer with a book about Queen Elizabeth I's ill-starred favourite, Robert, Earl of Essex. Godfrey immediately, and with palpable envy, dubbed him 'Robert Earl of Sex'.

In fact, the two members of our group who came closest to sex in Sarajevo were Mrs Susan Raven and me - although not with each other.

On our last night, as we all sat watching some god-awful Montenegrin Dance troupe, our interpreter, a melancholy-looking Serb, nudged me, indicated Mrs Raven and said, 'I like your friend.'

He then indicated a solidly-built young woman with peroxided hair who sat nearby, smoking a cheroot and glancing our way in a markedly rogueish manner. 'My friend … she likes you,' the interpreter said. 'We four go somewhere else? Make jig-jig?'

Mrs Raven, sublimely innocent as ever, was unaware of the proposition and my turning it down on her behalf as well as mine. Back in London, she'd recently begun learning Italian; now, having discovered that the interpreter's friend spoke it fluently, she was taking the opportunity to show off her progress.

Some among our party had taken the expedition seriously, and turned in both copy and photographs. But A Day in the Life of Sarajevo was never to appear in the *Magazine* for the pretty much predestined reason that Michael Rand didn't like it.

Its only written record was a 400-line verse epic by Nick Mason and myself entitled *Sketches by Bosnia* and sparing no drunken, gluttonous or lecherous detail, that was distributed around the office and to a few kindred souls in other departments like Philip Oakes and Michael Bateman.

While it was circulating, the usually imperturbable Nick suffered a fit of nerves over how Godfrey would react and, unprecedentedly, left his post as production editor and went home in the mid-afternoon.

Godfrey, of course, loved it; how much we never realised at the time. Years later at a *Magazine* reunion, he turned out to know almost the whole 400 lines by heart.

It was so like him not to have told me what the doctor suspected. I first got wind of it from the landlord's wife at a pub where he'd sited a fruit machine, the Tally-Ho in Newtown: 'You must be very worried about Dad. We hope everything'll be all right…' Just like when he'd married Joan, I was the last to know.

I had to piece together the story from Joan and my sister, Tracey, who now lived with them in Hungerford, in the row of three rustic cottages opposite the busy fish and chip shop.

'He's been having trouble swallowing,' Tracey said. 'It's got that he can't manage anything much more than scrambled eggs.' Joan was afraid to utter the awful word. 'He thinks it's … something, you know.'

The diagnosis of throat cancer came about a week later.

He'd always been a heavy smoker, twenty Player's a day at least on top of his pipe and Log Cabin tobacco, the inside of the second finger on his right hand permanently stained dark brown with nicotine, its smell always on his breath.

Yet I always felt a contributory cause was the death of Grandma Norman, three years before, from which he'd never recovered. It had taken away his small stock of *joie-de-vivre* from fly-fishing on the Kennet and 'jugging up' in pubs. Instead, he'd sit for hours in his sacred armchair, staring at the TV, flicking at his lower lip with both thumbs as if his own life was already over. It was hard to believe he was only halfway through his 50s.

When finally I phoned him to let him know I knew, I stammered something nonsensical and he cut across me impatiently with 'Oh, *I'm* all right, Phil!' I was paid a fortune to find the right words for the *Sunday Times*, yet still couldn't do it with him.

He started having treatment at the Radcliffe Infirmary in Oxford, just like his mother before him. Its only outward sign was a small red mark on his neck, the kind you see on meat carcasses in cold storage. But, as with her, no message of hope was forthcoming.

Every time I went down to Hungerford, he seemed to have got smaller, his face whiter and more strangely heart-shaped. Now he was coughing all the time, that unique sound I remembered from earliest childhood, like 'Buffalo! buffalo!', his unchanged dark widow's peak bucking and heaving over a handkerchief. He often repeated what a fellow-sufferer at the Radcliffe, an old lady, had said: 'It's like trying to bring up string.'

The drugs he was on gave him 'bad trips', as he surprisingly put it: 'All these horrible faces, swooping down at me.'

He continued to smoke as heavily as ever, though now giving up the pipe that had always been so essential to his ex-officer persona, so misleading a mark of stability and trustworthiness.

The government had just conceded that smoking could kill and Joan had instructions only to buy him Player's 'with the health warning' as it was a guarantee of new stock. He also watched racing on the TV obsessively and betted heavily; sometimes he'd tell me, 'I've had a terrible week,' meaning on the horses.

When my mother heard the news, she sent a message asking if she could come and see him. They had a friendly talk – it could well have been their first during my lifetime – in which he finally seemed to show her some respect, settled as she was with Gerald Davison and enjoying the social position for which she'd always yearned.

As she recounted it to me later, there was even some tacit recognition of the terrible life he'd once led her, even some humour. '"If you'd been like you are now, Irene," he told me, "I never could have handled you."'

September 1971 ushered in a glorious Indian summer; the river he had forsaken looked perfect and Hungerford's many gardens were full of overblown roses whose old-fashioned scent perfumed the breeze.

The town's little-used railway station was continually in the news, for a bizarre sequence of train derailments seemed to be almost systematically destroying its platform buildings, which still wore the brown livery of the old Great Western Railway. Each time I arrived on the branch-line from Reading, something else had gone: the waiting-room, then the station-master's office, then the gents' toilet.

When it became clear he had only a few weeks left, I went down there to stay. At the *Magazine*, only my shared secretary, Stephanie, Nick Mason and Brenda knew what was going on; no one else ever noticed my absence.

I arrived to find Joan's parents, whom I'd only ever known as Mr and Mrs Salsbury, already there, rallying round her. Mrs Salsbury, a stout woman with a plaintive, daffodil-shaped mouth, had always deeply disapproved of her involvement with my father and that had naturally extended to me. Mr Salsbury had the same grim expression as his daughter, but was a nice, if monosyllabic man. Their strong Birmingham accents had always made my heart sink as the soundtrack to my breaking home, and still did.

However, present circumstances brought out a softer side to Mrs Salsbury. 'Don't you remember we was here when Cloive got his diagnosis?' she said to Joan, dabbing her eyes. 'He went off to the doctor's by himself and come back with a lot of cakes he'd bought. Funny chap, bringing us all cakes at a toime loike that.'

He had long been bedridden in his and Joan's dark first-floor room in the main cottage (which, despite its steep-sloping eaves, still had a strange similarity to their 'secret' hideaway on Ryde Pier). I suggested moving him down to the middle cottage's almost unfurnished front sitting-room, where there was far more natural light and a companionable but not intrusive noise from outside, unless the bikers happened to be congregating outside the fish and chip shop over the road.

Like most of Britain, he hadn't yet graduated to colour television, so

I hired one for him as a surprise. The whole town knew of his situation by now and the electrical shop brought the set and fitted a new aerial in time for him to watch the colossal 2000th anniversary celebrations of the Shah of Iran's Peacock Throne.

Sometimes, it seemed to comfort him to think of the countryside from which he'd been so reluctantly torn to be a seaside showman, and even identify with the pheasants and partridge and rabbits and hares he'd once shot so promiscuously. 'It's what every wild creature wants, isn't it? Just to crawl away on its own and die...'

There were moments when we were closer than I'd ever imagined we could be, and I even managed the right words. Once, as I raised him up to give him some fizzy lemonade, the only thing that eased his throat, I said, 'Remember how Gran Norman always had fizzy pop under the bed?'

'Yes.' Almost a smile. Then: 'You're a lovely boy.'

'You're a lovely man,' I said.

Another day, after he'd begun to slip in and out of consciousness, he beckoned me close and began, 'When I pop off...' Dismissing my feeble protest, he continued, 'When I pop off, I don't want Joan to be chivvied.'

I guessed what was behind this cryptic utterance. He'd said many times that one of the cottages would be left to me, one to Tracey and one to Joan 'because she's worked so hard.' Which was indisputable: during their summers together at the Pier Pavilion, she'd more or less vanished into its kitchens in a white overall and on its gala nights had been his helper in the adjudication of knobbly-knee and cockle-eating contests.

So had there now been some rethinking on the subject? But he refused to go any further, only repeated himself with a flicker of his old accusing stare if ever he suspected me of *lese-majeste* towards her.

'I just don't want Joan to be *chivvied*.'

He died on October 24, 1971, his 57th birthday. My mother said that when they were married, he'd often told her he'd 'never make old bones.'

In the morning, he seemed to recognise the birthday cards Joan showed him but by midday he'd fallen into a coma, breathing as noisily as a tractor, just as his mother had done at the end.

I was sitting on one side of the bed, reading about the deranged teenager known as 'the Boy Jones' who broke into Buckingham

Palace and tried out Queen Victoria's throne – at the back of my mind, a half-memory of what a crime reading used to be amid the Pavilion's summer madness – when the tractor noise suddenly cut off.

'He's gone, Phil,' Joan said. At that very moment, an unknowing Mrs Salsbury came in with two cups of coffee. I'd never have believed how glad I could be to see her.

In the afternoon, I met Tracey in Newbury and broke the news. We'd spent very little time together, so there was no question of hugging; instead, I took her into town and bought her a dress.

By evening, the deathbed had been removed, the room was once more a rather bare front parlour with horse-brasses on its beams and I slept there on a Put-U-Up, not feeling a single qualm for he had gone away, utterly.

So, too, had Hungerford station. During the night, yet another runaway train slammed into and obliterated its last remaining building, the signal-box.

*   *   *

The usually silent Mr Salsbury found his tongue after glancing into the garden shed his son-in-law had used as a workshop for repairing and servicing fruit machines. 'So many tools in there,' he marvelled, 'and all of 'em beautifully sharpened.'

Joan kept to her bed – their old bed – for days afterwards, pale and red-eyed but never actually weeping. The small Brummie voice that I'd never heard raised underwent a remarkable change: she acquired exactly his tone of tired fatalism, even used his particular pet phrases. I was to encounter this same apparent absorption of a dead spouse by the surviving one 11 years later, when I interviewed Yoko Ono just after John Lennon's assassination.

But of all people the hardest hit, despite what she'd suffered with him, was my mother. Love is simply unaccountable.

The 'chivvying' warning was soon explained: he'd left all three cottages to Joan, along with his RAF pilot's logbooks and Norman family relics of no interest to her, like Grandma Norman's photograph albums and a giant Bible with a metal clasp, a flyleaf of which recorded her ancestors' births and deaths during the late 19th century.

Tracey's legacy consisted of a smallish cheque, as Joan put it, 'to buy some books for Christmas'; mine, of a Victorian china tobacco jar and Grandma Norman's brass bed (which I already had). Joan also offered me his gold signet ring with its family crest and motto ('Press Forward') but I said I would rather she wore it.

All this mattered little to me, cushioned as I was by Lord Thomson's fivers, but his treatment of the daughter who'd been the light of his life, and was about to leave school with an uncertain future, was disgraceful, though perhaps not so surprising. Nonetheless, Joan remained unchivvied.

He had wanted to be cremated and have his ashes scattered over the Kennet, but it turned out that human ashes are so voluminous, they deluge rather than scatter, and a personage known as 'the water bailiff' objected.

At the service, ending with the normal conveyor belt-style farewell, Joan looked like a Mafia widow in a broad-brimmed black hat, lots of chunky gold jewellery and dark glasses. From first to last, no gesture of affection had passed between us. And from that day on, I knew I'd never have to see her again.

*   *   *

20

You should have hung on to that sheep's eye, mate

In April 1972, I and two non-journalist friends were rowing up the Thames in Victorian blazers and straw boaters for a Magazine piece recreating the journey of Jerome K. Jerome's *Three Men In A Boat (To Say Nothing of the Dog)*. We moored our period camping skiff next to Skindles Hotel in Maidenhead to use the toilets and give our 'Montmorency' – a hysteria-prone Yorkshire terrier - a run on the riverbank, and I phoned the office for the first time in two days.

'Prepare yourself for a shock,' Brenda told me. 'Godfrey's going.'

I could only goggle at my 19th century reflection in the phonebox mirror. A *Sunday Times Magazine* without Godfrey Smith was as inconceivable as as coffee without double cream, Bucks Fizz without Bollinger or Christmas without Santa Claus - to say nothing of the Varsity rugby match, the Secretaries' Lunch and dancing on our desks.

'He's going to be in charge of the paper's Review front,' Brenda said. 'Peter's leaving as well, to run the Look pages.'

The whole affair was a victory for Harry Evans, less public but no less significant than his recent defiance of a government injunction and the threat of imprisonment to serialise the revelatory diaries of former Labour cabinet minister Richard Crossman.

He had always deeply resented that the *Magazine* was not under his control as editor of the paper and that the ideas he constantly sent it – all pursuant to his cherished ideal of 'reader service', to be illustrated by helpful charts, maps and graphs - were declined with only token politeness, if that. Yet, so long as it remained almost monotonously profitable and Godfrey enjoyed the protection of C.D. Hamilton, he could do nothing.

Then Providence had handed him two weapons. The first was a drop in the *Magazine's* advertising revenues, not large but deeply shocking after years of quantum rises; the second was 'A Day in the Life of Sarajevo'.

Normally, that costly, fruitless and badly-behaved interlude might never have come to management's attention. But by a bizarre coincidence, Yugoslavia's dictator, President Tito, was a friend of Lord Thomson's son, Kenneth. Tito had heard of the Sarajevo excursion, and of the facilities lavished on it, had seemingly waited impatiently to read about it in the *Magazine*, and finally complained personally about its non-appearance to Kenneth Thomson, who naturally told his pop.

Now, even Godfrey's special relationship with 'CDH' was of no avail. Harry could make the unanswerable case not only that the *Magazine* had brought the *Sunday Times's* name into disrepute at an international level but that it had lost its former golden touch and needed a totally new direction. That its profligacy had reached astronomical levels was evident simply in the charges to Room 701 at Sarajevo's best hotel.

So Godfrey had to go, Peter Crookston too, as his complicit deputy, and with them the *Magazine's* independence - for its next editor would be appointed by Harry.

Among my colleagues it was widely thought that, after so many years of waiting and intriguing, Mark Boxer might finally get back the job he had rashly ceded to Godfrey. There was unanimous dread that the appointee might be Ron Hall, Harry's shambling, curly pipe-puffing chief assistant editor, nicknamed 'Badger' by *Private Eye*, who made no secret of regarding all the *Magazine's* male personnel (and me particularly, I thought) as 'a load of poofters.'

But it was to be Magnus Linklater, who'd come from editing the *Evening Standard's* Londoner's Diary a couple of years earlier to run the paper's Spectrum features pages. He was the son of the Scottish novelist, Eric Linklater and, added to Francis Wyndham and James Fox, would bring the *Magazine's* Old Etonian count to three. The pessimism with which his staff-to-be greeted the news wasn't much less than if it had been Badger Hall. 'Don't expect him to have any backbone,' Mrs Susan Raven said, Cassandra-like. 'He's Harry's man, put here expressly to do Harry's bidding.'

He looked rather forbiddingly serious with his thick-framed glasses and black moustache, although, like me, he'd written a chapter of the multi-author porno novel *I Knew Daisy Smuten* (his a racy account of group sex in a frozen pea factory). The only time we'd ever spoken was when he asked me to sign his copy of the finished book along with its fifteen other contributors.

Godfrey accepted what was a major demotion with characteristic grace, telling us 'Magnus is thrilled' with an avuncular smile (for he was only 30, a year older than me, at Cambridge while I was on the *Cambridge News*) and taking him out to lunch to pass on such crucial advice as 'Never let the Overmatter get above £100,000.'

Peter Crookston was also sportsmanlike. Over their lunch at the Blue Lion, he spoke wistfully of special issues of the *Magazine* he'd always wanted to do, including one about human eccentricity in all its forms which, in his Geordie accent, sounded to the classically-educated Magnus like 'Non Sequiris Vox' but was actually 'There's Nowt So Queer As Folks'.

Just as a stout man could be elegant in behaviour, a slim, beautiful one could be the very opposite. For Mark Boxer's failure to win back the *Magazine* brought forth none of Godfrey's generosity of spirit. When he, too, lunched *a deux* with Magnus, it was for the sole purpose of bewailing Harry's poor judgement in choosing him and telling him in minute detail how unsuited to the job he was.

Some balm to Mark's injured pride was having a television documentary about him concurrently in preparation. It was for the BBC2 series *One Pair Of Eyes*, in which significant figures in the arts and media gave the viewer a glimpse into their busy, influential lives. Pursuant to this, he was being followed around by a four person film crew whose director he treated with Lady Bracknell-esque hauteur.

The usual *One Pair of Eyes* showed its subject both at work and play but after this one had been filmed drawing his cartoon for *The Times,* more blindingly floodlit than Norma Desmond, there remained precious little work to record. The rest of the programme therefore had to consist of stage-managed social events such as Mark attending a first night at Glyndebourne with his wife, Lady Arabella; turning out for the *Sunday Times's* cricket team in immaculate whites, languidly fielding at silly mid-off; and – a particular coup - playing croquet with Cecil Beaton.

The awkwardness of not once again being editor of the *Sunday Times Magazine*, as many people outside Thomson House believed, was circumvented with typical snakiness. Magnus Linklater, only just arrived in the job, was sitting at his desk when Mark walked in without warning followed by the BBC film crew, introduced him patronisingly as 'the new generation', then suggested a series on 'cross-generational nepotism'.

Magnus's on-camera surprise and mystification had the desired effect of making him appear totally out of his depth and Mark an oracular *eminence grise.*

However, after more than a month's shoot, his *One Pair of Eyes* still hadn't absorbed enough interesting material to fill a prime-time hour on BBC2. As a rather desperate last resort, the director took him back to Cambridge to reminisce about his celebrity as an undergraduate, in particular the editorship of *Granta* that culminated in his being sent down over a poem that rhymed 'God' with 'sod'.

It was decided he should be shown recalling those glory days while punting on the River Cam like a latter-day Rupert Brooke. A wooden platform had to be built on the punt's prow to take the extra weight of the camera crew.

As Mark propelled this top-heavy equipage past the college 'Backs', another punt appeared from the opposite direction with another platform, another BBC film crew and another former university superstar also reminiscing for another *One Pair Of Eyes*.

Godfrey's farewell dinner was at the Casserole in the King's Road. At intervals during the evening, he and Peter gripped each other emotionally (even though on the fifth floor they would continue working only a couple of rooms apart) and as he signed the last restaurant bill that almost touched the ground, our profound melancholy did not suggest the sunset of an editor so much as an empire.

Magnus had made no formal speech to the *Magazine* about his intentions and for some while I saw him only from a distance, usually closeted with Michael Rand. Then, early one evening after almost everyone else had gone, he suddenly walked into my office and began to talk to me, pacing up and down rather didactically but revealing a wonderfully dry, self-deprecating wit.

I was currently writing my Three Men In A Boat piece, although half-expecting him to axe it as too redolent of Godfrey's indulgent regime. Instead, he asked how many words I meant to write, inhaling sharply when I told him but making no objection. He also put his finger on the main problem I'd been having: how to evoke Jerome K. Jerome's comic voice without resorting to pastiche.

Not until later did it sink in that he'd been talking to me about my work understandingly and helpfully as only Nick Mason ever had before.

During Godfrey's last months, I'd decided I wanted to broaden my travels from just all over America and become the kind of roving foreign correspondent, or 'visiting fireman', for the *Magazine* that Nicholas Tomalin was for the paper.

There was seldom a Sunday that it didn't carry a major Tomalin dispatch, whether from Greece under its fascistic 'Colonels', being tailed by an inept secret policeman named Inspector Lambrou; or Lusaka, dining privately with the Zambian President Kenneth Kaunda; or witnessing what he termed 'a splendid shoot-out' between rival politicians and their supporters in the Philippines. Yet, although I devoured every word he wrote, and strove to inject his trademark wryness into my copy at every opportunity, we'd somehow never got to know each other.

The problem for this would-be visiting fireman was where in the world to visit first. Vietnam obviously suggested itself, but it was already crawling with people from the paper, every one in search of a scoop to match Tomalin's 'The General Goes Zapping Charlie Cong.' As in so many other matters, I turned to the omniscient Nick Mason, asking him to suggest somewhere not already deluged by rival visiting fireman where the latent Tomalin in me might flower 'You might try looking at the Middle East,' he said.

By that, of course, he meant the uneasy stalemate between Israel and its Arab neighbours since the Six-Day War following Israel's pre-emptive strike in 1967. I seized on the idea and, after a couple of days speed-reading cuttings and relevant reference books, easily got Godfrey's 'OK dear boy' for a profile of King Hussein of Jordan.

Even during (relative) peacetime, the King's life had been a perilous one. He'd inherited his throne at the age of 17 following a thoroughly British education at Harrow, then Sandhurst (where a parade ground sergeant-major once bawled him out as 'You 'orrible little King, you!') and had since survived innumerable assassination attempts, from ambushes of his official limousine to acid in his nose drops.

The Six-Day War had drastically shrunk Hussein's kingdom, with Jerusalem and the west bank of the River Jordan now under Israeli occupation, while his Arab neigbours Syria and Iraq both plotted his destruction for his pro-Western sympathies. To add further to his troubles, the Palestinian Black September movement had made Jordan their base, hijacking three foreign jumbo jets to a remote desert airstrip and holding the world stage for weeks until the Jordanian army managed to expel them.

I expected a country whose king had been at Harrow and Sandhurst to welcome the *Sunday Times Magazine* with open arms, and so it seemed. At the Jordanian Embassy, a gracious Georgian house in the leafiest part of Holland Park, a charming female diplomat assured me there would be 'no problem' about interviewing HM, as she called him; within 24 hours I had a visa granting me an indefinite stay in the Hashemite Kingdom of the Jordan.

As there were several weeks until my departure, I started to learn Arabic (on expenses) from an amiable Egyptian named Mr Gemery at a languages school in Oxford Street. Spoken Arabic had a harsh sound, like 'gh', alien to an English voice which gave me an almost instant sore throat. And the right-to-left script with its sweeping curves and hovering dots looked so like the Pitman's shorthand I'd learned as a cub reporter that I often tried to read it that way.

When Magnus became editor, I wondered whether the trip would be off, but instead its scope expanded alarmingly.

In 1969, Libya's King Idris had been deposed in a bloodless coup by a group of young army officers led by the modestly-ranked Colonel Muammar Gaddafi. Since then, as head of a military revolutionary command council, Gaddafi had set about eradicating all traces of Libya's past as an Italian colony, nationalised the American companies which for generations had been siphoning off its vast oil deposits and used the revenues to fund dissident movements as far afield as Northern Ireland's Provisional IRA, all without awarding himself a single promotion.

Two weeks before my departure, he announced a jihad, or holy war, against Israel: the first time most people in the West heard that soon-to-be-familiar word. Magnus came into my office – he never called one into his – and showed me the story in the *Telegraph*. 'Since you're going roughly in that direction,' he said casually, 'perhaps you should try to see Gaddafi, too.'

The new Libyan Arab Republic still maintained a conventional embassy in St James's Square although, as a mark of its radicalism, none of the male staff wore jackets or ties. There a dour press-attaché told me that Colonel Gaddafi had never given an interview to the British press, whom he regarded as pro-Israel lackeys, and would be even less likely to do so after the furore over his support for the Provisional IRA. Nonetheless, my request would be cabled to the Libyan capital, Tripoli.

The photographer booked to accompany me was Colin Jones, a slightly built 35-year-old with a mop of curly hair, a Cockney accent and a grin that threatened to split his face in two.

Before taking up photojournalism, he'd been a principal dancer with the Royal Ballet in the fabled era of Margot Fonteyn and Rudolf Nureyev, and for a time had been married to the Canadian prima ballerina Lynn Seymour. As one of the few straight men in the company, his life had been very pleasant, although extreme stage-fright prevented him reaching the topmost echelon.

His former profession still showed in the way he sat in airport waiting areas, feet at rightangles to his legs in a perfect straight line. He'd been included in the Sarajevo trip and one night, as our party trailed drunkenly back to our hotel, had entertained us by walking on his hands.

There was almost no country to which Colin went on assignment as a photographer that he hadn't already visited with the Royal Ballet, always to a rapturous welcome. His opinion of them all tended to be the same: 'Arsehole of the world, mate.'

I dreaded what awaited the two of us in angry fundamentalist Libya, where the combustible Colonel Gaddafi was almost guaranteed not to see me, but looked forward to an easy ride in Anglophile Jordan with its Harrow and Sandhurst educated king. Certain I would be invited to dinner at his palace, I made sure to pack a black velvet smoking-jacket.

'You are welcome in Jordan,' said the immigration officer who stamped our passports at Amman airport. The country was effectively under martial law, but with a markedly British accent: the mass of soldiers guarding the terminal wore khaki battledress and turned-down berets albeit some with unexpected pastel colours. Outside, men of the Arab Legion, King Hussein's personal elite force, in their red and white keffiyehs, sat behind machine guns mounted in open Land Rovers.

'You are welcome in Jordan,' said the taxi driver who took us to the Amman Intercontinental, a featureless grey wedge perched atop one of the city's seven hills. As I knew from Don McCullin, the hotel hadn't been so welcoming to him and the other media covering Hussein's campaign against Black September. 'We were all locked in the basement disco for days, with hardly any food or water. But when we checked out, the 15 percent service charge was still added to the bill.'

In both our rooms, the metal window frames had deep grooves and gouges. 'Bullet holes, mate,' Colin said. 'This place has had a right fuckin' pasting.'

Off the marble lobby was a 'Press Bureau' where a lone, chainsmoking man sat at a desk as empty as Godfrey Smith's but for a portable radio tuned to the BBC. After telling me I was welcome in Jordan, he said my meeting with HM would be delayed for a few days by the impending official visit of Sultan Qaboos bin Said, ruler of the Gulf state of Muscat and Oman and one of his few allies in the region.

We had our first sight of him the next day back at the airport, meeting his guest with a full-dress military display that Colin wasn't allowed to photograph. The king was short and conspicuously muscular, dressed like an ordinary soldier in beret and battledress; the Sultan was tall, young, fork-bearded and exquisitely-robed. Their formal embrace was the cue for a bagpipe band to play *Scotland the Brave*.

If Sultan Qaboos's visit kept me from my interviewee, at least it provided some background narrative. When Hussein took his guest into the desert to watch army manoeuvres, we were taken along in the official convoy. At the end, the Sultan in his tailored grey fatigues, looked just as immaculate as at the beginning.

I only wish I could have said the same. I had started out wearing a white suit and a black shirt, but after a day under broiling sun in an open car, travelling at top speed against the gritty desert wind, my suit was black, my shirt was white and my face scarlet.

HM had no other public engagements with the Sultan and until he could find time to see us, the man at the Intercontinental's Press Bureau arranged a series of what were little more than tourist excursions.

One day, we were driven to Wadi Rum, the desert valley 200 miles east of Amman where Lawrence of Arabia had been filmed. With us we took a teenage Desert Legionnaire in keffiyeh, ankle-length coat and crossed cartridge belts, to join the six others who garrisoned the little square fort with castellated walls, like something from a Victorian Christmas stocking, that still stood sentinel there.

Nearby were encamped the Bedouin Beni Sakr tribe, Lawrence's one-time ally against the Turks, who passed through here at the same time every year. Having danced in much of the Middle East, Colin knew something about Bedouin customs, specifically the strict purdah in which they kept their wives and daughters. 'You wait' he said as we walked towards the low-lying black tents. 'By the time we get there,

there won't be a single bird in sight.'

Indeed there wasn't – but, although none of the all-male company could speak English, we were hospitably received and invited to share a vast communal platter of mutton and rice. As an honoured guest, I was given one of the sheep's eyes, about three times the size one would expect and impossible to refuse without giving offence. But since we were seated cross-legged on rugs, I managed to bury it in the sand underneath mine.

'You should have hung on to that sheep's eye, mate,' Colin said later. 'It would have seen you through the week.'

We also were shown the River Jordan at a point where it formed the frontier with Israel. Here, the mystic flood, celebrated in hymns and spirituals, was little more than a choked-up stream. All my kindergarten Bible-study came rushing back as our guide pointed out Bethlehem on one misty horizon and the Dead Sea on another. Israel, viewed through binoculars from a Jordanian army bunker, looked almost shockingly green.

In London, I had learned just enough Arabic to get us into trouble. At the unending military roadblocks, I'd come out with a carefully prepared phrase and unleash a lengthy, incomprehensible reply. Passport checks were a particular problem: the two first names Philip Norman caused endless puzzlement and were frequently inverted, while 'Colin Jones' made a more fanciful transition into 'Joan Collins'.

After a week, there was nothing left for us to do but sit around the pool at the Intercontinental, drinking endless tiny cups of cardomom-flavoured coffee and waiting for the public address system to call Norman Philip or perhaps Joan Collins to the Press Bureau for the day and time of our royal audience if it ever really was going to happen.

We soon fell into conversation with some people who were there for most of every day; Jordanians allowed to use the hotel facilities thanks to varying degrees of celebrity. There was Hamid, a bald, musclebound hunk who'd once held the title of the Middle East's Third Most Perfectly-Developed Man, his beautiful girlfriend Nabila, Amman's premier belly-dancer, and the Jordanian air force's star fighter pilot, known as the Squadron Leader. Others had shot down Syrian or Iraqi MiGs in the periodic skirmishes with those fractious Arab neighbours, but only he had ever accounted for an Israeli Phantom.

He was tiny and fair-skinned, being of Circassian, or Russian, ancestry and had been trained in Britain by the RAF, whose slang he lovingly preserved. 'I was posted near Aberdeen,' he told me. 'Bloody freezing, it was up there. Real brass monkey time.'

The Intercontinental was exempt from Jordan's strict laws against female 'immodesty', and at the poolside bikinis and revealing halter-tops abounded. 'Oh, blimey!' the Squadron Leader would murmur rapturously. 'That chick over there's got a wizard pair of drop-tanks on her.'

When I said his combat-record must have made him a favourite with King Hussein, he winked and tapped the side of his nose. 'HM and me? You couldn't get a cigarette-paper between us.'

The call from the Press Bureau did finally come and I interviewed the King at his Basman Palace on the most commanding of Amman's seven hills. It was heavy going: he'd been through this a hundred times before and most of what he said I'd already read in cuttings. 'Israel must implement United Nations Resolution number 22 and effect an immediate withdrawal from the West Bank ...I will continue to do all that is in my power to procure a durable and lasting peace...'

His peculiarly automaton diction managed to bleach all drama even from the time Black September had waylaid his motorcade and he'd shot it out with them alongside his guards. Or as he put it: 'Eventually, we were able to extricate ourselves from the ambush that had been prepared.'

However, he played up for Colin, who photographed him on a terrace, revving up a giant Harley-Davidson in a black shirt with a cheroot gripped between his teeth. Afterwards, we were entertained to lunch at the palace. But not at the royal table, as I'd expected; we ate by ourselves in the kitchen.

So I needn't have bothered with that black velvet smoking jacket.

Even if the interview itself wasn't great, I had more than enough for my profile, what with Sultan Qaboos, the army manoeuvres, the trip to Wadi Rum and the sheep's eye. But I was long-conditioned by the *Magazine's* ethos that you didn't just interview someone; you *spent time with them*. And, maybe, subconsciously trying to delay moving on to the unknown terrors of Colonel Gaddafi's Libya.

After several vain entreaties to the Press Bureau for further access, I decided to ask the heroic fighter pilot who seemed such an Anglophile and close buddy of the King's to plead my case with him.

Colin and I met the Squadron Leader in the Intercontinental's basement disco which otherwise was deserted, in darkness and racked by the thunderous noise of Grand Funk Railroad. When he'd asked whether he could bring his brother, I expected someone equally tiny, but was introduced to a near-giant who was serving with Jordan's equivalent of the SAS.

'My bro is on sick leave,' the Squadron Leader explained. 'The silly bugger was fart-arsing around with a military rocket and it went off in his hands.'

While I bought relays of Chivas Regal and did my number on the Squadron Leader, his brother showed Colin the scars from this mishap, holding up his shirt and proudly illuminating each deep crater and runnel in his torso with a cigarette lighter. 'Here … and here … and look here…'

'… So I'm wondering if you could possibly help me,' I concluded.

The Squadron Leader nodded decisively and said 'Leave it to me. Now, you boys come back to my place for a nightcap.'

His huge brother came, too, and it was a long journey in his VW Beetle, over successive 'circles' housing government ministries and foreign embassies, all heavily guarded by the Desert Legion. At length we ascended yet another of Amman's seven hills and stopped outside a small semi-detached house that could just as well have stood on a British council estate. You walked straight into a room furnished with a three-sided leather couch, a low table and a 1950s gramophone with splayed, silver-tipped legs. Further accommodation lay behind louvred swing doors like a Wild West saloon's

The four of us sat around the couch, taking turns to inhale from a hubble-bubble pipe with a brown lump of hashish on top of its glass bowl, and the gramophone played the Platters' *Harbour Lights*, rather inappropriately as the overhead light was suddenly lowered

After a few minutes, the Squadron Leader disappeared through the swing-doors and returned wearing only a pair of olive-coloured pyjama-trousers several times too big for him. He sat back on the couch, this time uncomfortably close to me, but for a while occupied himself with pulling out his elasticated waistband to its full extent, gazing intently downward, as though checking his instrument panel before take-off, and letting it snap back again.

Then he put his arm around me. He had to reach up to do so.

'Please don't,' I said.

'Aw, Philip, come on,' he protested. 'Don't be a spoilsport.'

'I'm not … like that,' I said.

'You're not?' He seemed amazed.

'No.'

It didn't seem to spoil the party a bit. He just shrugged and went over to sit beside Colin while his outsize big brother shifted along the couch next to me.

As I'd noticed in Sarajevo, Colin had a way of instantly going from sobriety to a state of advanced drunkenness in which his grin almost bisected his face and physical co-ordination totally deserted him. I'd been too preoccupied to realise he was now in that state, although some co-ordination remained.

Leaning forward, he outlined the tumescence beneath the Squadron Leader's pyjama trousers with a finger a thumb and exclaimed, 'Gawd, look at that erection he's got, the dirty old sod!'

I was thrown into utter confusion. Wasn't this supposed to have been a *straight* ballet dancer? Had he always known this was on the cards and just let me walk into it? The silhouetting of the erection had made the Squadron Leader loll back with closed eyes and I had no doubt that matters would swiftly progress from there.

'I have to go,' I told the giant

'You have to *go*?'

'Yes.'

To my astonishment, he said 'Okay', then rose and politely held the front door open. 'Do you know the way?'

'Yes,' I lied.

As I left, I looked back and saw Colin being carried through the Wild West saloon doors in the Squadron Leader's arms, rather like Scarlett O'Hara in Rhett Butler's on the *Gone With The Wind* poster.

It took me two hours to reach the Intercontinental, walking the whole way down and up and down what seemed like all six of Amman's remaining hills and through its most closely-guarded districts. As I crossed each circle, shadowy heads in keffiyehs watched me suspiciously and automatic weapons were noisily cocked.

Next morning when I phoned Colin's room, I half-expected him not to be there, but he answered in his usual cheery way as if nothing untoward had happened. I couldn't bring myself to mention the previous night other than to ask what time he'd left the Squadron Leader's house.

'About ten minutes after you,' he said.

He was, after all, 100 percent straight, but years in the ballet had taught him to deal with advances from other men, using humour to prevent feelings being hurt or anger aroused. The Scarlett O'Hara moment had been a part of that, although he never explained just how. Then our two failed seducers had driven him back in perfect amity while I was blundering around the trigger-happy streets, so pathetically shocked and scandalised.

Incidentally, I never did get any more time with King Hussein.

*   *   *

21

Colonel Gaddafi says that's
so not cool

The sights on Tripoli's once-elegant seafront included a line of statues of ancient Romans in cloaks and togas, all with their heads neatly lopped off. Colonel Gaddafi's repudiation of Libya's former Italian masters clearly made no exceptions.

As we walked along on our first evening, looking at the vast oil tankers anchored out in the bay, Colin's curly hair drew repeated honks from the all-male occupants of passing cars. 'Don't tell me it's going to be like those camp Jordanians all over again,' he said gloomily.

Our stay initially looked to be a brief one. At the Libyan Arab Republic's ineradicably Italianate Ministry of Information, another dressed-down Gaddafi official (apricot shirt and flip-flops) said that no cable from London about my interview had been received and at present the Colonel was not in Tripoli.

Did that mean he'd gone abroad, I asked, quite prepared, and more than adequately funded, to pursue him if necessary. The official regretted that he could tell me nothing more.

I'd read about Gaddafi's periodic disappearances into Libya's trackless deserts for the purpose of prayer and meditation, but according to the BBC's World Service (that indispensable aid to all visiting firemen) none had ever lasted as long as this. There was speculation that he might have been deposed by his deputy on the Revolutionary Command Council, the equally modest-ranked Major Jalloud, and might now be under arrest or even dead.

'I don't think much of your timing, mate,' Colin remarked.

New to the game that I was, I thought the British Embassy in Tripoli might have some idea about what was going on. But when I telephoned for an appointment with the Ambassador, I was told he was too busy to see me and I'd have to talk to a Second Secretary named Bob Sharpe who 'dealt with the press', as if I were just another routine hack.

The Embassy was a handsome building on Tripoli's sea front, its front garden showing the marks of frequent invasions by anti-British demonstrators and ritual burning of Union Jacks, although in those days before embassies were stormed and diplomats held hostage, it had no kind of formal security.

My meeting with Bob Sharpe lasted barely ten minutes; indeed, from from the moment I sat down, I could sense his longing for me to get up again and leave. He told me that the Embassy knew nothing of Gaddafi's whereabouts and couldn't help me in any way. 'The situation here is extremely delicate,' he said, 'and if you insist on remaining in Libya, I must ask you officially not to do anything that might jeopardise the interests of my government.' Yes, *his* government.

I rejoined Colin downstairs to find he'd had an interesting talk with the British 'bird' at the reception desk.

'I'll tell you what they're all dead scared of here, mate – that Gaddafi will stop the diplomatic bags coming in. 'Cos in a Muslim country that's the only way they can get any booze.'

Unlike in Jordan, almost no one outside our hotel spoke English, so it was a stroke of luck to run across an elderly Yugoslav, working as a sub-editor for the Libyan state news agency, who'd spent many years living in London. Kindly and worldly-wise, he supplied background for the portrait that, it seemed increasingly likely, would never have a sitter.

For centuries past, Libya's deserts had been where other nations fought their wars, from Caesar's legions to the Eighth Army v the Afrika Corps. The Italians, otherwise the world's most charming nation, had been the worst of colonists, regarding its tiny population as still over-burdensome and pushing thousands to their deaths out of high-flying aircraft. Several members of Gaddafi's own family had suffered this fate.

What was seen by the outside world as his ranting and sabre rattling, Libya's two million inhabitants saw as finally putting them on the map as a nation. And after King Idris's dissolute and corrupt regime, he was loved for his humility – *de facto* president yet still plain Colonel Gaddafi - and simplicity. He still only drives a Fiat; the one Italian thing he tolerates. And when he wants to change it, he just goes to the dealership and waits in line.'

Yet even this insider from the state news agency had no clue as to his whereabouts. 'He might be somewhere in the desert, drinking sour milk with his Tuareg cousins. He might be on that next bench, listening in to us. You can find him everywhere and you can't find him everywhere.'

The one thing we got from the Ministry of Information was a visit to the nerve centre of Gaddafi's so-called 'cultural revolution', located in the ex-King's royal palace. And here we encountered what seemed to be Libya's one and only hippy.

His name was Sadeg, which I knew meant 'wise'; he was tall and slim, and wore a blue denim jacket and jeans, a purple T-shirt, several strings of beads, a silver neckband and American baseball boots. His hair was a tightly curled Afro and he spoke almost accentless English, smiling often with brilliant white teeth.

He was a poet and writer who'd lived much abroad, both in America and Switzerland. What part he played in Gaddafi's cultural revolution I never knew exactly, for we spent most of that first encounter talking about pop music. 'Do you like Crosby, Stills and Nash?' he asked. 'And Cat Stevens? Oh, man ...out of sight!'

I mentioned in passing that I was hoping for an interview with Gaddafi, but losing hope by the minute. 'I can arrange an appointment for you,' Sadeg said casually.

'Really?' For fundmentalist Islam and Cat Stevens hardly seemed to go together (Little did I know!).

'Yeah, no problem, man. Just give me a couple of days.'

When he invited us to his flat to see his album collection, Colin caught my eye and pulled an ''Ere we go again' face. When we found our way there, to be greeted not only by Sadeg but a friend even bigger than the Squadron Leader's brother in Amman, I could see him already casing the exits.

But our suspicions proved unfounded. The massive friend pulled back a heavy sideboard, unlocked a safe in the wall behind it and took out a bottle of the Libyan wine which had been rather famous pre-Gaddafi but possession of which was now punishable by death.

We drank the wine and listened to Cat Stevens's *Teaser and the Firecat* album, the lights undimmed, our virtue unthreatened. As we left, I asked Sadeg about the Gaddafi interview.

'Hey, man, don't worry,' he grinned. 'Just be cool for a couple of days and I'm sure the two of you will get to sit down and rap.' Colin was incredulous ('Pull the other one, it's got bells on!') but for some reason I believed it.

As the weekend was coming up, I persuaded him that we should hire a car and drive the 80-odd miles eastward to Leptis Magna, a Roman city so perfectly preserved in the sand that only the very top sections of its roofs are missing. Temples, streets, even public toilets look so pristine, one can almost hear a murmur of voices from them.

We were the huge site's only visitors and on the way round, my wallet fell out of my back pocket without my noticing. 'That's the last you've seen of that mate,' Colin said. But at the exit, it was handed to me, its contents intact, and the attendant who'd found it refused to accept any reward.

On the following Monday and Tuesday, we could only sit around our hotel and wait. It had neither pool nor decent public areas, so we spent the time in one or other of our rooms, both of which had the same view of two rusty-hulled oil tankers.

When my spirits burned low, as they increasingly did, I'd ask Colin to tell me a story from his time in the Royal Ballet with Margot Fonteyn and the great dancer-turned choreographer Robert Helpmann. Those solemn, smear-eyed beings who defied gravity onstage sure had been a riotous bunch in private.

My favourite was the one about their flight to South Africa before the era of pressurised cabins. 'When we hit some bad weather, the pilot had to gain height to get above it and both the stewardesses got so short of oxygen that they fainted. Helpmann dragged one of them into a toilet, put on her uniform and served lunch from the trolley.'

At about 6pm on Wednesday, I was alone in my room when the bedside telephone rang. 'He'll see you,' Sadeg's voice said, 'if you can come right now.'

Sadeg navigated our hired Volkswagen Beetle to the sprawling Aziza army barracks about three miles out of town. There his blue denim and curly Afro led us, unchallenged, through a succession of courtyards where adolescent soldiers in full equipment were being drilled by bellowing NCOs.

We went along an institutional green corridor and climbed a raw concrete staircase. As we neared the top, someone called out to Sadeg in an odd little chirruping voice and he turned to Colin and me with a broad grin. 'That was Muammar Gaddafi, saying "Hello,"' he explained.

The interview was to take place in a long conference room, its high windows full of a gorgeous flaming sunset. Halfway down, three figures sat on a low couch behind a coffee table and a row of microphones as if half the world's media were expected, but each one trailing a length of plugless flex.

Two of the trio, both strikingly youthful, were subordinate officer-members of the Revolutionary Command Council, Abu Bakr Unis and gold-toothed Bashir Hawadi. The third was a white-faced boy, no more than fifteen, with a stenographer's notepad open on his knee. To their right on a plastic chair sat Colonel Gaddafi.

Though not yet given to dressing like an Italian film star, he cut a dapper figure in his grey safari-suit and gave off a faint whiff of expensive cologne. The face I'd seen before only in smudgy newsprint, railing against something or other, was gauntly handsome, with deep grooves in his cheeks like black sickles reaching almost to his small, watchful eyes. He fidgeted continually, tapping a pencil on his chair arm, banging his knees softly together and shifting his elegantly-shod feet.

I knew he was believed to speak perfect English for, like so many of the world's dictators, he'd been trained by the British army, in his case on a signals course in Beaconsfield. However, he chose to answer my questions in Arabic in that strange chirruping voice, then getting Sadeg to translate. As a result, they came back to me in the lightweight jive-talk of Libya's only known hippie.

One concerned the latest of his verbal onslaughts on Israel, for bombing Palestinian refugee camps it alleged were giving cover to the terrorists who constantly threatened it. 'Colonel-a-Gadaffi says,' Sadeg translated, 'that killing women and innocent little kids ... that's so not cool.'

We'd been talking for only about five minutes when, without any warning, Gaddafi stood up and the trio on the couch did the same. Numb with dismay, I reviewed my last two questions, wondering what I'd said to offend him. Better not to have got here at all than to screw up so quickly.

But they simply walked to the other end of the room, took down some mats that were draped on a row of bentwood coat stands and knelt to say their evening prayers in response to a faint call through the deepening sunset. Then they all came back and resumed their former places.

So it carried on surreally, the windows flaming to deeper and deeper red, sweat overflowing my armpits and creeping up my back, the trio of boy revolutionaries watching impassively, Sadeg's bent

Afro murmuring hippy-speak, Gaddafi obviously understanding every word I said but sticking to Arabic - though he occasionally threw in an English word or phrase – and Colin with two clattering Nikons crawling around him, unchecked.

He could be humorous, as when I mentioned the Arab leader he was known to hate and despise above all others.

'King Hussein…' I began.

'Of Jordan?' Gaddafi chirruped almost archly.

His latest headline had been a proposal merger of Libya with Egypt, whose long-time president, Gamal Abdel Nasser – Britain's nemesis during the Suez Crisis of 1956 - had also started out as a Colonel. I asked how the westernised, cosmopolitan Egyptians could ever be one with the ascetic fundamentalist Libyans.

'Colonel-a-Gadaffi says that in your country, you have the English people and the Scottish people,' Sadeg translated. 'The Scottish are the only cats in your island who can pronounce the letter r. I have been in Britain and I saw how they were badmouthed by everyone. You make jokes about them. You consider them as Bedouin.'

That led to the unavoidable question of Gaddafi's offer to supply arms to the Provisional IRA – 'provisional' in this case meaning murderously permanent. The black sickles in his cheeks deepened into what one couldn't accurately describe as a smile.

'Colonel-a-Gaddafi says that the whole world is sending arms to the Jews and that's *so* not cool,' Sadeg translated, then added sotto voce, 'I don't want to hassle him any more on this.'

In the second hour, the atmosphere became noticeably friendlier. Orange juice was served in little glasses with a bluebird pattern and the formal 'Colonel-a-Gaddaffi says' was dropped.

'Do you dream?' I asked through Sadeg, but Gaddafi answered directly, in English. 'Why do you ask me this?'

'I've heard you dream of becoming as great as Nasser.'

The black sickles really did smile this time, and he returned to Arabic.

'I dream very little,' Sadeg translated.

Informality seeming to work best, I tried, 'What are your pleasures?'

'Talking with relatives. Talking with friends. Praying, Reading the Koran. The Koran gives me…' Sadeg paused and explained, 'This is what we say in Arabic, soul comfort. Because when you say 'All-ah', your soul will settle down in peace.'

'Are you afraid of anything?'

'No,' Sadeg translated. 'Because if you fear God, you can't fear anything else.'

Light-headed with relief, I was hardly aware of the drive back into Tripoli. When we dropped Sadeg at his flat, he chuckled and said, 'Didn't Muammar Gaddafi sit still and have his picture taken like a good boy?'

And that was the last we ever saw or heard of Libya's only hippie.

The next morning, as I was listening to the interview tape in my room, the telephone rang. 'Philip!' said a beaming English voice 'It's Bob.'

I was mystified. 'Bob?'

'Bob Sharpe, Second Secretary at the Embassy. I understand you've been successful.'

'I've seen Gaddafi if that's what you mean,' I said.

The mere mention of the name seemed to make him nervous. 'Quite … quite. The thing is, the Ambassador's having drinks beside his pool this evening and he'd be delighted if you both could join him.'

'How do you think they found out so quickly?' I asked Colin.

'Haven't the foggiest. But they're going to try and pick your brain about Gaddafi, aren't they?'

The drinks beside the Ambassador's pool couldn't have been nicer. All the other guests were Embassy staff who, in Tripoli's current volatile atmosphere, never went anywhere or met anyone else, yet put up a good show of not being sick to death of each other. The choice and quantity of the drinks suggested that Gaddafi hadn't yet obstructed the diplomatic bag. The Ambassador was mortified that I'd been in town for all this time without our having got together.

In a very little while, he and our new best friend Bob Sharpe got me and Colin into a corner and began questioning us about our encounter with Gaddafi, evidently thinking us both too simple to realise what they were doing.

It felt very like the scene in *Great Expectations* when Pip returns from his first visit to Miss Havisham to spin his gullible relations a wild fantasy about having seen giant dogs fight over veal cutlets from a silver basket. I didn't go quite that far, but I was irritated by their blatant two-facedness as well as slightly drunk from the diplomatic bag.

Although I'd agreed in advance with Colin to tell them only the bare minimum, I couldn't resist a few Pip-like embellishments, such as that

Gaddafi had worn imitation crocodile shoes (whereas Colin, from his vantage-point on the floor, had noted they were the real thing) and that the carpet under his feet had looked worn almost threadbare by their perpetual fidgeting.

The Ambassador and Second Secretary (Press) were all ears. I heard later that everything I told them – even the mock-crocodile shoes – had been reported to the Foreign Office in London and cc'd to other British Embassies throughout the Middle East.

We had two more days before the first available flight back to London and I was afraid that during that time Gaddafi might regret giving the interview and order the confiscation of my tapes and Colin's film. I was always looking over my shoulder to check if we were being followed by the mohabarat, or secret police (which had also functioned, under the same name, in supposedly democratic Jordan). I was certain our phones at the hotel had been bugged; when I called Magnus Linklater at the *Magazine* to let him know I'd got Gaddafi, I expressed myself so obliquely that he thought I was saying I hadn't.

The friendly Yugoslav at the state news agency agreed that Gaddafi's notorious unpredictability constituted a danger and advised us to keep as low a profile as possible for the next two days. 'Don't drink alcohol … don't have any kind of accident with your hire car.'

Rather than the mohabarat, our greatest hazard turned out to be Tripoli's traffic police with their automatic prejudice against all foreigners. An Egyptian friend of the Yugoslav's had recently halted at a red light in a Fiat 500 and been shunted from the rear by a Libyan in an open truck transporting two baby camels The Egyptian had been the one to be prosecuted, for carrying more than the permitted number of camels in a Fiat 500 – and been found guilty.

So we used the hired VW as little as possible, Colin always driving, as carefully as if it were a ballerina in his arms. Then on our last evening, we stopped at a light behind a silver Mercedes driven by an Indian woman in a sari. She turned round, looked straight at us, then backed into us, crumpling the VW's left wing.

The next morning, we drove to the airport hours before our flight, terrified that returning it in this state might provide an excuse to stop us leaving the country.

Circling the car hire office, we saw it was staffed by only one man who had a little boy, presumably his son, with him. We waited until the man was occupied with another hirer on the far side of the car park, then firmly returned the VW to his little boy, grabbed our bags and sprinted to Departures.

We thought we were safe at last as our plane taxied out to its runway and the pilot's voice began, 'Welcome aboard this Libyan Arab Airways flight to London Heathrow....' It caused a sudden commotion at the rear of the cabin; a male passenger jumped up and shouted, 'London! I don't want to go to London! I want to go to Rome!'

Today, it would have been just his hard luck. But in 1972, the pilot turned around and went back to the terminal to let him off.

'Well, Tripoli was a laugh, wasn't it?' Colin said when we were finally in the air. Coming from someone for whom foreign capitals usually competed to be 'the arsehole of the world', this was praise indeed.

* * *

22

Bowie's wonderful line about sitting in a tin can

Harry had given Magnus Linklater the *Magazine* simply to be an instrument of his own new power over it, curb the extravagance and arrogance of Godfrey's reign and turn it into a more modest, 'useful' component of the *Sunday Times*. Yet, to all our astonishment, something quite different happened.

In his first week as editor, Magnus wore a collar and tie, the way he had on the paper. But in his second, he wore a brown suede jacket with trendy raglan lapels, *not buttoned up*, and in his third a white T-shirt. That was how long he took, as we could say then, to go native.

For under his aegis, little about the *Magazine* seemed much different. Its overwhelming *raison d'etre* continued to be its visuals, determined by the boundlessly arrogant and extravagant Michael Rand and David King - hugely expensive Alan Aldridge or David Levine illustrations; running spreads of Don McCullin photographs undiluted by a single advertisement.

Nor were any other figures from the old regime moved elsewhere after Godfrey and Peter Crookston, however questionable their usefulness, now - or ever. George Perry carried on in the role describable only as Being George Perry; Mrs Susan Raven ditto. Mark Boxer also remained, still regarding himself as senior to the editor and expecting any idea he put up to be automatically green lit; if it were not, he'd follow Magnus around the office like an aggrieved wife, protesting, 'You don't *understand* …you've not been *listening* …'

Magnus must have been uncomfortably aware of how closely his performance was being studied, not least from inside his own office. Godfrey at the end had had two secretaries – a 'secretariat', as Mrs Raven caustically remarked – the brilliant Sheila McNeile joined by a tall, laconic young woman named Sarah Lewis, and this arrangement continued. 'Magnus is doing *really* well,' I overheard Sarah tell someone on the phone in the tones of a teacher to a worried parent.

He certainly was adept in handling one of the trickiest editorial teams in the business. Along with his dry wit and total lack of self-importance, he had a decisiveness that Godfrey had always lacked ('the editor's indecision is final,' we used to say.) And after Godfrey's self-deluding 'young rip' culture with its underside of bitchiness and backstabbing, Magnus was refreshingly upfront and no-nonsense. Across all the *Magazine's* cliques and factions, everybody - even the inscrutable Rand, even the tirelessly obnoxious King – soon came both to respect and like him.

Under Magnus, its editorial content was no longer entirely dictated by its private whims and enthusiasms but more connected to news and current affairs. V.S. Naipaul wrote about a chaotic election in the Rajasthani city of Ajmer. Bernard Levin (such a hero of mine when I was on the *Hunts Post*) wrote about the 1972 U.S. Democratic Party convention in Miami. Peter Gillman wrote about the first McDonald's to open in Britain. Magnus himself wrote about the demise of *Life* magazine after 50 years as the acme of photojournalism, whose last glory days I'd glimpsed when Dick Adler worked there.

Gone, too, were the enormous theme issues and series George Perry had managed (and usually mismanaged) under Godfrey. 'Magnus actually told George to piss off the other day,' I overheard Sarah Lewis proudly tell her unknown friend on the phone.

A few staff changes took place, the main result of which were two men on the *Magazine* named Bruce. One was a new picture editor, Bruce Bernard; the other was Bruce Chatwin, a new fine art consultant faced with the task of filling David Sylvester's giant shoes.

Bruce Bernard was the younger brother of Jeffrey, the columnist, Soho habitue and self-advertising drunk whose charm had always been lost on me, although he greatly amused Dick Adler: 'I'll always remember one of his columns that began 'While browsing in a surgical supplies store the other day.''

His sibling had found no such easy way into journalism and previously done various kinds of manual labour, including scene-shifting at the Royal Opera House. Although in his early 30s, he looked about 12, his shirt collar sticking up under his ears like Just William. But his taste in photography and photographers was impeccable and, once you penetrated his extreme shyness, he was charm personified.

Unfortunately, he had a thirst almost equalling Jeffrey's and so was never at his most alert after lunch, which tended to be when Michael

Rand would view the latest set of colour transparencies from some star like McCullin, projected onto a screen in a small side room with Bruce working the projector. The way he worked it in his woozy state made every shot look equally woozy.

Bruce Chatwin, too, had arrived by a roundabout route, having formerly worked for the auction house Sotheby's. Like the other Bruce, too, he looked younger than his early 30s; a lithe Christopher Robin in jeans with a golden flat-top haircut. He was plainly very clever but at that time it hampered his writing, which was convoluted to the point of unreadability.

Even so, he quickly progressed from art pieces to a series of lengthy essays on 'the Great American Families'. For he was another of those young writers – none of them, curiously, ever plain, proletarian or female – whom Francis Wyndham, also still in post, befriended, encouraged and promoted.

I had returned from the Middle East putting on ludicrous Lawrence of Arabia airs, wearing a safari jacket made by the Jordanian army tailor and bringing a bunch of fresh mint into the office every day to flavour my 'chai'.

Gaddafi's first interview with a British journalist, headlined 'Libya's Prophet With a Gun', was a cover-story illustrated by Colin's snatched black-and-white shot of that haggardly handsome face. For the King Hussein piece ('The King Who Shoots Back') I ended up writing 6,000 words. 'They're all in,' the sub, Dick Girling, told me, not at all to my surprise.

That summer of '72, Heinemann published my third book, *Wild Thing*, a collection of short stories recycling my *Magazine* articles on Motown, Nashville, James Brown, the Beatles' Apple Corps and Eric Clapton, and the first whose appearance didn't fill me with cringing shame.

The best stories had American settings, modelled on places I'd been lucky enough to visit, like the Apollo Theater in Harlem and Nashville's Grand Ol' Opry, with passages of dialogue I remembered verbatim. Many of the characters were black, among them a James Brown facsimile named Mr Movin and a Supremes-type vocal trio, the Ultimates. Back then, no white writer was ever attacked for 'cultural appropriation'. It used to be called versatility.

In the same vein, 'Blues Next Door', was a portrait of the great New

Orleans stride piano-player Champion Jack Dupree, who'd married a much younger white Yorkshire-woman and ended up living in a council house in Halifax. *Playboy* magazine, then a highly lucrative fiction market, bought it for $2,000, three times my advance for the whole book.

The novelist and academic Malcolm Bradbury said in *New Society* that I'd 'done more than most writers to take a cultural reading in a place [i.e. pop music] that compellingly matters.' However, in the *Spectator*, Auberon Waugh, who'd enthused about my dreadful novel, *Plumridge*, wrote that this time I had 'slobbered over the page.'

It's always risky to make one's characters too much like their real-life models (not that that's ever stopped me) and in *Fun House*, which drew heavily on my memories of the Beatles' Three Savile Row, the warring supergroup's charming, indiscreet, moustachioed press officer I named Rodney was obviously Derek Taylor, now no longer working for 'the Fabs' and a bigwig at Warner/WEA Records.

However, as I might have expected, he took it in good part, sending me a note referring only to the story's style but signed 'Rodney'.

My office mate and great friend Brenda Jones had recently left the *Magazine*, independently of the change at the top. She'd been invited to fill a senior vacancy on *Business News* by its editor, Peter Wilsher, a tousled elf of a man with a weird, creaky voice who was the paper's most respected figure after Harry. The money was much better and she'd be handling copy more challenging than Lanning 'Groper's' gardening page.

Brenda's desk had been taken over by James Fox, still the *Magazine's* only other staff writer, but in no sense my rival since our subject matter and *modi operandi* were quite different and we got on very well.

The tall, beautiful, aristocratic James had long been a recipient of Francis Wyndham's encouragement, but this hadn't yet encouraged him sufficiently to produce an article taking less than about six months. It would finally be handed in as a book-length pile of manuscript for Nick Mason and a team of sherpas with icepicks to chip out the 10,000-odd words that would appear.

Our neighbour, just across the narrow side-corridor, was Bill Cater, who'd originally been Peter Crookston's ace rewrite man, but somehow ended up as business manager. Bill's attitude to his job was ambivalent. At some moments, he seemed as protective of the *Magazine's* money as if it was his own, complaining bitterly that

Magnus was 'spending like a drunken sailor'; at others, the expenses-claims he was expected to pass without demur caused him sardonic amusement. He even instituted a contest for the title Expenseman of the Year, of which James was the first winner with a claim reading simply 'Taxi there. And back.'

I hadn't seen Harry since his apparent *coup d'etat* at the *Magazine*, although after the Gaddafi piece he'd sent me a Herogram about what he called my 'new role as a getter of scoops.' It was only at second-hand, mostly through Magnus – naturally a fertile source of gossip about the fifth floor – that I learned what an extraordinary change had come over him.

Dispensing with his chauffeur-driven car and, indeed, with his former low-key, conservative persona, he'd bought an enormous Harley-Davidson motorbike which he rode from his Highgate home to the office each day, clad in Hell's Angel black leathers, and parked in the lee of Thomson House for the commissionaires to keep an eye on. The term 'midlife crisis' was just coming into use, and this seemed to be a textbook example.

It was at about this time that the paper's Look pages ran a series of pieces by an unknown writer with the unassuming name Tina Brown about the months she'd recently spent living in New York. Their tone was satirical but also sexy in a pre-feminist way, as when she described being 'goosed on the Staten Island ferry' without apparent resentment.

From then on, Tina Brown was often seen at the *Sunday Times*, almost as if she were being formally shown around the place. I was introduced to her myself but registered only a blonde-haired 20-something who seemed as unassuming as her name and spoke with what I thought was an Australian twang, though in fact she was British, the daughter of the film producer George H. Brown.

According to Magnus, she was not always so unassuming. 'When Tina met Mark Boxer, she kissed him on the mouth and said, "*You're* the person here I most wanted to meet"' - which, in light of subsequent events, might not have been 100 percent accurate.

It then emerged that she'd been commissioned to write something for the *Magazine*: a profile of David Bowie, the most gaudy and sexually-ambiguous figure in the new Glam-Rock movement.

The copy duly arrived and Magnus, who affected a disdain for all pop music, passed it to me for judgement. It was not spectacularly good, but would pass after some cutting, the addition of a few further facts and rewriting of some rough patches. Tina made the additions and did the rewriting without protest, then sent back a new version with a note saying she was glad to have had another stab at it. The cutting was done by me.

Under the new order, the page-proofs were sent up to Harry. He'd never shown the slightest interest in David Bowie's increasing fame or pop in general, and I expected him to have nothing to say about this. Yet the proof came back covered with detailed comments in his high-speed italic hand. Somewhere between the Crossman Diaries and the Thalidomide campaign,he'd evidently taken a crash course in Ziggy Stardust, the Laughing Gnome and the lyrics of *Space Oddity*, from which he singled out 'Bowie's wonderful line about sitting in a tin can.'

Although, to my knowledge, he'd never seen Tina's original copy, he somehow knew which passages I'd cut out, told me quite sharply that they'd been 'fascinating' and ordered them all to be restored.

*   *   *

Magnus seemed happy for me to continue as a visiting fireman in the Nick Tomalin mould and November found me teamed with Colin Jones again and off on a five-week trip to India, principally to interview its Prime Minister, Mrs Indira Gandhi.

In those days, you didn't need a visa for India, only a pink booklet stapled into your passport, known as an All-India Liquor Permit. The country was under prohibition like America in the 1920s but there were 'permit rooms', mostly in the big hotels, where foreign visitors could booze to their hearts' content.

The Middle East was still an unknowable enigma to me. but India opened itself up instantly and uninhibitedly. Our first evening in what was still called Bombay ended with Colin and myself sitting in the waterfront brothel to which the *Sunday Times's* local 'stringer' had brought us, watching a troupe of girls no more than ten or twelve dance and sing to the clash of little cymbals between their fingers.

It was the queasiest of spectacles, so I turned and looked through the open window behind me. On the waterfront below, a line of wooden barrows had been parked overnight, all tilted at the same steep angle, each with an equally steeply-tilted human silhouette asleep on it.

Bombay was a bludgeoning assault on the senses with its ferocious heat; its clamorous, crazy traffic in which terrible accidents almost but not quite happened almost every minute; above all, the milling crowds whose endless flicker the eye could never escape (and with me brought on a sensation like travel sickness).

Most traumatising was its appalling poverty; the whole families who bedded down each night on open pavements with a heartbreaking air of domesticity, the beggars with every kind of awful disability, some supposedly inflicted by themselves or their families. I remember once passing a legless, one-armed man slumped on the ground, who then suddenly reappeared ahead of me with his one hand outstretched; he'd been sitting on a roller skate.

One never became inured to such things, but unless one developed a kind of tunnel-vision, it would have been impossible to go onto the streets at all.

We stayed at the colonial era Taj Hotel, overlooking the massive stone arch known as 'the Gateway of India', built by the British in 1924 even though by then it was clear they would soon be shown out through it. I thought of Grandad Bassill, here long before the sun showed any sign of setting on the Raj, with his wood-and-brass newsreel camera, his sola topi and hundred golden guineas in advance expenses.

Our first subject was Bombay's Hindi-language film industry – not yet called Bollywood or noticed much in Britain – which pumped out as many productions as Hollywood in its heyday, all enormously long due to their audience's demand for adventure, music and 'sacrifice' crammed into one story. Most of them used the plots of Shakespeare plays over and over, with *Hamlet* and *Macbeth* the favourites.

We spent a day with a top box office star named Dharmendra, who was making six films concurrently and admitted finding it hard to remember which one he was shooting at a given moment. On-set procedure followed. Hollywood's exactly, except that when the bell rang and the red light went on for a take, everyone present, including Dharmendra, shouted 'Silence!'

I had been warned to expect stomach trouble and armed myself with the 'kaolin and morphine' mixture that could still be bought over the counter in Britain. In fact, Indians suffered just as much in that area, and it was a perfectly permissible conversational topic. A ravishing actress named Mumtaz whom I interviewed told me in the lovely Victorian English almost everybody used she was 'just recovering from a smart attack of diarrhoea.'

As it turned out, my only ailment was mild conjunctivitis, caused by the studio arc lights and draughts from the giant electric fans.

Indira Gandhi was then the world's most powerful woman, her only rival Mrs Sirima Bandanaraika, the Prime Minister of Sri Lanka. I talked to her in her office in New Delhi, the Lutyens-designed ceremonial capital where government still went on largely on the British model. Outside the window, cavalry with plumed helmets and pennon-tipped lances were circling a sandy parade ground, just as Grandad Bassill would once have filmed them.

In a land of riotous colours, Mrs Gandhi was monochrome, clutching a nondescript shawl around her, speaking in a flat, passionless little voice with some kind of sweet or lozenge in one cheek: not the banality of evil but absolute power. Only the steel-grey plume that seemed to erupt from her uncoiffured hair suggested what lay beneath.

She seemed utterly bored by my questions and, fast running out of ideas, I asked which members of her cabinet I might usefully interview. 'You should talk to Mr Dixit,' she replied. In India, 'x' is pronounced 'ksh'. I heard a muffled gurgle from Colin on the floor with his Nikons but managed to keep going.

Much more visually rewarding was the early-morning reception in the garden of her private residence, when Delhi's balmy winter sunshine evinced a near-smile for the hundred or so vividly-attired people who'd travelled from all over India to see her.

Afterwards, the motorcade that took her to work dropped us off at our hotel in Old Delhi. In our particular car were three of her Sikh bodyguards and poking out from under its back seat a tommy-gun that Al Capone would have recognised. The same tommy-gun-toting Sikhs were to assassinate her in 1984.

Even in Mrs Gandhi's socialist, nationalist India, reminders of the British Raj ran too deep to be erased. Traffic signs still pointed to 'Civil Lines' and 'the Jockey Club'. An old-school Delhi journalist (and Oxford graduate) named D. F. Karaka took me to dinner at the latter; we ate roast beef and treacle pudding and in his every exchange with our liveried waiter, my host referred to me as 'the Sahib'.

For our final story, Colin and I had ourselves chauffeur-driven 200 miles eastward to Rajasthan, to stay in the palace of the Maharajah of Bikaner. The Maharajah, His Highness Karni Singh, was no longer in residence; Mrs Gandhi had stopped the generous pension that the British had paid his forebears and was taxing him at 125 percent. 'Now if I even want to offer you a cigarette,' he told me mournfully at his small bungalow in New Delhi, 'I have to sell something to pay for it.'

Bikaner Palace was a giant edifice of dark red stone in the castellated and domed Moghul style. Nearby stood a Moghul-style engine-shed – for the state railway had naturally started and ended at Karni Singh's father's door – and a Moghul-style garage containing a Rolls-Royce Silver Ghost, delivered overland from London sometime in the Twenties, and a pristine Royal Air Force biplane dating from the Great War.

We were the palace's only paying guests. As we walked to dinner down a long corridor lined with photographs of the old maharajah and his best friend, King George V, a bat swung companionably ahead of us.

Our meals were served in a cavernous trophy room lined with the heads of wild animals the old maharajah had shot in Africa as well as India, among them a rhino and a giraffe with its entire neck sticking out of the wall miraculously without overbalancing. In the adjacent kitchen, the enormous ranges hadn't been lit for years and our cook squatted at an open fire on the flagstones.

The district's other main attraction was the Temple of the Holy Rats, where the rodents were believed to be reincarnations of especially devout Hindus and enticed in, fed and sheltered. Anybody who accidentally killed one had to pay a weight of silver not equal to the rat but the person it represented. Across the road – literally – was a United Nations agency organising the subcontinent's largest rat-extermination programme. Even Colin, that jaded world-traveller in ballet-pumps, had to admit it was 'Unbelievable! Unbe-fucking-*lievable*!'

Unlike many first-time visitors to the country, I hadn't so far experienced any kind of religious transfiguration. But there was a moment when I lay on the marble floor of the palace courtyard after midnight, gazing up into the Indian heavens, as crammed with stars as the streets with people, murmuring 'God… Oh, my God!'

Christmas would soon be upon us and Colin wanted to get home to his wife, Priscilla, and their new baby daughter. (It had never crossed my mind what Priscilla must think of me for taking him away so much.) I set little store by Christmas, having spent too many on the end of Ryde Pier, so I decided to stay on until January, when Mrs Gandhi would be addressing her Congress party's conference in Calcutta.

On Christmas Eve, I went to a circus in a traditional big top, with clowns, acrobats, elephants – of course – and a red-coated, top-hatted ringmaster. You could tell this was India only when the trapeze act started and *four* people up there were clinging to one bar.

On Christmas Day, carols were piped throughout the hotel and a plate of mince pies appeared in my room. To get completely away from it, I went for a long walk through the heart of Old Delhi. At one point, the ceaseless flicker of the crowds brought on that travel-sick feeling and I looked upward to see an enormous green ape swinging along from rooftop to rooftop as if it was following me.

*　*　*

23

Why didn't I bring him back his shirts?

For those who'd experienced the incredible second childhood of the Sixties, becoming 30 was more than usually difficult. I remember when I was 27 being at a dinner party composed of people I assumed were all my age until one of them, a man, confessed to having already crossed that awful threshold. The rest of us listened sympathetically as if he'd been diagnosed with a fatal illness.

However, my 30th on April 13, 1973, came and went almost without my noticing, for I was in Memphis, Tennessee, researching a *Magazine* cover story on soul music.

I had begun two weeks earlier with Stevie Wonder, the former Motown child prodigy who'd escaped from Berry Gordy's aural auto -plant to develop at age 22 into the greatest soul performer since Ray Charles.

I met him in the lobby of New York's Hotel Barbizon, escorted by his brother and road-manager, Milton. Like Ray, his music kept him in a state of perpetual rapture, his head constantly turning to and fro to invisible melodies so that the dark glasses which should have registered the blank tragedy of blindness from birth were instead full of shifting sunlight.

Outside, a limo waited to take him to a theatre show in Philadelphia and Milton motioned me into the back seat beside him.

Straight away, his fingers began pressing the buttons on an outsize tape-recorder to play me new songs in progress. 'This one's called *Shine in the Night*. All the people rise up to put an end to the bad things in the world, and they shine in the night …The words to this one go, "I took a worthless trip down life's avenue. Take a chance on your mind, you'll be surprised what you find ..." Man, I love Latin music! I have to get some Spanish words for that one.'

In Philadelphia, Milton was tied up with arrangements at the theatre and, as no one else seemed available, I took on the role of looking after Stevie. He accepted it naturally and, indeed, it was hardly an imposition, for no sweeter, less troublesome young man could have been imagined.

So I led him to the rehearsal with his 15-piece soul-funk band, my reward an exclusive performance of *Uptight*, *For Once In My Life*, *Superstition* and the about-to-be-released *You Are The Sunshine of My Life*.

From there, I led him to the not-very-plush hotel room where he received a stream of visitors, all wanting something from him – his signature on an album or his name on a charity – all treated with the same charm and patience; in the end, I'd be the one to butt in with 'Sorry but Stevie needs a little time to himself now…'

In the whole day, he ate nothing, only sucked lemon-wedges for the sake of his voice. Never was there a sign of drugs or alcohol, though he did admit a fondness for the Portuguese rose wine that Americans pronounced 'Mat-oose'. I even helped him into his stage-clothes, the pink tweed three-piece suit, butterfly bow and big floppy cap of which he was hugely proud despite being unable to see them.

I couldn't stay for that night's show (although I'd catch it later in Chicago and was totally overwhelmed) so my last duty was to lead him into the wings, say 'Good luck' and send him out into the red, purple, orange and gold spotlights. All the way back to New York, I worried about how he'd get on without me to look out for him.

Other bits of the story almost touched that level, as when I had breakfast with the electric blues master B. B. King at his house on the Lower East Side. Suitably enough, B.B. wore a dressing gown of pale blue silk; I remember his fingers indenting it in the region of his heart when I mentioned Django Reinhardt. For the dignified African American who picked the elegant minimum of guitar notes hero-worshipped the three-fingered French gipsy who played the frantic maximum.

Ben E. King, the velvet-voiced lead singer of the Drifters' *Save the Last Dance For Me*, took me sightseeing around Harlem in his open Thunderbird. I saw the classically-trained Roberta Flack sing at Madison Square Garden with an orchestra directed by Quincy Jones, then (on the *Magazine* principle that one interview was never enough) flew with her to Seattle in the far northwest to continue our conversation while she rehearsed.

In Memphis, I walked down Beale Street, where a country boy named Elvis Presley had soaked up the influence of black performers, later to unleash the resulting musical hybrid as rock 'n' roll; I visited the pioneeringly bi-racial Stax record label and met Steve Cropper of Booker T and the MGs, Isaac Hayes and Rufus Thomas. In nearby Brownsville, I found the ancient bluesman Sleepy John Estes, living in a dirt-floored cabin, too impoverished to buy dark glasses to hide his blindness.

In many other locations, always with the same informality, I talked to Wilson (*Mustang Sally*) Pickett. Curtis Mayfield, William Bell, Arthur Conley, Eddie Floyd and Gladys Knight. It was wasting material on a heroic scale: I had enough for about 10 separate profiles but threw everything into one 5,000-worder.

By way of contrast, I was also profiling Senator Edward Kennedy, who had seen his brothers, John and Bobby, both struck down in the era of so-called love and peace.

'Teddy' had been expected to seek the Presidency in his turn until 1969, when he'd accidentally driven his car off the bridge from Chappaquiddick island in Massachusetts. The Senator had managed to escape from the submerged vehicle but left his companion, a young woman named Mary-Jo Kopechne, to drown. Now, as the Watergate scandal rapidly turned the Nixon White House the colour of ordure, Chappaquiddick receded from public memory and Democratic hopes were reviving that the last Kennedy brother might fulfil his manifest destiny.

I spent four days with Teddy, watching him campaign in the Kennedy heartland of Boston and rural Massachesetts. Afterwards, he invited me to the Kennedy Center in Washington DC, endowed in memory of Jack, where some journalism awards were to be presented in memory of Bobby. During the evening, he introduced me to their mother, Rose, a tiny woman with the bravest of all smiles, in the black dress she would wear for the rest of her days.

At one point, he told me of the death threats he continually received from madmen seeking to complete the full set. When I asked if he was brave, he smiled in the way that at some moments was so like Jack, at others so like Bobby. 'Hell, no,' he said.

Before flying home from New York, I called in at the *Sunday Times/ Times* office on Lexington Avenue with its grandfather clock and framed photographs of Winston Churchill and the Queen. The manager, Bob Ducas, ever the perfect Wodehouse clubman, beckoned me into his office.

'Your colleague, Nick Tomalin, was in town a couple of weeks ago,' he told me.

'Really?' I said rather stiffly, for by now I felt almost proprietorial about New York.

'Yes, on something to do with Watergate. The thing is, he had some shirts made at Brooks Brothers which weren't ready when he went back so they had to be delivered here. He's asked if you'll take them for him.'

My mind instantly went back to my first encounter with Tomalin in 1963, when he was editor of *Town*, a magazine so very much about shirts. I could picture the American kind he would favour; no pattern, or hardly any, with button-down collars. Definitely button-down collars.

It was a small enough favour to do the man who'd first told me I had a chance of making it in journalism without a university degree like his. But, *Magazine* big-shot that I felt, it annoyed me. Working my guts out (as I now characterised the past four thrilling weeks to myself) had left me no time to buy shirts. I told Ducas I hadn't enough room in my case.

Two days after I returned to Thomson House, Tomalin came in to my office with the slightly sidelong gait that, to me, still somehow signalled 'Cambridge' and asked whether I'd got his shirts.

'No, I haven't,' I said.

'You *haven't?*' he repeated.

'No… sorry.'

He said nothing more, just gave a wince of vexation, turned and walked out.

On October 6, 1973, war broke out in the Middle East again. Egypt's President Anwar Sadat chose Yom Kippur, the Jewish Day of Atonement, to launch a surprise attack on Israel aimed both at avenging his and his Arab allies' humiliation in the 1967 Six-Day War and taking back the territories they had lost. The famously tough Israeli army had grown slack and complacent in the interim and for some days it looked as though Sadat's gamble might succeed.

I rushed into Magnus and said I should cover the war for the *Magazine*. After all, with King Hussein and Gaddafi under my belt, wasn't I now an old Middle East hand? And an Arabic speaker (of sorts) to boot?

He agreed at once but, under the new order, would have to clear it with Harry Evans. Meantime, he told me to get my inoculations, pack and be ready to fly to Tel Aviv at a moment's notice.

Late that evening, he phoned me at home. 'Better unpack, I'm afraid,' he said. 'Harry has decided the *Sunday Times* is sending only one person to the war – and it's going to be Nick Tomalin for the paper.'

A few days later, as I was passing his office, I saw him in a huddle with several executives from the fifth floor, among them Ron Hall and Peter Wilsher. Seeing me, he beckoned me to join them.

'We've just had some terrible news,' he said. 'Nick Tomalin has been killed by a Syrian rocket on the Golan Heights.'

My immediate thought, even before 'It could have been me' - and recurring to this day - was '*Why* didn't I bring him back his shirts?'

*   *   *

January 1974 saw Colin Jones and me set off on another long trip, this time to the Far East. In Jakarta, Indonesia, we investigated the world's most hellishly crowded city: in Bali, we spent a week living in a straw hut on the beach and drinking rum from whole green coconuts; in Hong Kong, still securely under British rule, we ventured (with a heavy police escort) into the Walled City of Kowloon, an anomalous enclave belonging neither to Britain nor mainland China whose two main products were Christmas crackers and heroin.

We also had visas for Vietnam, where the war continued to drag on, but I decided to change course to the Philippines (where Colin, of course, had already been several times with the Royal Ballet) and add further to my collection of despots by interviewing President Ferdinand Marcos and his wife, Imelda. That was to be the end of our travels together and of the *Magazine's* golden age.

From 1974 on, the Seventies meant increasing economic and social chaos as the Arab oil-producing nations doubled and redoubled the price of their product in reprisal for the West's support of Israel. In Britain, the addition of a miners' strike and problems with food-imports led to galloping inflation, constant unpredictable blackouts and the imposition of a three-day working week.

As a result, the *Magazine's* advertising revenues slumped dramatically. And that, together with Magnus's refusal to jump to Harry Evans's bidding, led to his removal from its editorship in the most brutal way in 1975.

He had become so popular that the whole staff, in an unprecedented show of unity, sent a memo to Harry, protesting at his treatment. Harry responded in a typically disarming way, going round to each signatory of the memo and personally apologising to them. But the decision was irrevocable. At Magnus's leaving party, Michael Rand threw inscrutability aside in a speech about how 'desperately sorry' everyone was to see him go.

His successor was to be Hunter Davies, a former Atticus columnist and Look pages editor, whose chirpy faux-naivete had always seemed very much of the Sixties but in the Seventies was beginning to wear thin; for instance, his habit when signing a letter or memo of drawing a little face, smiley or frowny as applicable.

When Hunter addressed his new staff, he told us that until now we had all been 'under-achieving', which, translated from faux-naïve chirp, meant we were rubbish but he was going to sort us out.

This time, Harry had left nothing about his coup to chance; with Hunter came the paper's art director, Edwin Taylor, while Michael Rand took over Taylor's far less powerful job on the paper. In at the same time came a ready-made 'front-of-the book' department named Lifespan, headed by Michael Bateman, to supply the reader-service features so dear to Harry's heart on subjects like real ale and dental hygiene, with plenty of maps, graphs and charts.

Nick Mason, the production editor and the *Magazine's* most essential component would be staying on, as would the more debatably so Mrs Susan Raven, George Perry and Meriel McCooey. The picture editor, Bruce Bernard, left after a couple of meetings about the *Magazine's* photographic content with Hunter, whom thenceforward he described as 'the Philistine from Carlisle.' Bruce Chatwin lost his contract as fine art consultant and went off to write *In Patagonia* and found a new cult of travel writing (more's the pity.)

My own future looked uncertain. I still had a piece commissioned by Magnus to write – about sailing on the 'Jazz Ship' from Florida to the Bahamas with Sarah Vaughan, the Woody Herman Orchestra and Stan Getz – but something told me that under the new regime it would never go in, so not to bother. There was also the fact that every conversation about writing I had with my new editor brought back my favourite Wodehouse quote: 'Had his brains been constructed of silk, they would have been hard put to it to make a canary a pair of camiknickers.'

Then Harry called me upstairs and said 'Philip, I'd love you to be Atticus.' The prize he'd dangled in front of me on my first visit to Thomson House had finally arrived.

*   *   *

Epilogue

The characters pop off the page with some verisimilitude

I stayed on the *Sunday Times* for six more years, simply because there was nowhere else I wanted to be. During that time, I had offers to join both the *Observer* and the *Daily Mail*, but never seriously considered either, any more than I did the idea of turning freelance. The Thomson Organisation had breastfed me for too long.

My year as Atticus soon cured me of my languorous *Magazine* ways. Writing its 2,000-word, half-page single-handedly – for I dispensed with the traditional assistant – meant no more poring over my prose at leisure like a monk illuminating a manuscript. Faced with a weekly deadline, I had to re-learn to write almost as fast as I used to on the *Northern Echo*. And the two celebrity interviews per column had to be one-offs, seldom longer than 45 minutes.

I then became a general feature writer, usually doing the 'page 5' piece which, with its outsize photograph, filled almost the same space as Atticus.

I can't say I made many new friends on the paper, where having come from the *Magazine* stigmatised me as incurably effete and precious. But at least Magnus was back there as news editor and, as always, I got on well with the photographers, particularly the charming Michael Ward, the bit part-player in British war films who always addressed me, Navy-style, as 'Number One'.

After Hunter Davies moved on from the *Magazine*, to be succeeded by the more silky-brained Phillip Clarke, my byline reappeared in it, supplementing pieces on the paper's Look, leader and sometimes even sports pages. True, I no longer virtually commuted to and from the States or roamed Asia at will, but the pink slip for advance expenses remained a constant comfort.

During the mid-Seventies, I was the only *Sunday Times* writer who regularly crossed the covered footbridge into *The Times'*s building. With Derek Jewell still clinging to his Sunday 'jazz/pop' slot in the

Weekly Review, I volunteered myself to *The Times's* arts editor, John Higgins, as its first-ever rock critic. For a few drunk-with-power years, I would review rock stars' performances in *The Times*, then interview them in the *Sunday Times*.

American rock 'n' roll pioneers, now all but forgotten in their homeland, still had devoted followings in Britain, so I got to meet almost every one who'd lightened the bleak winters and summers of my adolescence - Fats Domino, Neil Sedaka, the Everly Brothers, even the daddy of them all, Bill Haley. I covered the rise to superstardom of Fleetwood Mac, the Eagles, Queen, and Bob Marley, whom I saw record *No Woman No Cry* live at the Lyceum ballroom through a green fog of ganja-smoke, feeling even hotter than I had in the Jordanian desert.

I interviewed Bob Dylan for an hour at his press-conference at the National Film Theatre by refusing to yield to any other questioner, heard Little Richard sing *Bama Lama Bama Loo* to me down a telephone line and took Bruce Springsteen shopping for Scotch wool pullovers at Harrods.

The moment of moments came with Beach Boys' visit to London in 1977. It was their first tour since Brian Wilson, their crewcut mini-Mozart, had rejoined the lineup after a decade of psychiatric problems belied by his odes to sun and surf like *Fun Fun Fun*, *Wouldn't It Be Nice* and *Good Vibrations*. I was allowed to watch them rehearse, Brian at the piano with his personal therapist massaging his shoulders and bribing him with cigarettes to hit all his old choirboy high notes.

Then, suddenly, they struck up *Barbara Ann* - the Beach Boys with Brian Wilson playing just for me. I lay awake half that night, still saturated in it.

It was during these years that Harry Evans won his long and vastly expensive campaign for the child victims of Thalidomide, exposing its manufacturers, the Distillers Company, as callous and duplicitous, irrespective of the fact that their whisky-producing division were major advertisers in the *Magazine*. Both as a moral crusade and example of an editor's commitment, stamina and nerve, it probably will never be equalled.

Also during these years, Harry left his wife, Enid – a distinguished educationalist whom few of his staff had ever set eyes on – for Tina Brown. 24 years his junior. From then on, his hair grew down over his ears, he took to wearing tieless floral shirts and pastel-coloured safari jackets in the composing-room and his social circle widened exponentially for, despite her youth, Tina was a networker of genius.

He could still send me a Herogram which made me feel, as freckled Mike Corner had put it long ago in Darlington, that 'I'd go through hell for him.' But it was very different when I upset one of his celebrity friends; indeed, a reprise of the Richard Attenborough episode back when Godfrey still ruled the *Magazine*.

The anarchic Michael Bateman, who now ran its new Lifespan section - and was increasingly straying outside Harry's reader-service brief – had commissioned me to write some satirical verse-portraits of prominent personalities, illustrated by the likes of Ralph Steadman and Luck and Flaw. One was of the broadcaster Melvyn Bragg, whom Harry now saw socially; it earned me a shrivelling Anti-Herogram that began, 'These verses are not doing you or the paper any good ...'

Throughout the late 70s, the *Sunday Times* increasingly suffered what was now termed 'industrial action' by its powerful print unions that prevented publication so often, it became known as 'the Sunday Sometimes'. By 1979, even the benign Thomson Organisation had had enough and shut down the paper for a year, while still keeping the whole editorial staff on full salary.

I used the time to write a biography of the Beatles, despite heavy discouragement from colleagues and friends who told me that everyone already knew everything there was to know. The publishers obviously half-expected this to be case, for my advance was minuscule. It was Harry who financed the research that took me back to New York and LA, as well as Hamburg and repeatedly back and forth to Liverpool, as a payment on account of future serialisation rights.

Ten days after I delivered the manuscript, John Lennon was assassinated in New York. Consequently, *Shout! The True Story of the Beatles* (incorporating the precious eyewitness material at Apple Corps to which Dick Adler had steered me 12 years before) became a bestseller in Britain and the US and was duly serialised in the *Magazine*. My third novel, *The Skaters' Waltz*, finally getting my father and Ryde Pier between hard covers, had recently put me into the first Top 20 Best of Young British Novelists, but hereafter I was fated to wear the less becoming tag of 'rock biographer'.

In 1980, the Australian media tycoon Rupert Murdoch, who already owned the *Sun* and the *News of the World*, began discussions with the Thomson family about adding the *Sunday Times* and the *Times* to his tucker-bag. We on the *Sunday Times* were aghast at these overtures from the man *Private Eye* called 'the Dirty Digger', the more so when we discovered that in the negotiations our paper was being portrayed as a chronic loss-maker like *The Times* whereas, despite the current economic recession, it continued to turn a healthy profit. Harry shared our concern and became actively involved in a search for an alternative buyer – *any* alternative buyer.

For a time, it seemed that Murdoch's plan might be thwarted because of the large slice of the British press he already controlled. However, a secret deal with the Prime Minister, Margaret Thatcher, saved him from going before the Monopolies Commission in exchange for giving her struggling Tory government his papers' unqualified support.

Murdoch did for Harry by flattering him out of his *Sunday Times* stronghold and making him editor of *The Times*, where the knives were out for him from the start. I witnessed one example first-hand on March 30, 1981, after John Hinckley fired several shots at President Ronald Reagan as the President was getting into his limo in Washington DC.

The news reached *The Times* in the early evening, while Harry was with Tina at my publication dinner party for *Shout!* Yet no one bothered to phone him at the restaurant until almost midnight. His tenure was to last only a year longer.

It soon became apparent that what Murdoch called 'journos' ranked very low in his estimation and that a perhaps subliminal factor in his wish to acquire the *Sunday Times* was to take its particular pampered journos down a few pegs. One of the senior features' editors, John Barry, accurately forecast that, once he owned it, he'd 'soon start pulling the wheels off.' Its great feature writer Peter Dunn, who'd tried to rally opposition to the Murdoch takeover, compared the lot of his staff to that of a bed of mushrooms. 'You're kept completely in the dark and every so often, someone comes and pours shit over you.'

Murdoch began pulling the wheels off by giving the editorship to Frank Giles, who'd been passed over for it in Harry's favour 14 years earlier. 'He can't believe it,' Dunn said. 'He missed the boat in 1967, but it's come back again. His face has got this weird glow like a Hallowe'en lantern.' But no chalice could have been more poisoned; it was said that Murdoch used to look across from his office in the *Times* building at Giles behind his desk at the *Sunday Times* and make as if to draw a bead on him with a rifle.

The proceeds from *Shout!* allowed me to take severance from the paper in 1982 to write my biography of the Rolling Stones and spend a year in America. I was granted an 'H' visa, entitling me to stay there indefinitely if I chose, on the basis that *Shout!* had added significantly to the national culture.

 The New York lawyer handling my application needed to tell the U.S. Immigration Service where I'd 'been at college'. When I confessed that I hadn't, he said not to worry as my career made me the equivalent of an Oxford or Cambridge graduate. So I did finally reach that pinnacle, albeit only theoretically and 22 years too late, in a fifty-fourth-floor office in the Chrysler Building.

That meant I was living in rural Long Island in 1983 when Rupert Murdoch forced Frank Giles to serialise the infamously inauthentic *Hitler Diaries* in the *Sunday Times*, having refused to let its Insight team investigate them first. Disengaged and far-away though I was, I felt the paper's worldwide humiliation, still not dissipated to this day.

In the years of Murdoch-isation that followed, every echo of what the *Sunday Times* had been was to disappear - except one. Even after once-beautiful copper-fronted Thomson House had been abandoned and razed to the ground and the paper moved to its new proprietor's grim labour camp in Wapping, an insidious frisson still lingered of Godfrey's guffaw, of ideas lunches, ideas breakfasts, desk-top dancing and 'jollies' to Twickers and Sarajevo. Successive Murdoch editors came in with one fixed objective above all: to control the *Magazine*.

Two major figures from its good old/bad old days, somehow escaped the wholesale sackings, redundancies and intricate personal humiliations that characterised the Murdoch era. The first – perhaps not surprisingly, given his thin man's lightness on his feet - was Godfrey himself. For several years afterwards, he had a column on the paper's leader page, holding forth as benignly from his weekly 800 words as he once had from behind his desk-cum-lunch table. He was fond of setting his readers little literary competitions for which the prize was always 'a bottle of fizz.' They were now his young rips.

The second survivor, astonishingly, was George Perry, whose future had been said to be hanging by a thread when I arrived on the *Magazine* in 1966.

As the years passed, George's resilience took on almost an epic quality, like that of some wild Atlantic cape battered by centuries of storms yet eternally looming through the fog and spray. Until well into the Nineties, he served as the *Sunday Times's* film expert, as distinct from critic; the man who knew that John Wayne had been born Marion Morrison and how much Erich Von Stroheim's *Greed* had cost to make and how to spell Darryl F. Zanuck and what the 'F' stood for.

In 1995, I took a break from rock biography to write *Everyone's Gone to the Moon*, the cartoonish tale of a Sunday broadsheet in the Swinging Sixties, its charismatic editor, Jack Shildrick, and his vain efforts to curb its irresponsible, spendthrift colour magazine.

Harry and Tina were by now based in New York, she much the greater journalistic influencer as editor of The New Yorker, he president of the publishers Random House. My British publishers were a division of Random House and when my commissioning editor there read *Everyone's Gone to the Moon*, she was seized by double terror of a libel suit and losing her job.

Harry not only published the book in the U.S., but sent me a note about it, saying that 'the characters pop off the page with some verisimilitude.'

It almost felt like a Herogram - and after all the years, it still gave me a glow.

A few months back, I went to an exhibition of Don McCullin's photographs at Tate Britain. As well as the images on the walls, there were display cases showing his work in the *Magazine* during the 80s and 90s. By then, it had been repeatedly cut down from the heroic dimensions of Godfrey Smith's era, but still looked enormous compared with the impoverished little booklet it is today.

Many young journalists whom I tell how it used to be simply don't believe me. I sometimes find it hard to believe myself.

*　　*　　*

Biography

Philip Norman has an international reputation as a chronicler of pop music and culture. *Shout!*, his ground-breaking biography of the Beatles, first published in 1981, has remained continuously in print, selling more than one million copies, and was recently listed by Waterstones bookshops as one of the 100 best biographies in any genre.

He has since written acclaimed books about the Rolling Stones, Elton John, Buddy Holly John Lennon, Mick Jagger, Sir Paul McCartney, Eric Clapton and Jimi Hendrix. Philip is also an award-winning fiction-writer (included among the first Top 20 'Best of Young British Novelists') and a playwright whose works have appeared on BBC2 and Radio 4. He has written two musicals, *This is Elvis: Viva Las Vegas* and *Laughter in the Rain: the Neil Sedaka story*.

*   *   *